Sunset

New Zealand
TRAVEL GUIDE

By the Editors of Sunset Books
and Sunset Magazine

Lane Publishing Co. • **Menlo Park, California**

Book Editor: **Cornelia Fogle**

Design: **Cynthia Hanson**
      Kathy Avanzino Barone

Illustrations: **Joe Seney**

Maps: **William Dunn & Joe Seney**

Photographers

Betty Crowell: 94. **Lynn Ferrin:** 11, 35.
Cornelia Fogle: 19, 27, 38, 75, 78, 103, 119.
Chris Gilbert: 3, 22, 62, 67, 83, 86, 111.
Libby Mills: 51. **Bruce Moss:** 54, 59, 91.
New Zealand Tourist Office: 6, 14, 30, 43, 46, 70,
106, 114. **Jim Rearden:** 122, 127. **Richard Rowan:** 98.

Cover: Clear waters of Lake Matheson mirror the
snowy peaks of Mount Tasman (left) and
Mount Cook (right) in Westland National Park.
Photographed by Chris Gilbert.

Come with us . . .

to New Zealand, a land of rugged, scenic beauty and
warm, hospitable people. Share with us a wealth of
rewarding travel destinations and activities. And join
with us as we explore and learn about a very special
country and its people.

We deeply appreciate the many individuals and
organizations in New Zealand who helped in the preparation of this book. In addition to the invaluable assistance of the New Zealand Tourist Office, especially Mike
Damiano, we also gratefully acknowledge the information provided by tourism officials throughout the
country.

And a special thank you to Fran Feldman for her
careful copy editing of the manuscript.

Editor, Sunset Books: David E. Clark

Second printing January 1986

CONTENTS

Cricket players dressed in traditional white garb bring a touch of England to Auckland Domain.

Special Features

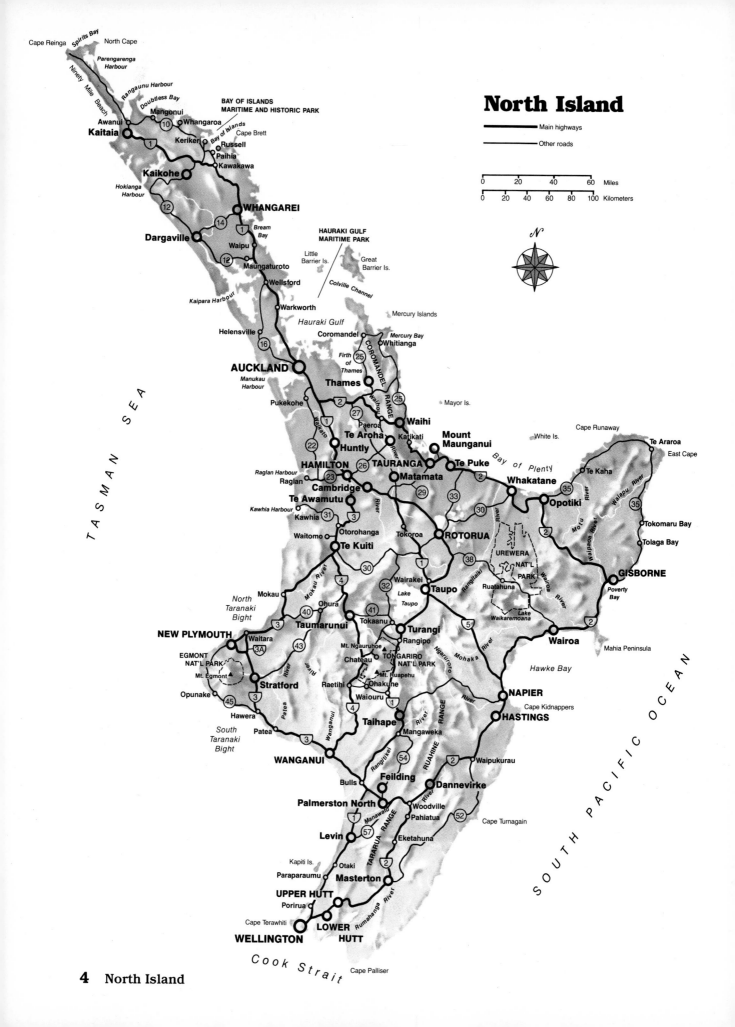

North Island

Main highways
Other roads

Miles
0 20 40 60

Kilometers
0 20 40 60 80 100

TASMAN SEA

Cape Reinga Spirits Bay North Cape
Parengarenga Harbour
Ninety Mile Beach *Rangaunu Harbour*
Mangonui *Doubtless Bay*
Awanui (10) Whangaroa *Bay of Islands* BAY OF ISLANDS MARITIME AND HISTORIC PARK
Kaitaia Kerikeri *Cape Brett*
(1) **Russell**
Paihia
Kaikohe Kawakawa
Hokianga Harbour (12)
(14) **WHANGAREI**
Dargaville (1) *Bream Bay*
Waipu HAURAKI GULF MARITIME PARK
(12) Maungaturoto Little Barrier Is. Great Barrier Is.
Kaipara Harbour Wellsford *Colville Channel*
Warkworth Mercury Islands
Hauraki Gulf
Helensville Coromandel *Mercury Bay* Whitianga
(16) *Firth of Thames* (25) Cape Runaway
AUCKLAND Thames • Mayor Is. Te Araroa
Manukau Harbour (25) East Cape
Pukekohe (2) White Is.
(1) (27) Paeroa **Waihi** *Bay of Plenty* Te Kaha
(22) **Te Aroha** Katikati **Mount Maunganui** Te Kaha (35)
Waikato **Huntly** **TAURANGA** **Te Puke** Opotiki
HAMILTON (26) **Matamata** (2) Tokomaru Bay
Raglan Harbour (23) (29) (33) **Whakatane** (35) Tolaga Bay
Raglan **Cambridge** (30) *Motu River* *Waipaoa River*
Te Awamutu UREWERA NAT'L PARK **GISBORNE**
Kawhia Harbour (31) Kawhia (3) Tokoroa **ROTORUA** (38) *Poverty Bay*
Waitomo Otorohanga (1) Ruatahuna (2)
Te Kuiti Wairakei *Lake Waikaremoana*
Mokau River (30) (32) Taupo (5) **Wairoa**
Mokau (4) *Lake Taupo* **Taupo** *Mahia Peninsula*
North Taranaki Bight (40) Ohura (41) Tokaanu (5)
Taumarunui **Turangi** *Ngaruroro River* *Mohaka River*
NEW PLYMOUTH Waitara (43) Rangipo
EGMONT NAT'L PARK (3A) Mt. Ngauruhoe TONGARIRO NAT'L PARK *Hawke Bay*
Mt. Egmont Chateau Mt. Ruapehu **NAPIER**
Opunake **Stratford** Raetihi Ohakune Cape Kidnappers
(45) (3) Waiouru (1) **HASTINGS**
Hawera (4) *RUAHINE RANGE*
South Taranaki Bight Patea *Wanganui River* **Taihape** Waipukurau
(3) Mangaweka (2)
WANGANUI (54) **Dannevirke**
Bulls **Feilding** *RANGITIKEI* (2)
Palmerston North Woodville (52) Cape Turnagain
(1) Pahiatua
Kapiti Is. **Levin** (57) Eketahuna
Paraparaumu Otaki *TARARUA RANGE* (2)
Rumahanga River **Masterton**
UPPER HUTT
Porirua
Cape Terawhiti **LOWER HUTT**
WELLINGTON
Cook Strait Cape Palliser

SOUTH PACIFIC OCEAN

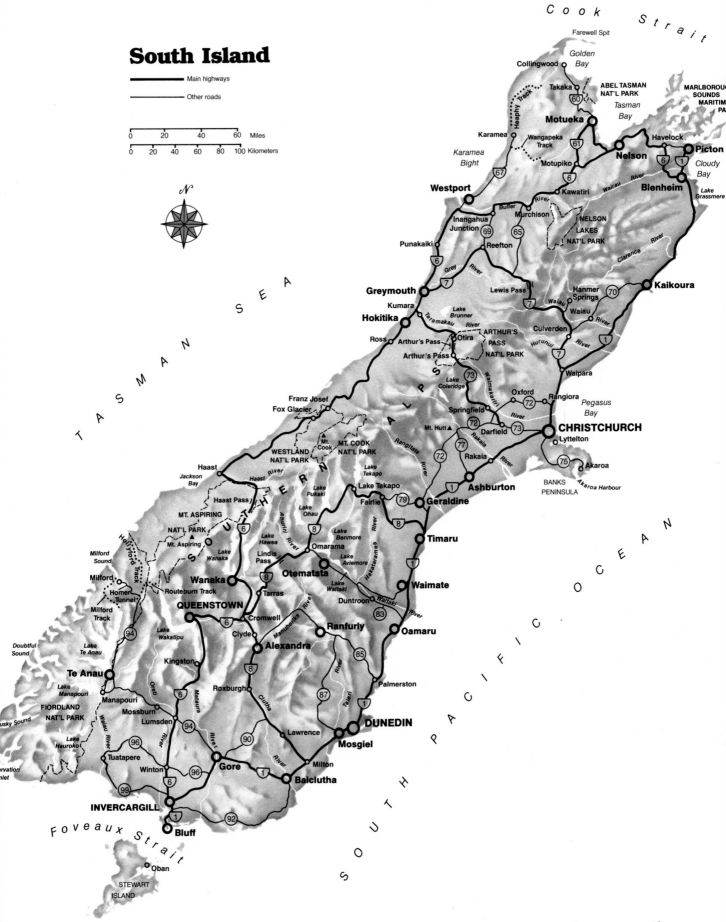

South Island

— Main highways

— Other roads

0 20 40 60 Miles
0 20 40 60 80 100 Kilometers

N

C o o k   S t r a i t

Farewell Spit

Golden Bay

Collingwood

Takaka — 60

ABEL TASMAN NAT'L PARK

Tasman Bay

MARLBOROUGH SOUNDS MARITIME PARK

Karamea

Wangapeka Track

Motueka

61

Havelock

Nelson

6 — Picton

1

Cloudy Bay

Heaphy Track

Motupiko

6

Karamea Bight

67

Westport

Kawatiri

Wairau River

Blenheim

Lake Grassmere

Inangahua Junction

69

Buller River

Murchison

NELSON LAKES NAT'L PARK

Clarence River

Punakaiki

65

Reefton

Kaikoura

6

Grey River

Hanmer Springs

70

Greymouth

7

Lewis Pass

Waiau

Waiau

Kumara

Lake Brunner

7

Culverden

Hokitika

Taramakau River

1

Ross

Arthur's Pass

Otira

ARTHUR'S PASS NAT'L PARK

Hurunui River

Arthur's Pass

Waimakariri

73

Waipara

7

Lake Coleridge

Oxford

Rangiora

72

Pegasus Bay

Franz Josef

Springfield

72

CHRISTCHURCH

Fox Glacier

Mt. Hutt

Darfield

53

Lyttelton

WESTLAND NAT'L PARK

Mt. Cook

MT. COOK NAT'L PARK

72

77

Rakaia

Akaroa

Rangitata River

Rakaia

75

Haast

Haast River

Lake Tekapo

Rakaia River

BANKS PENINSULA

Jackson Bay

Lake Pukaki

Lake Tekapo

1

Akaroa Harbour

Haast Pass

Fairlie

79

Ashburton

MT. ASPIRING NAT'L PARK

Lake Ohau

Geraldine

8

Mt. Aspiring

Ahuriri River

Lake Hawea

8

Lake Benmore

Hakataramea River

Timaru

Hollyford Track

6

Lake Wanaka

Omarama

Milford Sound

Lindis Pass

Lake Aviemore

1

Milford

Wanaka

Otematata

Lake Waitaki

Waimate

Routeburn Track

Tarras

Waitaki River

Milford Track

Homer Tunnel

QUEENSTOWN

Cromwell

Duntroon

83

Oamaru

Doubtful Sound

Clyde

Manuherikia River

Ranfurly

Lake Te Anau

94

Lake Wakatipu

Alexandra

85

Te Anau

Kingston

8

Roxburgh

Palmerston

Lake Manapouri

Manapouri

6

87

1

FIORDLAND NAT'L PARK

Mossburn

Clutha River

Lawrence

DUNEDIN

Dusky Sound

Lumsden

94

90

Mosgiel

Lake Hauroko

96

Milton

servation Inlet

Tuatapere

Winton

96

Gore

1

Balclutha

99

6

92

INVERCARGILL

1

F o v e a u x   S t r a i t

Bluff

Oban

STEWART ISLAND

T A S M A N   S E A

S O U T H E R N   A L P S

S O U T H   P A C I F I C   O C E A N

INTRODUCING NEW ZEALAND

British heritage joins with Maori culture in this land of scenic wonder

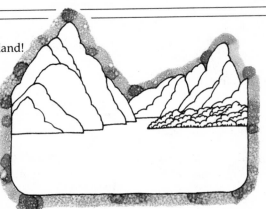

Haere mai! Welcome to New Zealand!

Isolated by vast southern seas, New Zealand is a land of awesome scenic beauty—a spectacular coastline indented by tree-rimmed bays and inlets; magnificent glacial mountains upthrust above fiords, lakes, and streams; volcanoes towering above arid desert and subtropical forest. Its remote location has shaped its self-sufficient people.

Along with Australia, New Zealand is one of only two South Pacific countries peopled predominantly by immigrants of European origin. Coupled with its British heritage is New Zealand's Maori culture, which adds an underlying Polynesian graciousness to the country.

New Zealand is a young country with frontier vitality; the first British colonists arrived less than 150 years ago. Natural barriers—rugged mountain ranges and dense bush—confined early settlement largely to the coast, and today most major cities border the sea. Much of the land is sparsely populated and used mainly for farming and grazing. Meat, wool, and dairy products are the country's principal exports.

Outside the population centers is the real New Zealand, a land of clearly defined districts, each with a distinct character, molded by its landscape and its settlers.

The land and its people

New Zealand lies about 10,400 km/6,500 miles southwest of San Francisco, a similar distance south of Tokyo, and about 1,920 km/1,200 miles southeast of Sydney.

New Zealand's two main islands extend about 1,600 km/ 1,000 miles along a diagonal fault line. To the west lies the Tasman Sea; to the east, the South Pacific Ocean. Narrow Cook Strait separates the two islands. Though relatively small in area, the country encompasses an amazing variety of geological and climatic conditions.

Both Auckland, its largest city, and Wellington, its capital, are situated on North Island. Important South Island cities are Christchurch and Dunedin.

Glaciers and volcanoes shaped the land

Dominating the topography is a magnificent snow-capped mountain range—the Southern Alps—extending some 650 km/400 miles along the western side of South Island. Often obscured by clouds, this mountain chain was probably the reason the Maoris called New Zealand *Aotearoa* — the long white cloud. From the high peaks, glaciers gouged out long, slender mountain lakes and coastal fiords.

Volcanic action shaped much of North Island; ash and lava showering over the central part of the island buried vast forests and dammed river valleys to create the Rotorua lakes. Two volcanoes are still active: Mount Ngauruhoe in Tongariro National Park and White Island in the Bay of Plenty. From Rotorua south to Taupo, thermal activity has created geysers, boiling pools, steam vents, and silica terraces.

Indenting the country's coastline are deep-water harbors, glacier-carved fiords, and "drowned" river valleys invaded by rising seas at the end of the Ice Age. Wooded headlands shelter curving bays and sandy beaches. Vast tracts of scenic wilderness have been preserved in ten national parks and three maritime parks.

As New Zealand's land forms vary, so do its rainfall patterns and climate. Prevailing westerlies drop most of

Jet boat skims along the Kawarau River near Queenstown on a golden autumn afternoon. Early snowfall dusts the Crown Range to the north.

Tuning in to Kiwi conversation

shout BUSH *pakeha* *Tramp* Petrol CUPPA SMOKO **?**

Colorful expressions and breezy slang—some borrowed from their British and Australian cousins—brighten the conversation of most *Kiwis* (New Zealanders). Subtle humor, an independent tradition, and the outdoor life influence many of the words and phrases you'll hear.

For many men, social life revolves around the local pub, where they meet their *mates* (male friends) and *shout* (treat) a round of beer. Families may spend the weekend at a *bach* or *crib* (country cabin or house), go for a *tramp* (hike) on a *track* (trail) through the *bush* (woods, forest), or perhaps *hire* (rent) a *caravan* (camper or trailer) for their *holiday* (vacation).

Personal contacts. If you have a friend-of-a-friend to contact, find a *call box* (phone booth) and *ring up* (telephone) the *bloke* (fellow). If his wife invites you to their *flat* (apartment) for tea, check the time of the invitation; tea is not only a beverage, it's also the evening meal.

If you eavesdrop in a pub, you may hear a worker say he's *brassed off* (angry, frustrated) about his job, co-workers, or *screw* (salary). When you hear talk about a *hooker*, it's a rugby player they're discussing. If someone's called a *Pommie*, he's an Englishman; a *pakeha* is a person of European descent. You don't understand? Don't worry. It'll all *come right* (be O.K.).

On the road. If you drive a car during your travels, you'll put your luggage in the *boot* (trunk), clean your *windscreen* (windshield), stop for *petrol* (gasoline), and peer under the *bonnet* (hood) if you hear a strange noise.

For major problems, you may need to ring up a *break-down truck* (tow truck), *locker* (locksmith), or *panel beater* (car body mechanic).

You'll drive on *sealed* (paved) and *metalled* (graded gravel or crushed rock) roads. Warning signs you'll encounter include the following: *collision corner* (dangerous intersection), *greasy if wet* (slippery if wet), *hump* (bump), *give way* (yield), *no exit* (dead end), *change down* (shift into low gear), *no overtaking* (no passing), *road works* (construction), *special care* (caution), and *uneven surface* (rough road).

Touring tips. When traveling by motorcoach, passengers take a break at the *wee-tea stop* (comfort stop); elsewhere, excuse yourself to *spend a penny*.

If you're motoring and get thirsty, stop for a *cuppa* (cup of tea or coffee), a *fizzy* (carbonated beverage), or—at the end of the day—even *spirits* (liquor). When you want to picnic, buy food supplies or ask your hotel to prepare a *cut lunch* (packed lunch) for you. Then, when you feel *peckish* (hungry), you can find a pleasant site beside the road or in a *domain* (park).

If you stay on a sheep station, you'll see flocks in the *paddocks* (fields). Shearers stop for a *smoko* (coffee break), then work *flat stick* (at maximum effort).

On back-country trips, it's customary to *boil the billy* (heat water in a small can over a campfire for tea). Trampers should take along some *sticky plaster* (adhesive tape) in case of blisters and a *torch* (flashlight) if it's an overnight trip. If someone tells you to *get cracking* or *rattle your dags*, they want you to hurry up. When the weather turns cool, pull on a *jersey* (pullover sweater). Try not to *grizzle* (complain) if it starts to rain. On the beach, you can stop to *natter* (chat) with a fellow *fossicker* (beachcomber).

You'll like New Zealand. Its people are *smashing* (terrific) and the country's a *beaut!* And we're not *having you on* (pulling your leg). Cheerio!

---

their moisture along the western slope of the high mountains. Depleted of moisture, dry winds fan over the warm eastern slope.

Temperatures are never excessively hot in summer nor uncomfortably cold in winter. Ranges are more extreme on South Island; here you'll find the wettest and driest regions of the country, as well as some of its warmest and coldest weather.

Seasons are reversed in the Southern Hemisphere.

Luxuriant forests and bright wildflowers

New Zealand's isolation and diverse geography and climate are reflected in its unique plants. Tree ferns and palms flourish in subtropical rain forest within sight of snow. Flowering trees and tiny alpine wildflowers bloom in colorful displays.

Native and introduced trees. In the northern region of North Island, kauri trees tower over lower-growing trees and shrubs. The crimson-blossoming pohutukawa tree—called "New Zealand's Christmas tree" — brightens the northeastern coast and other areas in December.

In luxuriant lowland forests, tall podocarps (conifers) such as rimu, totara, and kahikatea — all valuable commercial timber — rise above lower broadleaf trees. Among native varieties are tawa, miro, hinau, puriri, kohekohe, towai, and the red-flowering rata and rewarewa trees. Ferns and mosses thrive beneath the forest canopy.

Twining through the treetops are the scarlet-blooming rata vine and the clematis, with its fragrant, starry white flowers. In early spring, golden cascades of kowhai blossoms blanket river banks and open areas.

Beech forests abound in cooler mountain areas;

undergrowth is usually sparse. In areas where rainfall is heavy, such as Fiordland, trees may be festooned with beardlike mosses and scarlet-blooming mistletoe.

British colonists planted many European trees on their homesteads and along roads. In April, these trees produce glorious displays of autumn color, at its best in Canterbury and Otago. You may also see plantings of Monterey pine, Douglas fir, and even redwoods.

Other plants and wildflowers. In regions too dry to support forests, shrubby manuka often blankets entire hillsides with its starry white flowers. Tufted tussock grasses spread across much of South Island's high inland hill country.

Other distinctive plants you'll see are the silky, ivory-colored flowerheads of toetoe and the swordlike leaf clumps of New Zealand flax. The Maoris used tall dried toetoe stems for *tukutuku* paneling (page 48) and flax fiber for clothing, ropes, and baskets.

In late spring and early summer, alpine wildflowers — snow grounsel, mountain gentian, mountain buttercups, mountain daisies, and New Zealand edelweiss — put on a brief but colorful show. Lupine varieties brighten mountain slopes and coastal areas.

Forest wildflowers include kotukutuku (the pink-flowering native fuchsia) and flamboyant red kakabeak. More than 60 native orchid species grow in moist grasslands and perch on tree trunks and branches in the rain forests.

Unusual birds—but few animals

The New Zealand bush teems with native birds. Best known is the flightless kiwi, a wingless, tailless, nocturnal bird with grey brown plumage and a long, tapered bill. It has given its name to New Zealanders, who are called Kiwis the world over. Another flightless bird is the weka, a smaller relative of the kiwi.

Other birds you may spot in the bush are the bellbird, whose sweet song resembles the chime of silver bells; the tui, another songster recognized by a tuft of white feathers at its black throat; friendly bush robins and fantails; the tiny rifleman; the bright-eyed tomtit; and wood pigeons. The morepork, a small owl, is active after nightfall.

In wet, swampy places you'll often see the colorful pukeko, a long-legged swamp hen. Similar in appearance is the rare takahe, thought for many years to be extinct. Inhabiting South Island mountains is the shrill-voiced kea, a mountain parrot.

Shore and sea birds, such as penguins, petrels, shags, gannets, shearwaters, gulls, and terns, are abundant along the coast. You can visit a royal albatross colony east of Dunedin and a heron colony at Okarito Lagoon, north of Westland National Park.

New Zealand has no native animals. All of its wild animals are descendants of imported animals brought here for food, sport, fur, or as predators.

Europeans follow Maoris to New Zealand

New Zealand's earliest inhabitants—called "moa hunters"—were peaceful nomads who roamed the islands as early as 750 A.D., stalking the flightless moa birds for food. When and where they came from remain a mystery.

According to Maori tradition, Polynesian voyager Kupe sailed south about 950 A.D. from the legendary Maori homeland called Hawaiki, thought to be in eastern Polynesia, and discovered a land he called *Aotearoa*. Eventually, he returned to Hawaiki and passed on sailing instructions to the land of the long white cloud. Four centuries later, a number of canoes journeyed south to Aotearoa, guided by the sun and stars. It is from these ancestral canoes that most Maoris claim their descent.

The Maoris introduced tropical food plants, especially the kumara, a variety of sweet potato. They depended on fish and birds for meat. At the time the first Europeans arrived, most Maoris were living in the northern and central areas of North Island, where their agricultural society thrived in the warm climate. Intertribal battles were common.

Exploration and exploitation. Europeans had long speculated that a great unknown continent existed in the South Pacific before 1642, when Abel Tasman was dispatched by the Dutch East India Company in search of new trade opportunities. He sailed along the western coast of South Island, anchoring in Golden Bay near the northern tip. Several of his sailors were killed in a clash with Maoris, and Tasman departed without landing.

Captain James Cook sailed to the South Pacific on a British scientific expedition. Mission completed, he turned south in search of the unknown continent. On October 7, 1769, he sighted the eastern coast of North Island and landed 2 days later at Poverty Bay.

Sailing north along the coast, Cook passed in a storm the ship captained by French explorer Jean de Surville. During the next 6 months, Cook circumnavigated both islands, charting the coast and recording information on the flora and fauna and on the Maori people. After his report was published, New Zealand became known to the world. Cook returned on two more voyages, making his base at Ship Cove in Queen Charlotte Sound.

Interest in the South Pacific and its resources increased. In the 1790s, sealers arrived to slaughter seals by the thousands. A decade later, whalers seeking provisions began calling at the Bay of Islands, which soon became the center of European settlement. In the 1830s and '40s, whaling stations sprang up on bays all along the coast south to Foveaux Strait.

While sealers and whalers plundered the seas, timber traders were razing the great kauri forests. Mill settlements mushroomed along Northland harbors and rivers.

Maoris reeled under the impact of the sailors and traders, who brought contagious diseases and firearms that permanently altered Maori life. The missionaries who began arriving in the Bay of Islands in 1814 attempted to protect the Maori people from exploitation.

Annexation and settlement. The ravaging of the country's natural resources, threat of annexation by France, land speculation, and insistence by the impatient London-based New Zealand Company to colonize exerted pressure on the British to annex the country. Britain reluctantly decided to negotiate with Maori chieftains. On February 6, 1840, Captain William Hobson concluded the Treaty of Waitangi with leading Northland chiefs, and New Zealand became part of the British Empire (now Commonwealth). Maori land rights were protected, and Maoris were granted equal citizenship status with European settlers.

Once the treaty was signed, shiploads of Europeans—most of them British—began arriving to establish planned settlements on both islands. Sheepherders imported large flocks to graze on the vast grasslands. Misunderstandings inevitably arose between Maoris and European settlers over land purchases. In 1860, conflicts in Taranaki spread throughout much of North Island, and the Land Wars continued intermittently for 20 years.

Meanwhile, South Island was gripped by gold fever. After gold was discovered in Central Otago in 1861, the stampede was on. Able-bodied men deserted the towns for the diggings, and prospectors poured in by the thousands. Almost overnight, Dunedin became the country's richest and most influential city.

In the late 19th century, the introduction of refrigeration opened a new industry—supplying meat-hungry British markets with frozen lamb. Dairy herds yielded butter and cheese for export. Agriculture expanded as rivers were rechanneled to irrigate new areas.

New Zealand's government

An independent member of the British Commonwealth, New Zealand is governed by an elected, single-chamber Parliament modeled after Britain's House of Commons. Since 1865, Wellington has been the nation's capital.

Queen Elizabeth II is represented in New Zealand by her appointed Governor-General, who each year appears at the opening session of Parliament in full formal regalia to read the royal Speech-from-the-Throne that officially opens Parliament.

Parliament has one chamber, the House of Representatives, composed of 92 members (including four Maori legislators elected directly by Maori voters) elected for 3-year terms. The country has two main political parties, the National and Labour parties. The leader of the party winning a majority of seats in Parliament becomes the Prime Minister. Members of the Cabinet are selected from among the parliamentary membership of the winning party. Legislation is enacted or amended by a simple majority vote in Parliament.

Until World War II, New Zealand automatically followed Britain's lead in international affairs. Since that time, though, it has established close alliances with the United States and Australia and has taken a leadership role among the nations of Polynesia and the South Pacific.

Self-reliant, friendly people

Throughout its history, New Zealand has attracted people who wanted to make a fresh start. Self-reliant, hard-working, and independent, the Kiwi is an amiable, friendly companion.

About 90 percent of New Zealand's 3.2 million people are of British descent; Maoris make up about 9 percent of the population. Nearly three-quarters of the people live on North Island. *Pakeha* (persons of European descent) intermingle freely with Maoris, who have largely adopted the European life style while preserving their own traditions and culture.

Life here has a solid quality. Most people work a 5-day week. They treasure their weekends and actively pursue all kinds of sports and outdoor activities.

Traveling in New Zealand

Numerous international airlines — including the country's own Air New Zealand — serve Auckland International Airport. Flights from Australia and the South Pacific land in Wellington and Christchurch as well. Several steamship companies cruise between New Zealand and international ports.

Public transport links cities and towns

Getting around the country is a pleasure. Whether you travel by plane, train, motorcoach, car, or ferry, you'll appreciate New Zealand's comprehensive and dependable transportation network.

Air service. Air New Zealand, Mount Cook Line, Newmans Airways Ltd., and several small regional airlines provide scheduled flights between the country's main cities, provincial towns, and resort areas. Charter planes are based at many airports.

Trains. New Zealand Railways provides passenger rail service between the larger cities and towns on both islands. Fast, comfortable trains feature adjustable seats, smoking and non-smoking sections, buffet cars, and refreshment service.

North Island's main line runs between Auckland and Wellington, passing west of Tongariro National Park. Two express trains link the cities: the deluxe Silver Fern daylight train, which runs daily except Sunday, and the overnight Northerner, which operates daily.

On South Island, train routes branch out from Christchurch—south along the coast to Invercargill, west across Arthur's Pass to Greymouth, and north to Picton. The Southerner daylight express train links Christchurch, Dunedin, and Invercargill daily except Sunday.

Interisland ferries. Passenger/vehicular ferries steam across Cook Strait several times daily, providing sched-

Milford Track hikers cross a rushing stream on a metal suspension bridge. On organized trips, trekkers carry only personal gear.

uled service between Wellington, at the southern tip of North Island, and Picton, in South Island's Marlborough Sounds. The trip takes about 3 hours and 20 minutes.

Ferry service also links Bluff, at the southern tip of South Island, and Stewart Island.

Motorcoaches. Long-distance motorcoaches of Railways Road Services cover the country from Kaitaia, near the northern tip of North Island, to Invercargill, at the southern end of South Island. Scheduled service connects most of the country's places of scenic, historic, and cultural interest. Reservations are necessary on all Railways Road Services routes, but no seats are assigned; if you purchase your ticket 72 hours ahead, your seat is guaranteed. If you want a window seat, try to be near the head of the boarding line.

Mount Cook Line also operates a network of long-distance motorcoach lines on both islands, with brief stops in small towns along its routes. Newmans Coach Lines and H & H Travel Lines Ltd. also provide scheduled regional service.

Travel passes. Independent travelers should investigate the various travel passes available from Air New Zealand, New Zealand Railways, and Mount Cook Line. Check with your travel agent or the New Zealand Tourist Office (page 12) for information. All passes must be purchased prior to arrival in New Zealand, but no reservations can be made until after you arrive.

Tour packages— with a group or on your own

Many travelers appreciate the convenience of seeing New Zealand's highlights as part of a group. Your travel agent can provide brochures on a variety of tour packages, some covering the duration of your New Zealand visit and others just a portion. Tours range in length from 3 days to 3 weeks and depart throughout the year. Additional information is available from offices of international carriers flying to New Zealand.

If you prefer touring independently, ask about fly-drive or fly-coach touring plans. Offering a more flexible

Information for travelers

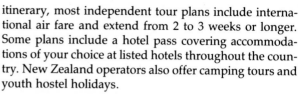

New Zealand government tourist offices are happy to provide visitors with general and specific travel information and to answer your inquiries, both before you go and after you arrive in New Zealand. Travelers planning an extended stay need a visa, obtainable from the nearest New Zealand embassy or consulate.

While you're in New Zealand, contact visitor information centers in the large towns and resort areas for specific information on the locale you're touring.

Planning your trip. In North America, you'll find a New Zealand Tourist Office in these locations:

Los Angeles, CA 90024: Suite 1530, Tishman Building, 10960 Wilshire Boulevard

New York, NY 10111: Suite 530, 630 Fifth Avenue

San Francisco, CA 94111: Suite 970, Alcoa Building, 1 Maritime Plaza

Vancouver, B.C., Canada V7Y1B6: Suite 1260, IBM Tower, 701 West Georgia Street

U.S. citizens planning a visit longer than 30 days or Canadian citizens staying longer than 6 months can apply for a visa at the nearest embassy (in Washington or Ottawa) or consulate (same cities and buildings as the New Zealand Tourist Office).

Australian branches of the New Zealand Tourist Office are located in Brisbane, Melbourne, Perth, and Sydney.

London, Frankfurt, Tokyo, and Singapore also have branches of the New Zealand Tourist Office.

After you arrive. Once you land in New Zealand, the staff in the offices of the Government Tourist Bureau (G.T.B.), located in Auckland, Rotorua, Wellington, Christchurch, Dunedin, and Queenstown, can help you obtain accommodations throughout the country; they also make travel arrangements and provide tour information.

In cities and larger towns, check the local public relations offices (P.R.O.) and visitor centers for information on local attractions and special events.

In the main tourist centers, look for free tourist publications; these feature seasonal events and special attractions, restaurant listings, and shopping suggestions.

Motorists who belong to an automobile club can obtain motoring information, maps, accommodation guide books, and route-planning assistance at offices of the Automobile Association in larger towns. You'll need to present your home auto club membership card.

itinerary, most independent tour plans include international air fare and extend from 2 to 3 weeks or longer. Some plans include a hotel pass covering accommodations of your choice at listed hotels throughout the country. New Zealand operators also offer camping tours and youth hostel holidays.

After you arrive, you'll find many short fly-drive and fly-coach holidays available from Auckland and Christchurch to main tourist areas.

Traveling by car

If you enjoy touring leisurely, one of the best ways to see the countryside is by rental car or camper. For tips on driving in New Zealand, see page 56.

Major rental car companies include Mutual-Avis, Tasman-Hertz, and Budget. All three have branch offices and representatives in major towns and tourist areas throughout the country. Companies offer a variety of plans, including one-day rates, one-way hire, unlimited kilometer rates, fly-drive trips, and plans where a car awaits you at the wharf or railway station. Rental cars are not transported between the islands.

Campers or motor vans can be rented in Auckland, Wellington, and Christchurch. Vehicles come in several designs and accommodate up to 6 persons. Generally, campers are equipped with sleeping and limited cooking facilities, but no toilet or shower. (Most New Zealand campgrounds have communal kitchens and centralized shower and toilet facilities. For more on camping, see page 15.) Usually, you rent by the week; rates include unlimited mileage and insurance. Summer travelers should make rental arrangements well in advance.

In the main centers, you can arrange for a chauffeur-driven automobile, with a knowledgeable driver-guide to show you the sights.

Taxis and local bus service

Reliable and inexpensive public transportation makes sightseeing easy in the major cities. City bus service connects the central districts with outlying suburbs; Wellington also has electric commuter train service to its northern suburbs. Bus fares vary by the number of sections of the route traveled.

Taxis in cities and towns operate from taxi stands or on call. Rates vary throughout the country, but are normally charged on a per-kilometer basis, with extra charges for night and weekend trips and for extra luggage. You can arrange an hourly rate for sightseeing.

Enjoying your visit

In the cities and resort areas, you'll find tourist accommodations in all different price ranges. Facilities may be more limited in the countryside, but you'll find a warm welcome awaiting you wherever you go.

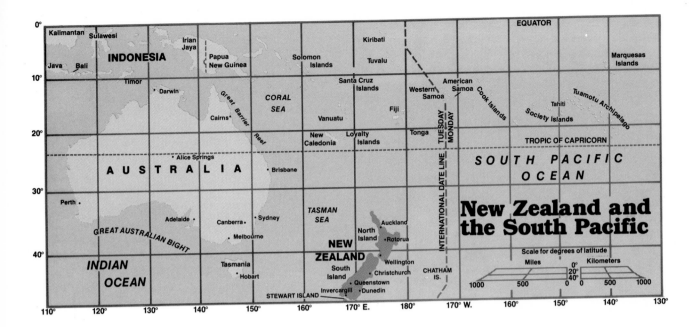

Hotels and motels

In recent years, numerous hotels, motor inns, and motels have been built in New Zealand, and many existing facilities have been upgraded. The cities offer choices ranging from modern high-rises to older, small hotels with a gracious charm. Country hotels are generally small, with friendly, old-fashioned atmosphere. Motels are situated throughout the country.

The main travel season extends from November through April. Peak demand occurs from mid-December through January and again during the Easter holidays, when New Zealanders take to the road; early reservations are recommended during these school vacation periods. Some hotels and motels apply a small surcharge for one-night stopovers. During the off-season, reduced rates may be available.

For current information on facilities and rates, consult your travel agent or the *New Zealand Accommodation Guide,* available from the New Zealand Tourist Office (page 12). In New Zealand, the Automobile Association publishes the *Accommodation and Camping Guide* for its members; it contains a detailed listing of hotels, motels, and motor camps.

Comfortable hotels. In addition to independent hotels, several chains maintain hotels throughout the country. The government-operated Tourist Hotel Corporation (THC) provides excellent resort accommodations on both islands. Other major operators include Hyatt Kingsgate, Sheraton, Travelodge, and Vacation hotels; Lion and Dominion Breweries (DB) also have hotels throughout the country. Older refurbished hotels make up the hostelries in the Establishment chain.

Rooms usually have tea and coffee-making facilities, telephone, and television. Some hotels provide daily newspapers, room refrigerators, and laundry facilities.

Hotels need licenses to be able to serve drinks on the premises. A hotel ranks as fully licensed (liquor can be sold to the public), tourist licensed (liquor available to hotel guests only), or unlicensed (no liquor sold).

Well-equipped motels. New Zealand's modern motels offer excellent value. Flag Inns and Best Western operate motels throughout the country, but most small motels are independently owned.

Motel flats provide fully furnished accommodations with kitchen facilities, refrigerator, cooking and dining utensils, and nearby laundry facilities.

Serviced motels are motorists' hotels with tea and coffee-making facilities but no kitchens. Breakfast is often available; larger motels have a restaurant on the premises.

Fishing lodges and golfing holidays

If you'd like to break your journey with several days of trout fishing or a few rounds of golf, you may want to seek out one of the special hostelries catering to your sport.

Some of the more expensive lodges are quite luxurious and take only a few guests. Others are comparable in price and comfort to an excellent first-class hotel; a few are extremely simple. For information, consult the *New Zealand Accommodation Guide.*

Your travel agent can help you arrange such a vacation. If you write to a hotel for a brochure, it's a good idea to enclose an international postal reply coupon to assure a prompt response.

Fishing lodges. Several North Island lodges offer fishing and hunting in a scenic or wilderness setting. Among those to consider are Solitude Lodge, perched on a peninsula near Rotorua overlooking Lake Tarawera; Waikato River Lodge, near Reporoa midway between Rotorua and Taupo; Huka Lodge, on the Waikato River north of Taupo;

Fattened Wairarapa lambs, bound for the freezing works, funnel through a loading chute at Pirinoa. Other flocks await their turn in the paddocks.

Tongariro Lodge, at the mouth of the Tongariro River near Turangi; and Wilderness Lodge, on the Ripia River in the mountain wilderness southeast of Taupo.

Deep-sea anglers might consider Kingfish Lodge Hotel, facing Whangaroa Harbour and accessible only by boat. Rustic cabins are available on Mayor Island, under the auspices of the Tauranga Big Game Fishing Club (P. O. Box 501, Tauranga).

If you're looking for a South Island retreat and are willing to put up with some inconveniences, try one of the fishing lodges or guest houses in the Marlborough Sounds (page 80); some are accessible only by boat or float plane from Picton. Another place fondly regarded by many Kiwis is family-run Mitchells, a fishing lodge on the shore of Lake Brunner on the West Coast.

Golfing holidays. Nearly 400 golf courses dot this small country, and many New Zealanders take to the links with enthusiasm.

In the Bay of Islands, you can walk to the excellent Waitangi course from the THC Waitangi Hotel. Built overlooking the island-studded bay, the course has a number of very good holes.

Near the trout-fishing center of Taupo, you can spend your daylight hours on the greens of the Wairakei International Course and your evenings enjoying the hospitality of the fine THC Wairakei Hotel.

Many excellent golf courses are located near cities and large towns. For more information about golfing in New Zealand, see page 16.

Home hospitality

A highlight for many travelers is spending a night or two in the home of a New Zealand family. You have your own room (and frequently, a private bath) and join the family for a leisurely home-cooked dinner, informal social activities, and a full breakfast. If you prefer, you can arrange bed-and-breakfast accommodation only, or lunches on request. Host families are scattered throughout both islands, in cities, in towns, and on farms. For more on farm visits, see page 124.

If you're looking for something more luxurious, consider one of the country's unusual dwellings that host a few paying guests. Overlooking Auckland's busy harbor is Ellerton Lodge, a restored colonial home in Devonport. Muriaroha is a gracious Rotorua home, filled with antiques and art and surrounded by gardens.

Your travel agent can make reservations for you through the New Zealand Tourist Office. In New Zealand, stop at an office of the Government Tourist Bureau (page 12) or make arrangements directly through New Zealand Home Hospitality Ltd., P. O. Box 309, Nelson; phone (54) 85-727. Some regional organizations also arrange home stays; local tourist offices can provide more information. Usually, advance payment in full is required, so only a voucher changes hands between you and your host.

Budget accommodations

You don't need a big budget to enjoy a New Zealand holiday. You'll find a wide range of moderately priced accommodations in small hotels and motels, guest houses, and cabins. Visitors can also stay in youth hostels or campgrounds.

Small hotels and guest houses. Moderate and low-priced licensed hotels offer clean rooms and good food without elaborate amenities. Guest houses and private hotels have no liquor licenses, and their rates vary according to their facilities. Rooms may or may not have a private bath, but most contain a sink and electric heater.

Youth hostels. The Youth Hostel Association offers its members an extensive chain of hostels throughout the country. Dormitory accommodation is available at moderate cost; you must provide your own sleeping bag. Communal cooking facilities are provided at each hostel, and stopovers are limited to 3 nights at any one place.

For information on membership and hostel locations, write the Youth Hostel Association of New Zealand, P.O. Box 436, Christchurch.

Campgrounds. During holiday periods, New Zealanders flock to the beaches and lakes, to the mountains, and to the country's national parks. Serving these travelers is a vast network of campgrounds, motor camps, and cabin and cottage accommodations. Many economy-minded overseas visitors have also discovered these facilities. It's a fine way to see the country and meet friendly Kiwi families.

Campgrounds are crowded during the December-January school holidays, but they're seldom full the rest of the year. Most campgrounds have a modern communal kitchen and dining room, laundry facilities, and centralized shower and toilet facilities. Some even offer a swimming pool, spa, children's play area, TV room, boat rentals, or barbecue facilities. You'll meet other campers easily; chatting and swapping experiences as you relax or do your chores are part of camping, New Zealand style.

General camping information is available from the New Zealand Tourist Office (page 12); detailed descriptions of campsites, motor camps, and cabins are provided in the Automobile Association's guide (page 13). Another helpful guide is the *Mobil Camping and Caravanning Guide;* look for it in New Zealand bookstores.

Eating and drinking, Kiwi style

In general, meals in New Zealand are substantial, no-frills affairs. But you can find continental finesse in both cooking and service in top city restaurants. Home entertaining is usually informal and hearty.

Food specialties. New Zealand lamb is world renowned and needs no introduction; you'll also find beef, pork, and poultry on restaurant menus. Venison and wild pork are available at restaurants specializing in wild game.

New Zealanders are very partial to what the Maoris call *kai-moana*—food from the sea—and it is superb. Rock lobster (crayfish) is most plentiful in spring and early summer. Tiny whitebait, netted in coastal rivers as they migrate upstream in the spring, are served in crisp, batter-fried fritters. Rock oysters are excellent, as are the succulent Bluff oysters scooped up from the chilly waters of Foveaux Strait. Scallops and mussels have distinctive yet delicate flavors. The rare toheroa usually goes into a rich soup; other creamy seafood soups feature the tuatua clam and the paua (abalone).

On restaurant menus you'll see a variety of ocean fish, including snapper, flounder, grouper, John Dory, and the sea perch called orange roughy. But if it's trout you want, you'll have to catch it yourself; trout fishing is strictly a sport, and none is caught commercially.

New Zealand fruits are superb in season, but you won't always find them on restaurant menus. In addition to familiar varieties, look for kiwifruit, passion fruit, feijoa, and tamarillo (tree tomato). The country's traditional dessert is pavlova, meringue with sliced fruit and whipped cream; it's best when prepared in New Zealand homes.

Among New Zealand cheeses you'll discover are a local blue vein, several types of cheddar, and others based on favorite international varieties.

In Rotorua, you can sample Maori-style cooking, with meat and vegetables cooked by steam in an underground oven (page 46).

Teas, lunch, and snacks. Morning and afternoon tea (or coffee) breaks are widely observed, both at home and at work. Along with your hot beverage you can enjoy scones, biscuits (cookies), thin sandwiches, or a "sweet."

In "takeaways," milk bars, coffee lounges, and other informal food centers, you can get a quick between-meals snack, such as fish and chips, thin sandwiches, or warm savories. Many hotels feature smorgasbord lunches with an array of hot dishes, cold meats, salads, and desserts.

Picnicking is a pleasant alternative when you're touring. Just be sure to plan ahead in areas such as the West Coast or Fiordland where facilities are widely scattered. You can pick up bread, cheese, fruit, and beverages for an informal repast; or, if you request it the previous night, your hotel may pack a lunch for you.

Beverages. Beer is the favorite drink, and spirits are also available. Among friends it's customary to take your turn "shouting" a round. Bars are open daily except Sunday, Christmas Day, and Good Friday. Licensed hotels serve drinks from 11 A.M. to 10 P.M. (to 11 on Saturday night) in bars, lounges, and licensed restaurants; guests staying in a licensed hotel can be served any time.

Licensed restaurants serve liquor, beer, and wine. Informal restaurants may be unlicensed (you can call ahead and inquire); if you want, you can bring your own wine and pay a modest corkage fee. Bottled wine, beer, and liquor are available in bottle shops.

Restaurant wine lists offer diners a growing selection of New Zealand table wines, as well as limited imports from Australia, the United States, and Europe. It's customary to pay the wine steward separately for wine and drinks.

Join the Kiwis in outdoor sports

Spurred on by the country's invigorating climate and inexpensive, easily available facilities, almost every New Zealander participates in one sport or another. On every fair-weather weekend, you'll see families heading for the beach, sailing in sheltered bays and harbors, and walking forest trails.

Many sports enthusiasts savor the tranquility of a favorite fishing stream or the camaraderie of play on the local golf course. Others seek the excitement of the racetrack or stadium, where they follow enthusiastically the fortunes of horse racing and team competition. Kiwis are renowned—not without reason—for their dedicated pursuit of "racing, rugby, and beer."

Visitors who join in outdoor activities gain special insight into the Kiwi life style. You can plan your travels to include hiking on one of New Zealand's scenic tracks (trails), skiing on its challenging slopes (page 52), or fishing in its clear lakes, streams, or offshore waters (pages 36 and 47). Pause for a while to watch a Saturday cricket match or a game of lawn bowls, or join the crowds cheering on a favorite horse or rugby team.

Golfers find challenging courses charging only modest fees; though weekends are busy, fairways are uncrowded mid-week. Motorized golf carts are not used, but you can rent a trundler (caddy cart) for a small fee. You'll find public and private courses throughout the country. Visiting members of overseas clubs are usually accorded guest privileges at private golf clubs; bring a letter of introduction from your home club secretary. You'll find more about the sport and a listing of some of the country's top courses in *Golf in New Zealand*, available from the New Zealand Tourist Office.

Tennis has thousands of enthusiasts—even some farms and sheep stations have a private court for family and guests. Visiting players can often arrange a tennis match with local players by contacting the regional secretaries of the New Zealand Lawn Tennis Association.

Evening entertainment

Much of the night life revolves around the hotels, where musicians entertain and bands play for dancing. Some towns have weekend cabaret entertainment.

Touring national and overseas artists visit the major centers, and local theater groups perform in the larger cities. Civic and university groups also offer music and drama. The New Zealand Symphony Orchestra, the Ballet, and the Opera Company tour on both islands. Maoris entertain in their traditional style in Rotorua.

For information on current entertainment, check local tourist publications and daily newspapers.

Shopping for New Zealand crafts

Shop craft centers and other stores for handcrafted articles and quality souvenirs. In country areas, it's fun to visit the general store—the local "sell everything" retailer.

Woolly sheepskins and lambskins—by-products of the export meat industry—are converted into rugs, car seat covers, toys, and wearing apparel. Other wool products include hand-knitted sweaters, weavings, car robes, and blankets (some in Maori designs). Suede clothing, leather goods, and opossum fur articles are also popular.

You'll see the work of New Zealand's excellent potters and woodworkers throughout the country. Native woods used singly or crafted in inlaid patterns are shaped into bowls, candleholders, trays, and other items.

New Zealand jade, called greenstone, is fashioned into traditional *tiki* pendants and contemporary jewelry. Iridescent paua shell is used handsomely in jewelry, trays, ashtrays, and boxes. Other pieces show off fine metalwork or New Zealand gemstones.

If you're interested in Maori culture, look for records of Maori music and Maori-carved wooden articles in traditional designs.

Festivals and annual events

Carnivals, festivals, flower shows, and sports events dot the New Zealand calendar. Summer is the busiest time, but you'll find activities in all seasons. Events mentioned below and those noted elsewhere are only a sampling of those you can attend. The New Zealand Tourist Office publishes an annual listing; you may find more events mentioned in local newspapers.

Spring (September through November) heralds the flower show season. Bulbs, rhododendrons, azaleas, and blossoming trees put on magnificent displays in botanic gardens. Alexandra salutes its commercial fruit industry with a September blossom festival. From October to April, lively and colorful A & P shows (page 123) are held at dozens of sites around the country.

In summer (December through February), many towns and resorts celebrate during the Christmas-New Year holidays with festivals, carnivals, regattas, parades, horse races, and other sports competitions. At Waitangi, an annual twilight ceremony on February 6 commemorates the signing of the Treaty of Waitangi in 1840.

Autumn (March through May) brings the Golden Shears sheep shearing competition in Masterton, Maori canoe races and other contests in Ngaruawahia, and the Highland Games in Hastings. National and international artists perform in Auckland's Festival of the Arts, in the Festival of Wellington, and in Christchurch's annual Arts Festival. Trout and game-fishing competitions are highlights of the autumn sports calendar.

In winter (June through August), Tauranga hosts a Citrus Festival and gathering of Scottish clans. Skiers take to the slopes, while ice skaters and curling enthusiasts head for South Island's frozen lakes and outdoor rinks.

Know before you go: tips for travelers

Documents, customs regulations, currency— this brief checklist will answer many of your questions as you prepare for your trip.

Entry/exit procedures. Passports are required of all overseas visitors except Australian citizens, and citizens of other Commonwealth countries who have been granted permanent residency in Australia and who are arriving directly from that country. Passports must be valid at least 6 months beyond the date the visitor intends leaving New Zealand.

Visas are not necessary for U.S. citizens (except American Samoans) staying 30 days or less, or for Canadian citizens visiting for 6 months or less. Visitors planning a longer stay can obtain visa application forms at U.S. consular offices in Washington, D.C., New York, Los Angeles, or San Francisco; or at Canadian offices in Ottawa or Vancouver.

Visitors do not need any inoculations to enter New Zealand unless they're arriving from South America or Asia.

All persons are required to complete passenger declaration forms on both arrival and departure. International air passengers pay a departure tax of NZ $2.

Customs. Visitors may bring in a limited amount of personal effects, which must be declared on entry and taken out of the country when the visitor leaves. Each adult may bring in duty-free six 750 ml bottles (4.5 liters total) of wine, one 1125 ml/40 oz. bottle of spirits, and 200 cigarettes (or up to 250 grams of tobacco or up to 50 cigars). Full details on customs limitations and restricted or prohibited imports may be obtained from the nearest New Zealand Government overseas representative.

Time. New Zealand is located just west of the International Date Line and has a single time zone—12 hours ahead of Greenwich Mean Time. Based on Standard Time, Auckland is 17 hours ahead of New York and 20 hours ahead of San Francisco. The country observes daylight-saving time from the last Sunday in October to the first Sunday in March; clocks are advanced 1 hour during this period.

Business hours and holidays. Offices and businesses are open on weekdays from 8 A.M. to 5 P.M.; post offices observe the same hours. Banking hours are from 10 A.M. to 4 P.M. Monday through Friday.

Shops and stores are usually open from 9 A.M. to 5:30 P.M. on weekdays (to 9 P.M. on late shopping nights). Many shops are open on Saturday morning.

Nationwide holidays include New Year's Day, Waitangi Day (February 6), Good Friday, Easter Monday, Anzac Day (April 25), Queen's Birthday (first Monday in June), Labour Day (fourth Monday in October), Christmas Day, and Boxing Day (December 26). Most attractions close on Good Friday and Christmas Day. Each province also celebrates an annual holiday.

Schools are closed from mid-December through the end of January (the main family holiday period), for 2 weeks in May, and again in August.

Currency. New Zealand operates on a decimal currency system based on dollar and cent denominations. A visitor may bring an unlimited amount of foreign currency and travelers checks into New Zealand, but government restrictions limit the transfer of New Zealand funds outside the country. Banks are located in all international transportation terminals and throughout the country.

Tipping. Employed persons in New Zealand do not depend on tips or gratuities for their income. You are not expected to tip for normal service; light tipping is done only for special service or attention. Neither service charges nor taxes are added to hotel or restaurant bills.

Medical and emergency facilities. Medical and hospital facilities provide a high standard of care. Hotels usually have a doctor on call for medical emergencies. Water is safe to drink, and there are no snakes or dangerous animals in the country.

In large towns, an emergency system (phone 111) brings immediate contact with police, fire, or ambulance service.

Climate. New Zealand lies in the temperate zone; its climate ranges from subtropical in the north to temperate in the south. Average midsummer temperatures range from 25° C/77° F in the Bay of Islands to 18° C/65° F in Invercargill. Average winter temperatures range from 15° C/59° F in the Bay of Islands to 8° C/46° F in Queenstown. Rainfall varies (it's heaviest on North Island and the West Coast of South Island), but rainy days are distributed throughout the year.

Seasons are reversed from those in the Northern Hemisphere. The busy summer holiday season extends from December to February; late spring and autumn are delightful times to travel in New Zealand.

Miscellaneous. Since New Zealand operates on the metric system, you'll find distances expressed in kilometers, elevations in meters, rainfall in millimeters, weights in grams and kilograms, and temperatures in Celsius.

Electrical current in New Zealand is 230 volts, 50 cycles AC. Most hotels and motels provide 110-volt AC sockets (20 watts) for electric razors only. Appliances that normally operate on a lower voltage require a converting transformer. Most New Zealand power sockets accept three-pin flat plugs (top two pins angled); you'll need a special adapter plug to use most appliances manufactured outside New Zealand.

NORTH ISLAND

Cities, rolling farm lands, volcanic peaks, fishing lakes, and a varied coast

More than 70 percent of New Zealand's 3.1 million people live on North Island. Auckland, the country's largest city, has a population of about 770,000. Wellington, the capital, is home to about 320,000 people. Outside the metropolitan areas are rolling farm lands dotted with grazing sheep and cattle, as well as widely spaced farm towns and coastal settlements. Major inland towns are Hamilton, Rotorua, Taupo, and Palmerston North. Other large towns lie near the coast.

Most of New Zealand's 280,000 Maoris live on North Island, primarily in the northern and eastern districts. Maori legends and customs are still strong here. As you travel around North Island, you'll become aware of the roles played by the missionaries, colonists, and farmers who developed and shaped this young country.

An island overview

Stretched out in the shape of an elongated diamond, North Island extends some 825 kilometers/515 miles from Cape Reinga in the north to Cape Palliser, southeast of Wellington, in the south. Narrow Cook Strait separates the island from neighboring South Island.

North Island's mountain backbone reaches from Wellington northeast to East Cape, a continuation of the alpine fault that created the Southern Alps on South Island. Isolated peaks and ranges mark the land.

Lake Taupo, the Rotorua lakes, and a trio of volcanoes mark the inland plateau. Volcanic activity has shaped this region: eruptions showered ash over the land, and lava flows dammed river valleys forming the Rotorua lakes. You'll see signs of geothermal activity throughout central North Island, from Tongariro National Park north to White Island in the Bay of Plenty.

From forested mountain watersheds, numerous rivers flow into the lakes or to the sea. During earlier years, many lowland rivers served as water highways for Maori canoes and coastal sailing ships. Longest of the nation's rivers is the Waikato, main source of North Island's hydroelectric power.

Along the coast, rugged capes and deep harbors add drama. Long, sandy beaches curving along many bays attract vacationing families, and pleasure boats cruise protected waters.

Only widely separated pockets remain of the vast forests that covered much of North Island when Captain James Cook sailed along these shores. In the early 1800s, kauri timber became the country's chief export; later, settlers cleared lands for farming. Today, fruits, vegetables, and many flowers thrive in North Island's rich soil and mild climate.

Exploitation marked the early years

According to tradition, ancestors of the country's Maori inhabitants sailing in canoes from Polynesia arrived in New Zealand in the 14th century.

Dutch navigator Abel Tasman skirted North Island's southwest coast in 1642, but no European set foot on New Zealand soil until Captain Cook and his party landed at Poverty Bay (near the present site of Gisborne) in 1769.

After accounts of Cook's discoveries were published, interest blossomed. Sealers and whalers roamed the southern seas; by the early 1800s, the Bay of Islands had become their major provisioning and repair base — and New Zealand's first European settlement.

Missionaries, who began arriving in 1814, established mission stations along the coast. Colonizing groups settled at Wellington, Wanganui, and New Plymouth, and timber speculators razed the extensive kauri

Grazing sheep roam the rolling green hills of the King Country southeast of Taumarunui. In New Zealand, sheep outnumber people 20 to 1.

forests. Trading and mill settlements mushroomed on harbors and along navigable rivers.

Maori tribes, who traditionally had battled among themselves, reeled under the impact of European development. To help keep the peace between land-hungry Europeans and the Maoris, the British Government reluctantly annexed New Zealand in 1840 when representatives of the British Crown and Maori chiefs signed the Treaty of Waitangi.

Misunderstandings and ill feeling soon arose over land purchases. In 1860, fighting erupted in Taranaki between Maori warriors and government troops and spread across the central part of North Island. Referred to as the Land Wars, the fighting continued for more than 20 years; it was not until formal peace was declared in 1881 that immigrants could expand into fertile new farmlands south of Auckland.

In the early years, population centered in the Bay of Islands. As settlement increased, the capital was moved southward—from the Bay of Islands to Auckland in 1840, and finally to Wellington in 1865.

Touring North Island

From the main tourist centers to remote, secluded beaches, North Island offers an array of intriguing destinations and activities. Both Auckland, New Zealand's largest city, and Wellington, its capital, are attractive, bustling cities situated on scenic deep-water harbors. Highlights in Rotorua include fascinating thermal attractions and a look at Maori life.

Three national parks and two maritime parks preserve areas of special beauty. Visitors enjoy alpine activities and bush walks in Egmont National Park. You can ski, hike, or explore the varied terrain at Tongariro Park's volcanic preserve. Urewera offers a pair of lovely lakes and trails through dense forest. In the Bay of Islands and the Hauraki Gulf, you cruise amid scattered islands.

If the sea attracts, you'll find busy summer resorts or quiet hideaways along the coasts of Northland, the Coromandel Peninsula, Bay of Plenty, East Cape, Hawke Bay, or along the Tasman Sea. Big-game fishing lures deep-water anglers to warm Pacific waters off Northland and the Bay of Plenty. To sample some of New Zealand's fabled trout fishing, head for Lake Taupo, the Rotorua lakes, or their tributary streams.

You can walk through kauri forests, visit mission stations and colonial dwellings, learn about Maori culture and pioneer history, gaze on thermal attractions, soak up the sun on coastal beaches, fly over active volcanoes, or go fishing or skin diving in the island-studded sea.

Excellent highways cut through the interior of the island and border both the Pacific and Tasman coasts.

Place names reveal a nation's heritage

New Zealand place names reflect the colorful heritage of its Maori people, the navigators and mountaineers who sailed its coastline and explored its mountains, and the settlers who colonized and developed the land.

Early explorers named places for themselves—Cook Strait, Tasman Sea, D'Urville Island, Haast Pass; members of their party—Young Nick's Head, Banks Peninsula; their patrons—Egmont; daily events—Cape Runaway, Cape Kidnappers, Cape Turnagain, Preservation Inlet, Cape Foulwind, Cape Farewell; or geographical landmarks—Bluff, Bay of Islands.

Settlers frequently honored heroes, such as Wellington, Marlborough, Nelson, Hamilton; illustrious statesmen or settlers, including Palmerston, Auckland, Fox, Russell, Lyttelton, Masterton; or their European origins—Norsewood, Balclutha, Dunedin, New Plymouth. Miners and sheepmen added colorful names such as Pigroot and Drybread.

Descriptive Maori names identify many settlements as well as geographical landmarks. These may reflect legendary happenings or actual events, or describe the appearance of the land. Among words often used in Maori place names are these:

Ahi (fire); *ao* (cloud); *ara* (path, road); *aroha* (love); *ata* (shadow); *atua* (god, demon); *awa* (valley, river); *haka* (dance); *hau* (wind); *hui* (assembly); *huka* (foam); *iti* (small); *iwi* (people, tribe); *kai* (food, eat); *keri* (dig); *kino* (bad); *ma* (white, clear); *ma* or *manga* (tributary, stream); *mata* (headland); *maunga* (mountain); *moana* (sea, lake); *motu* (island); *muri* (end); *nui* (big, plenty); *o* (of, the place of); *one* (sand, beach, mud).

Other words include *pa* (fortified village, stockade); *pae* (ridge, resting place); *pai* (good); *papa* (ground covered with vegetation, earth); *po* (night); *puke* (hill); *rangi* (sky); *rau* (many); *roa* (long, high); *roto* (lake); *rua* (cave, hollow, two); *tahi* (one, single); *tai* (coast, sea, tide); *tangi* (sorrow, mourning); *tapu* (forbidden, sacred); *te* (the); *tea* (white, clear); *wai* (water); *whanga* (bay, inlet); *whare* (house, hut); *whenua* (land, country).

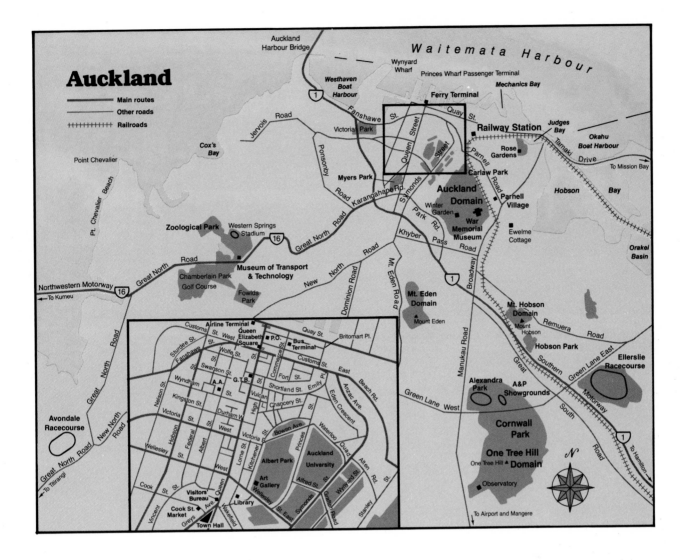

Highway 1 begins at Awanui, north of Kaitaia, and runs the length of the island through Auckland, Hamilton, and Taupo to Wellington. Highway 2 follows the eastern coast along the Bay of Plenty past Poverty Bay and Hawke Bay, then moves inland to its terminus in Wellington. Highway 3 skirts the west coast through the Taranaki and Wanganui regions. Other roads link the main routes and offer scenic alternatives for leisurely motoring.

Cosmopolitan Auckland

Sprawling across a narrow isthmus, Auckland and its far-flung suburbs separate two magnificent harbors.

To the east, at the city's downtown doorstep, lies sparkling Waitemata Harbour, guarded by Rangitoto Island; beyond spread the waters of the Hauraki Gulf and Pacific Ocean. West of the city, the shallow turquoise waters of Manukau Harbour funnel into the Tasman Sea. Protruding from Auckland's landscape are the cones of numerous extinct volcanoes, many of which were once

fortified by Maori tribes. Northwest of the city rise the forested Waitakere Ranges.

New Zealand's largest city, Auckland contains nearly a quarter of the country's population. It's the country's commercial and industrial center, North Island's transportation hub, and the arrival point of most overseas visitors. Enhancing the city's cosmopolitan flavor are a large Maori community, immigrants from various European and Asian countries, and Pacific Islanders attracted by employment and educational opportunities.

New waterfront development and modern shopping and office complexes distinguish Auckland's downtown. In the older suburbs, restored Victorian buildings provide nostalgic contrast. The city's most striking manmade structure is the Harbour Bridge, arcing dramatically across Waitemata Harbour and linking the city with the fast-growing North Shore.

No one lives far from the water, and Auckland's balmy year-round climate (though often hot and humid in summer) encourages water-oriented recreation. On weekends, families flock to the beaches, and hundreds of yachts cruise the sheltered harbors and gulf waters.

Towers of Auckland's commercial district rise against a blue backdrop of Waitemata Harbour. Sailboats dot the water on weekends.

Unlike the country's three other main cities, Auckland was not settled by organized, closely knit colonizing groups. After Auckland became the country's capital in 1840, government officials, tradesmen, and laborers migrated here, but no immigrant ships arrived until 1842. To protect the young town from hostile Maori tribes to the south, four military settlements of the Royal New Zealand Fencible Corps were established on the isthmus at Onehunga, Panmure, Howick, and Otahuhu.

As Auckland's population increased, land-hungry settlers coveting the rich Maori lands to the south soon embroiled the province in the Land Wars. Auckland lost its role as capital in 1865 to Wellington, but commerce generated by the Thames gold fields in the late 1860s helped to revive the city's economy.

Today's wealth comes from development of Northland and Waikato farm lands and industrial expansion on the city's outskirts.

Getting settled in Auckland

Queen Street is downtown Auckland's main thoroughfare. From the Ferry Terminal on Quay Street to Karangahape Road, its route is lined with offices, stores, pedestrian malls, and shopping arcades.

Auckland offers a broad choice of entertainment. For current evening attractions and sporting events, check tourist publications, available at your hotel or from the Visitors' Bureau, or the daily newspapers.

City buses link the downtown district with most tourist destinations (page 24); bus information is also noted in some tourist publications.

Shopping. Serious shoppers will appreciate the city's impressive array of excellent stores and shops, many of them specializing in quality New Zealand crafts.

A leisurely walk through the main shopping district offers many places to pause. Queens Arcade, at the corner of Queen and Customs streets, houses a delightful collection of shops in a setting enhanced by natural light, plants, marble, and mirrors. At 22 Customs Street West, the renovated Old Auckland Customhouse has a new lease on life as a handsome shopping emporium. Shoppers can browse in an Edwardian atmosphere along Strand Arcade.

Shops are generally open from 9 A.M. to 5 or 5:30 P.M. on weekdays, and from 9:30 A.M. to noon on Saturday; some shops in the Downtown Airline Terminal are open daily. Queen Street shops stay open until 9 P.M. on Friday; Thursday is "late night" on Karangahape Road.

Just minutes from Queen Street, Victoria Park Markets re-creates the spontaneous atmosphere of a lively European village food and craft market; it is open daily from 6:30 A.M. to 11 P.M. in renovated buildings on Victoria Street West opposite the park. Near the Town Hall, the Cook Street Market bustles with shoppers on Friday from 9 A.M. to 9 P.M. and on Saturday from 10 A.M. to 4 P.M.

Some delightful shopping areas are located in the suburbs. In Parnell, Victorian buildings along Parnell Road have been transformed into boutiques and specialty shops. In Remuera, one of the city's oldest and most select suburbs, modern arcades vie with fascinating older stores to tempt passersby. Interesting shops dot Ponsonby, one of the long-established western suburbs. In the casual atmosphere of Karangahape Road, you'll find bargains, variety, and a glimpse of Polynesia.

Entertainment. For an evening out, Aucklanders and visitors alike can enjoy dinner and dancing, a cabaret show, musical acts, or a theater restaurant.

Most concerts and recitals take place at the Town Hall. Touring shows, ballet, and stage plays are presented at His Majesty's Theatre; local casts perform at the Mercury Theatre and several smaller theaters. Western Springs Stadium and the Auckland Showgrounds on Greenlane Road in Epsom host special events.

In addition to the City Art Gallery, which features the art of New Zealand, Auckland has numerous downtown and suburban galleries offering changing exhibitions.

Sports and special events. Horse racing takes place at Ellerslie Racecourse and Avondale Racecourse, and night trotting at Alexandra Park Raceway. Spectators can watch Rugby Union games and cricket test matches at Eden Park, Rugby League games at Carlaw Park in Parnell, soccer at Newmarket Park, and men's hockey at Hobson Park in Remuera. Basketball games and wrestling and boxing matches are held at the YMCA Stadium.

The beaches and bays of this city on the water attract thousands of bathers and boaters from November through March. Throughout the summer, yachts sail across harbor waters and amid the islands of the Hauraki Gulf. On the Monday nearest January 29, everyone heads for the Waitemata shore to watch the colorful Anniversary Day Yachting Regatta.

Largest of the country's A & P shows is the New Zealand Easter Show, held at the Auckland Showgrounds in Epsom. An annual event in July is the Auckland International Film Festival. Biennially in March, in even-numbered years, the Auckland Festival highlights all facets of the visual and performing arts.

On foot in downtown Auckland

Queen Street is Auckland's pulse — the district where people go to work, eat, shop, and walk. A leisurely walking tour along Queen Street from the waterfront to Town Hall and back through Albert Park will help you get acquainted with the city.

Between Quay and Customs streets, Queen Street is a pedestrian mall — Queen Elizabeth II Square, marked by a fountain and statues. A few blocks farther up the street, pause to enjoy the greenery and benches in Vulcan Lane; blacksmiths once plied their trade here.

At the Visitors' Bureau in Aotea Square, you can learn about inner city walks and obtain leaflets with maps showing a variety of suggested routes.

Town Hall. Topped by a clock tower, the 1911 Town Hall stands on Queen Street opposite Wakefield Street. A magnificent kauri slab, cut from a 3,000-year-old tree, dominates the foyer; kauri timber was used to panel the city council chamber. The building also houses a large auditorium and a concert hall.

Nearby is Myers Park, a secluded reserve known for its many grand Phoenix palms.

City Art Gallery. A 19th century building at the southwest corner of Albert Park (Kitchener Street and Wellesley Street East) is home for the country's most complete collection of New Zealand art, recording the entire history of European settlement in New Zealand. A modern collection includes representative works by living New Zealand artists. The art gallery is open from 10 A.M. to 4:30 P.M. on weekdays, to 8:30 P.M. on Friday, and from 1 to 5:30 P.M. on Saturday and Sunday.

Albert Park. This peaceful retreat — a lunchtime haven for city office workers — crowns a low hill a few minutes' walk east of Queen Street.

Students from the nearby University of Auckland relax on the lawns, and mothers bring children here to play. Beneath towering trees, a statue of Queen Victoria keeps a watchful eye on the park's fountain, flower beds, and floral clock. On summer Sundays, you can enjoy afternoon band concerts here.

Supreme Court. One of Auckland's first public buildings, this fine example of Gothic revival architecture was built in 1868 at the corner of Waterloo Quadrant and Anzac Avenue. Modeled after England's Warwick Castle, the turreted building is ornamented with stone gargoyles and likenesses of historic figures. Public galleries in the courtrooms are usually open to visitors.

Strolling along the waterfront

Wide and busy Quay Street skirts the downtown waterfront. Just steps from the shopping district, you can observe ocean-going ships maneuvering in and out of berths and watch yachts and other small boats sail across the broad harbor.

At the foot of Queen Street, the gracious old brick Ferry Terminal is a harbor landmark. From here, a small ferry chugs across Waitemata Harbour to Devonport on the North Shore. Launch trips to the Hauraki Gulf islands depart from nearby wharves, and passenger liners tie up at Princes Wharf. Amphibian planes leave from Mechanics Bay at the east end of the downtown waterfront.

Walking west along Quay Street, you'll see fishing boats moored in Freemans Bay. Early risers can catch the activity at the produce markets and seafood bazaar,

Auckland—the essentials

Auckland, New Zealand's largest city, lies between two large harbors. All transportation lines converge here, making it a popular departure point for excursions to all parts of North Island.

Getting there. Most overseas visitors arrive at Auckland International Airport, located at Mangere, about 20 km/13 miles south of the city center. Air service links Auckland with cities throughout New Zealand.

Auckland is the northern terminus of North Island rail service, and daily passenger trains connect the city with Wellington and intermediate points. A network of motorcoach routes links Auckland with North Island's larger towns and tourist destinations. Cruise ships dock at Princes Wharf on Quay Street.

Accommodations. Auckland visitors can choose from a full range of downtown and surburban accommodations.

Leading city hotels are the Sheraton-Auckland, on Symonds Street; Hyatt Kingsgate Auckland, at Waterloo Quadrant and Princes Street; the Regent of Auckland, at Albert and Swanson streets; Auckland City Travelodge, on Quay Street overlooking the harbor; South Pacific, corner of Queen Street and Customs Street East; and Town House, on Anzac Avenue adjacent to Constitution Hill Park.

Smaller, centrally located Auckland hotels include the Royal International, on Victoria Street West; DeBrett, at High and Shortland streets; and Grafton Oaks Courtesy Inn, on Grafton Road near the Domain.

Among the large suburban hotels are the White Heron Regency and Rose Park Hotel in Parnell, Vacation Hotel at One Tree Hill, and Mon Desir Motor Hotel in Takapuna on the North Shore. Near the airport, accommodations include the Auckland Airport Travelodge, Gateway Lodge, and Airport Inn. The suburbs also offer an excellent choice of motels, small private tourist hotels, and guest houses.

Hauraki Gulf accommodations are available on Pakatoa, Waiheke, and Great Barrier islands.

Food and drink. Auckland's cosmopolitan population is reflected in the variety and quality of its more than 200 restaurants. Choices range from elegant to informal settings in restaurants featuring New Zealand seafood and game, continental cuisine, or ethnic fare from many parts of the world. Some restaurants occupy historic buildings; others offer views rivaling the cuisine.

Getting around. Taxis are available at all terminals and on Customs Street West just off Queen Street, or ask your hotel porter to telephone for one. Rental car offices are located at the airport, downtown, or in the suburbs, but avoid city driving if you can—Auckland has one of the highest traffic-to-population ratios in the world.

Buses of the Auckland Regional Authority (ARA) and suburban companies provide public transport throughout the metropolitan area. You can obtain route information by phone (797-119) or from the Bus Place, 131 Hobson Street. Buses depart from several downtown points; the Downtown Bus Centre is located on Commerce Street behind the main post office. Shuttle buses transport passengers between the railway station and Karangahape Road via Queen Street and Greys Avenue (exact change required, varying by zone).

The ferry to Devonport, on the North Shore, departs from the Ferry Terminal on Quay Street. Launches to Hauraki Gulf islands also leave from the waterfront.

Several companies operate half-day and full-day sightseeing tours; longer excursions are also available. Flightseeing trips take off from Mechanics Bay.

Tourist information. The Auckland Visitors' Bureau, 299 Queen Street at Aotea Square, has information on attractions and walking routes; maps and guidebooks are also available. A Travellers' Information Centre at the airport aids incoming visitors and will book Auckland accommodations. To make travel arrangements, schedule tours, and reserve accommodations throughout New Zealand, visit the Government Tourist Bureau, 99 Queen Street. Motoring information is available to members at the Automobile Association office, 33 Wyndham Street.

---

tucked between Sturdee Street and the fishing boat basin. Auctioning starts at about 6 A.M. on weekdays and ends before 10 A.M.

Hilly parks and formal gardens

Numerous extinct volcanic cones jut above Auckland's flat landscape. Most were once fortified by Maori tribes, who terraced the slopes and strengthened their stockades with ditches, earthen ramparts, and wooden palisades. Today, sheep graze and children play on the grassy terraces. You can ride in comfort to these hilly summits for panoramic views over Auckland and its twin harbors.

Other parks and gardens scattered throughout the city present seasonal flower displays and other attractions.

Mount Eden. Auckland's highest point (196 meters/ 643 feet), Mount Eden offers the city's finest view—over the city and water to the distant Waitakere Ranges.

Eden Garden, on Omana Avenue off Mountain Road, is rich with native and exotic trees and shrubs.

One Tree Hill and Cornwall Park. Crowned by an obelisk, One Tree Hill is the city's most striking feature. This *pa*-terraced volcanic cone rises above Cornwall Park between Manukau Road and the Great South Road. In Cornwall Park is Acacia Cottage, Auckland's oldest surviving wooden building (1841).

Mount Albert. Located southwest of the downtown district, Mount Albert is reached via New North Road and Mount Albert Road. You can picnic in a grassy crater.

Alberton, a restored Victorian homestead built in 1862, is open daily at 100 Mount Albert Road. The scene of many parties, it was the social center of Mount Albert in colonial days and still contains many Victorian heirlooms. Indian-style towers and verandas were added to the house in the 1880s; other notable features include the ballroom, the kitchen, and a brick-lined well.

Other parks and gardens. Formal gardens at Ellerslie Racecourse attract visitors even on nonracing days.

Jellicoe Park, off Manukau Road in the southern borough of Onehunga, contains a military blockhouse built in 1860 to protect the settlement from anticipated Maori attacks. A small museum displaying colonial furnishings and other memorabilia is housed in a replica 1840s Fencible cottage; it's open on weekend afternoons.

Auckland Museum crowns a hill

Overlooking the city and Waitemata Harbour from a grassy hilltop in Auckland Domain, the outstanding Auckland War Memorial Museum contains a fascinating collection of exhibits on New Zealand and the Pacific Islands.

Dominating the museum's Maori Court is an impressive war canoe, handcarved about 1835 from a huge totara tree. Other Maori exhibits include tribal buildings, clothing, tools and weapons, personal ornaments, and historic portraits of tattooed chiefs and maidens.

Natural history exhibits show off New Zealand's native birds, trees and plants, sea life and shells, animals, geology, and paleontology. Other exhibits feature the peoples of the Pacific and articles from their daily life, decorative and applied art, and maritime and military memorabilia. Replicas of Queen Street shops of the 1860s line the museum's Centennial Street display. Planetarium shows are presented on Saturday and Sunday.

From the expansive Domain grounds surrounding the museum, you look across Waitemata Harbour to the North Shore. The Cenotaph in front of the museum honors those who served in two World Wars. Down the slope, near the kiosk and duck pond, tropical and subtropical plants flourish indoors in the Winter Gardens.

The museum is open Monday through Saturday from 10 A.M. to 5 P.M. (to 4:15 P.M. in winter), and on Sunday from 11 A.M. to 5 P.M. A free map guides you through the exhibits.

Skirting the harbor on Tamaki Drive

Bordering the city's downtown waterfront, this 11-km/ 7-mile scenic drive follows the shore of Waitemata Har-

bour through the eastern suburbs to St. Heliers Bay.

You'll pass Okahu Bay, a popular anchorage for pleasure boats. Farther on is Savage Memorial Park, honoring New Zealand's first Labour Prime Minister. From Bastion Point, site of wartime harbor fortifications, you can watch maritime activity.

At Mission Bay is the Melanesian Mission Museum, currently closed for reconstruction. Built of Rangitoto stone, it contains relics from the era of bishops Selwyn and Patterson (1842–71), as well as artifacts from Melanesia and the Solomon Islands. Night-lighted Trevor Moss Davis Memorial Fountain is a memorable feature of an evening drive along the harbor.

Mission Bay is a favorite with bathers, as are Kohimarama and St. Heliers. The sheltered beach at St. Heliers vies in size and popularity with Takapuna Beach on the North Shore.

Ponsonby's charming Renall Street

One of a network of narrow streets lacing the northern slopes of the Ponsonby district, northwest of the downtown area, Renall Street retains pleasing traces of the atmosphere and individuality that characterized 19th century Auckland. Preserved along this steep, slender street and forming an intimate community are about 20 wooden cottages, most originally occupied by artisans.

The compact houses sit primly on narrow lots, separate from, yet in harmony with, their neighbors. Verandas adorn the dwellings and picket fences add a unifying touch. Some cottages enjoy views of the harbor. Near the bottom of the angled street is Foresters' Hall, the site of community gatherings during Auckland's early years.

The Auckland City Council has designated Renall Street as a conservation area to ensure the preservation of the buildings. Privately owned and occupied, they're not open to the public. At the Visitors' Center in Aotea Square, you can obtain a leaflet describing some of the dwellings and the neighborhood's development.

Browsing in historic Parnell

One of Auckland's oldest districts has been imaginatively restored to create a lively shopping area that retains the charm of a small town. Within walking distance of the Parnell shopping district are several historic buildings and a handsome rose garden.

To avoid an uphill walk, begin your excursion above the Parnell shops. Seek out the distinctive buildings that appeal to you, then stroll down Parnell Road to enjoy the neighborhood's appeal.

Historic buildings. At the top of the slope, near Parnell Road and St. Stephen's Avenue, are Anglican church buildings associated with Bishop Selwyn, a missionary who arrived in 1842. "Selwyn churches" in the Auckland area are characterized by simple Gothic design, steep shingled roofs, exterior bracing timbers, and diamond-shaped leaded windows. St. Stephen's Chapel, built in

1857 as successor to an earlier chapel, is located off St. Stephen's Avenue at the end of Judge Street; many pioneers are buried in the churchyard. Spired and churchlike Selwyn Court was formerly the bishop's library.

Continuing south on Parnell Road, you'll pass St. Mary's Church, a Selwyn building completed in 1898 and notable for its excellent Gothic design.

On Ayr Street, two fine old 19th century dwellings are now open daily to the public. Kinder House, 2 Ayr Street, was built in 1857 as the home of Rev. Dr. John Kinder, a distinguished churchman and artist. Outside, roses bloom in a Victorian garden.

Shingle-roofed Ewelme Cottage at 14 Ayr Street is also set in a garden. Built in 1863-64 by the Rev. Vicesimus Lush, the kauri-wood dwelling housed his descendants for more than a century. The restored home, open daily, contains many of its original Victorian furnishings.

Parnell's shops. Rejuvenated Victorian dwellings and stores along Parnell Road now house boutiques, jewelry and craft shops, restaurants and food stores, antique furniture shops, and art galleries. Near the top of the hill, Parnell Village is a delightful complex of small shops.

Rose gardens. Hundreds of roses are in peak bloom from November to March in Sir Dove-Myer Robinson Park on Gladstone Road. Mature trees and native shrubs frame a view across Waitemata Harbour, and a walkway leads down to sheltered Judges Bay. Nearby is Parnell Baths, a large salt-water pool open from October to April.

Vintage cars and kiwis in Western Springs

In the Western Springs district, you can visit a transportation museum and pioneer village, and see kiwis in Auckland's zoo.

Pioneer transport. Mechanically minded visitors of all ages delight in the fascinating collection of vintage motor cars, steam locomotives, and aircraft at the Museum of Transport and Technology on the Great North Road, about 5 km/3 miles from central Auckland. The museum is open daily from 9 A.M. to 5 P.M.

An electric tram and a double-decker bus shuttle visitors around the grounds. One exhibit depicts the development of calculating machines, from the abacus to the computer. Other displays highlight agriculture, printing, and photography. Old buildings have been restored and assembled in Pioneer Village.

Zoological Park. Auckland's zoo is one of several places in the country where you can see the kiwi, a flightless nocturnal bird that occupies a special place in the hearts of New Zealanders. In the dim light of the zoo's kiwi house, you watch these unusual birds in a bush setting.

Animals, birds, reptiles, and fish are shown in near-natural settings. Three trails winding through the grounds link the exhibits and a children's zoo. Zoo hours are 9:30 A.M. to 5:30 P.M. daily.

Epsom's Highwic mansion

South of Auckland Domain in Epsom is Highwic, the elegant mansion of Alfred Buckland, a 19th-century Auckland business magnate and landowner. Buckland took over the property in 1862 and constructed the spacious dwelling to house his large family. After his death in 1903, his descendants maintained the property until 1978.

Built in the English manner, the house has vertical boarding, latticed casement windows, and steep slate roofs. Interior details include an elegant staircase, pointed Gothic panels on the doors, and fireplaces enhanced by marble mantels. Surrounded by lawns and gardens, the mansion manages to retain an aura of serenity and seclusion despite its proximity to industrial activity.

The house is open daily from 10:30 A.M. to noon and from 1 to 4 P.M.

New Zealand Heritage Park

Visitors can experience New Zealand's unique culture and life style in a new theme park in a southeastern suburb of Auckland. Just a 10-minute drive from downtown, the park is located off the Ellerslie-Panmure Highway on Harrison Road, about 1½ km/1 mile southeast of the Southern Motorway. It will be open daily from November through March, and from Wednesday through Sunday the rest of the year.

The park consists of three main sections: Natureworld, featuring native plants, a walk-through aviary, and trout pools; Agriworld, highlighting the importance of agriculture, with shearing and milking displays, farm animals, and other exhibits; and Cultureworld, presenting Maori entertainers, craftspeople, and audio visuals on the country's scenery and development. You can try your hand at Maori-style carving, milking a cow, or panning for gold.

Excursions from Auckland

The good beaches rimming the Auckland coast in all directions are a popular weekend destination for many. But other attractions beckon visitors, as well. On day trips from Auckland, you can explore the scattered islands of Hauraki Gulf Maritime Park, visit colonial Howick and rural Clevedon, ride a vintage train near Glenbrook, go wine tasting in the Henderson Valley, or tour the Hibiscus Coast north of Auckland.

Guided motorcoach excursions take visitors through the Auckland countryside; southeast to Coromandel, Waitomo, and Rotorua; and north to the Bay of Islands. Day cruises visit some of the Hauraki Gulf islands.

Flightseeing trips departing from Mechanics Bay on the Waitemata waterfront offer aerial views of the city, harbors, and gulf islands. Flights also serve Pakatoa, Waiheke, and Great Barrier islands.

Shopping is delightful in historic Parnell, where refurbished Victorians now house shops, boutiques, and restaurants.

The beach scene

On fair weather weekends, Aucklanders head for the nearby beaches and bays that provide much of the city's ambience. Most can be reached by public transportation.

Fine beaches abound on the North Shore, bordering Hauraki Gulf. West of Auckland is the more untamed, hilly expanse along the Tasman coast. Closer-in beaches include Okahu Bay, Mission Bay, and St. Heliers, and others southeast of Auckland on Tamaki Strait.

North Shore. From the Ferry Terminal on Quay Street, Devonport is just a short ferry ride across Waitemata Harbour. The town's sheltered shore is backed by a grassy picnic reserve.

Devonport's North Head, a recreation reserve within Hauraki Gulf Maritime Park, offers glorious views of the gulf. Entrance to the reserve is from Takaraunga Road.

Adults enjoy strolling along a water-level trail, while children explore abandoned tunnels and gun emplacements of a former military fort. In January, guides lead walking tours; for information, phone Auckland 771-899.

Takapuna is one of the district's most popular strands. Many homes border beaches along the East Coast Bays, a series of coastal resorts stretching from Milford north to Long Bay. More fine beaches rim the Whangaparaoa Peninsula and Hibiscus Coast near Orewa.

West coast beaches. Along the rugged Tasman coast, great sandy beaches sprawl at the foot of steep forested hills. From roads above the beaches, many trails wind through trees down to the sand. Surfcasters fish from the rocks, and picnickers and hikers roam the beach and bluffs. Ocean surfers ride the waves at Piha and Muriwai Beach; Karekare and Bethells Beach are also popular.

Boating holidays— by yacht, raft, or canoe

Sailing through island-studded waters or sleeping on a yacht anchored in a deserted bay is a dream vacation well within your reach. Increasingly popular in recent years, boating holidays offer a relaxing opportunity to explore another fascinating facet of New Zealand. In the maritime parks, it's the only way to really see the country.

If a more active vacation beckons, you can raft or canoe down scenic rivers. For information on operators and excursions, contact the New Zealand Tourist Office.

Yacht charters. You can explore the coastline and islands at your own pace when you charter a yacht through a commercial operator. You'll cruise leisurely across sheltered gulfs and bays, past verdant islands and golden sand beaches. You stop when you wish for a swim, a barbecue on a lonely stretch of beach, or a bit of fishing or snorkeling. Usually your boat provides accommodation as well as transportation.

Depending on your sailing skills, you can hire a yacht with skipper or arrange for a bareboat charter (without skipper). A boat with skipper is more expensive, but it's relatively hassle-free. The skipper will know where the best beaches and fishing spots are, and how to get the stove to work. Bareboat chartering means that you do your own sailing; your operator will teach you the essentials before you depart.

Most of the charter boats cruise the waters of Auckland's Hauraki Gulf, the Bay of Islands, Lake Taupo, and the Marlborough Sounds. Charter yachts also sail off the Coromandel coast, around the Mercury Bay-Mayor Island area, along the coast of Abel Tasman National Park north of Nelson, and on Lake TeAnau. For information on operators, contact the New Zealand Tourist Office or the New Zealand Charter Yacht and Launch Owners Association, P.O. Box 3730, Auckland.

The main boating season runs from November to Easter; you'll have the largest selection of boats in February and March, when New Zealand children are back in school after their midsummer holidays.

Cruising operators. If you prefer not to charter a boat but still want to enjoy a holiday afloat, you'll find several excursions where you can go along for the ride. You may even be able to learn the ropes and then practice by helping to handle the vessel.

In the Hauraki Gulf, Trans Tours Gray Line (P.O. Box 3812, Auckland) offers a 2-day cruise exploring the bays and rugged coastline of Great Barrier Island. Passengers are expected to help sail the schooner.

If you want to cruise in Fiordland waters, you can take a 3 or 6-day cruise operated by Fiordland Cruises Ltd. of Manapouri. Your boat is a 48-foot-long houseboat, specially designed for cruising the fiords; its shallow draft allows passengers to go ashore in areas that don't have wharf facilities.

Canoeing and rafting. Several commercial companies offer canoe or raft trips down New Zealand's scenic rivers. Canoe and kayak safaris range from a short trip on the Kawarau River to an extended excursion on the Wanganui River or Lake Tarawera.

Also available are rafting trips lasting anywhere from a half-day to 5 days; trips operate on a number of rivers on both islands. Your guide will know the course of the river, the history and geology of the area, and the best camping and fishing spots. For information on excursions, write to the New Zealand Tourist Office.

Hauraki Gulf Maritime Park

For a pleasant day's outing, explore Hauraki Gulf Maritime Park, just off Auckland's eastern coast. The park encompasses all or part of several dozen scattered islands, from the Poor Knights Islands northeast of Whangarei to the Aldermen Islands off the southern part of the Coromandel Peninsula.

On several islands, vacationers can enjoy walks, swimming, boating, and deep-sea fishing. Other islands, inhabited only by wildlife, are remote and hard to reach.

Blue Boat launches leave Auckland's waterfront on scheduled trips to several of the larger islands, including Rangitoto, Motutapu, and Motuihe; ferry service also links Auckland with Waiheke Island. Day cruises depart from the city waterfront for Pakatoa Island. North of Auckland, a ferry departs for Kawau Island daily at 10:30 A.M. from Sandspit, east of Warkworth. During peak holiday periods, additional cruises are available. For a longer trip, consider chartering a yacht.

Amphibian planes take off from Mechanics Bay in Auckland on regular flightseeing and charter trips.

Accommodations are available on Pakatoa, Waiheke, and Great Barrier islands. For more information about park activities, contact the Hauraki Gulf Maritime Park Board, P.O. Box 5249, Auckland 1 (phone Auckland 771-899).

Rangitoto Island. A landmark of Waitemata Harbour, Rangitoto's sloping cone stands sharply against the sky. A favorite picnic spot, the island is a short 40-minute launch trip from the city. A bus meets the boat and takes passengers on a tour. You'll find a tearoom and swimming pool at the wharf and a store and sandy beach at Islington Bay, near the causeway to Motutapu Island.

One of the few peaks not fortified by the Maoris, Rangitoto has little soil and no permanent source of water; yet vegetation thrives in apparently barren conditions. Walkers can stroll from the wharf to Wilson's Park, Flax Point Bridge, and McKenzie Bay. It's a steep 4-km/2½-mile climb to the summit, where you have unsurpassed views of the gulf and city.

Motutapu Island. Linked to Rangitoto by a causeway, this island is farmed by the Department of Lands and Survey. A walkway crosses the farm.

Motuihe Island. Less than an hour from Auckland by boat, Motuihe is a popular day outing. Sheltered picnic grounds, safe sandy beaches, and walking trails abound.

Waiheke Island. Largest of the islands, Waiheke is dotted with small farms. Its lovely bays and beaches attract boaters and anglers. Hotel and motel accommodations are available on the island, accessible by launch or amphibian plane.

Pakatoa Island. Reached by launch from Auckland, Pakatoa has been developed into a resort, open from August through June. The island's beaches and fine views are popular with honeymooners.

Great Barrier Island. Largest of the offshore islands, Great Barrier has a rugged coastline bordered with pohutukawa trees. Deep-sea fishing is a big attraction, with hapuka, kingfish, and snapper the major catches. Guest houses are located at some of the bays. Access is by chartered launch or amphibian plane.

Kawau Island. A summer haven for yachters, Kawau fascinates naturalists and those with a yen for history. A ranger is stationed at Two House Bay (phone Kawau 892).

In 1862, Sir George Grey, an early governor of New Zealand, purchased the island and built his home here. He transformed Kawau into a subtropical paradise of imported trees, plants, and animals. Governor Grey's Mansion House has been restored, and visitors see the house and gardens much as they were in Grey's time. Mansion House is open daily from 9:30 A.M. to 3:30 P.M. (3 P.M. on Friday). Wallabies and kookaburras still inhabit the bush. Cottages and mineshafts date from the 1830s and '40s, when copper and manganese were mined here.

Colonial history in Howick

Dairy farms surround the seaside town of Howick, a colonial settlement that's managed to retain some of its village atmosphere. Located 23 km/14 miles southeast of the city, Howick was the largest of the Fencible settlements (page 22) established in 1847 to defend settlers from possible Maori attack. Buses to Howick depart from Auckland's Downtown Bus Centre.

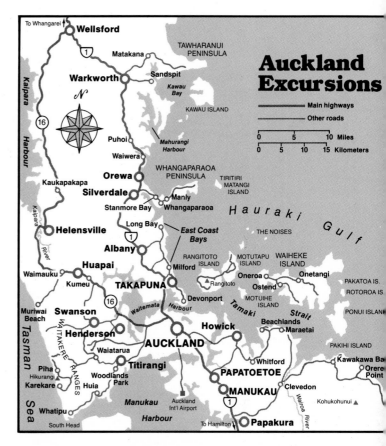

Nineteen colonial buildings from the 1840–1880 era are on display in Howick Colonial Village. Located in Lloyd Elsmore Park on Bells Road, off the main Pakuranga-Howick Highway, the village is open daily from 10 A.M. to 4 P.M. A small kauri plantation features trees and plant varieties popular in Victorian times, and an herb garden flourishes near the village pond.

Stockade Hill commands a view over the countryside and harbor. On Selwyn Road you'll see All Saints' Anglican Church, one of the distinctive "Selwyn churches" and the town's oldest building, dating from 1847. Near the beach is Shamrock Cottage; originally the Fencibles' canteen and later an inn, it's now a tearoom.

In the Garden of Memories on Uxbridge Street are more historic buildings; a small museum is open on Saturday and Sunday afternoons.

Golden beaches and rural villages

If you're driving, continue south to Whitford, then turn east and follow Maraetai Road to a chain of magnificent golden beaches that face Tamaki Strait.

In the village of Clevedon is the Clevedon Woolshed, a wool and craft shop that carries an extensive range of New Zealand products, including spinners' supplies, handspun yarns for weaving and knitting, and hand-crafted articles. Clevedon Country Explorers can arrange tours, farm visits, and demonstrations.

A regional botanic garden is located near Manukau.

A vintage railway

Southwest of Auckland, history buffs can ride on a vintage train and learn about the early settlement of the area.

South of Papakura, Highway 1 passes through fertile rolling farmlands as it ascends toward the Bombay Hills. Near Drury, turn west to Glenbrook and Waiuku.

On Sundays from October to June, locomotives and passenger cars from the early 1900s attract visitors to the Glenbrook Vintage Railway; you can board a train here for a nostalgic journey through the green farm lands.

Nearby Waiuku began as a portage settlement on the South Auckland trade route between Manukau Harbour and the Waikato River. During the 1860s, this area was the scene of conflicts between Maori warriors and settlers. The Waiuku Museum on King Street is open on weekend afternoons.

Market gardens near Pukekohe yield vegetables and fruit in abundance. For a splendid view, drive up Pukekohe Hill southwest of town; you'll gaze over the patchwork of gardens north across Manukau Harbour to Auckland and south to the mouth of the Waikato River.

Wine touring in the Henderson Valley

To become acquainted with New Zealand wines, spend a day touring and tasting in the Henderson Valley northwest of Auckland, heart of New Zealand's wine country. More than a dozen wineries are concentrated here, tucked into valleys at the foot of the Waitakere Ranges. Others are located a bit farther north near the towns of Kumeu, Huapai, and Waimauku.

Neat rows of vines sweep across the land, and huge fig trees cast welcome summer shade. The oldest vineyard in this region is Corbans, established in 1902 on its present site on Great North Road, just outside Henderson. Most of the wineries were established by Dalmatian settlers who originally came from Yugoslavia to work in Northland's kauri gumfields; many are still family operations, run by descendants of the founders.

Most wineries are open Monday through Saturday for tours and sampling. Often you'll talk to the winemakers themselves. Some tours include a winery stop; if you're touring independently, inquire at the Auckland Visitors' Bureau in Aotea Square for directions.

West of Henderson, the 50-km/30-mile Waitakere Scenic Drive follows the crest of the Waitakere Ranges, between Swanson and Titirangi. Bordered by lush tree ferns, the route affords spectacular views over Auckland and its two harbors. A side road leads to the Cascades reserve and Kauri Park. Signposted trails wind through native bush to waterfalls and stands of kauri trees.

Along the Hibiscus Coast

Bordering the Hauraki Gulf north of the Whangaparaoa Peninsula, the Hibiscus Coast is a favorite summer and weekend destination. You drive through rolling green farmlands to Orewa, a leading coastal resort and mecca

Under full sail, yachts race in a strong breeze on Auckland's Waitemata Harbour. The Anniversary Day Regatta takes place here in late January.

for summer campers. Visitor attractions border the beach; ocean surfers frolic in the waters offshore.

Waiwera, about 48 km/29 miles north of Auckland, is noted for its hot mineral spring pools where bathers soak away aches and cares. Visitors can picnic nearby and hike in the surrounding woods. Just north of Waiwera is Wenderholm Regional Park, a beach and riverside reserve.

The farming community of Puhoi retains customs brought by Bohemian immigrants in 1862. Warkworth, on the Mahurangi River, is the site of a giant dishlike antenna linking New Zealand to the worldwide satellite telecommunications system. The Kawau Island ferry departs from nearby Sandspit.

Historic and scenic Northland

If you want to relax in scenic splendor and in a balmy climate, head north! Northland's tourist mecca is the lovely Bay of Islands, cradle of New Zealand's early European settlement. But the region offers far more.

You can picnic on sheltered bays rimmed with crimson-flowering pohutukawa trees, go deep-sea fishing or cruising among scattered islands, or walk along windswept beaches or amid towering ancient kauri trees.

Here you'll find links with explorers Tasman, Cook, and de Surville, as well as tales of Maori conflicts and bawdy whaling days. Anglican and Catholic missionaries set up mission stations here; other settlements thrived on the kauri timber and gum trades.

Whangarei, Northland's port city

The region's commercial and industrial hub is the thriving port city of Whangarei, on the eastern coast. Its sheltered, deep-water harbor has attracted a number of large industries, including the country's only oil refinery and first oil-fired power station.

During holiday periods, coach tours depart from Whangarei for the Tutukaka Coast, the Bay of Islands, and Cape Reinga. Scenic flights can also be arranged.

City attractions. Stop at the City Public Relations Office on Rust Avenue for a map and tourist literature. A 48-km/29-mile scenic drive begins here; it winds through business and residential areas and several parks. Savor the view over city, countryside, and harbor from the summit of Mount Parahaki, then continue east to the suburb of Onerahi.

As it flows along the city's eastern border, the Hatea River cuts through several fine parks, including Whangarei Falls, A. H. Reed Memorial Kauri Park, and Mair Park; here, the river broadens into a natural swimming pool. Trails wind through the forest, and picnic sites abound.

Amid the rose gardens in Whangarei's Cafler Park you'll find the Clapham Clock Museum, containing some 600 clocks of varying age, origin, and design.

On pleasant days, the tree-bordered Town Basin bustles with waterfront activity. You can hire a dinghy, charter a launch, or watch youngsters fish for "tiddlers" off the wharf. Water-skiers skim across the harbor, and families stroll and picnic on nearby beaches.

Whangarei Heads. For an enjoyable outing, take the 35-km/22-mile scenic drive along the harbor's north shore to Whangarei Heads and Ocean Beach. Along the way you'll pass the Parua Bay boat harbor, majestic Mount Manaia, and numerous picnicking, swimming, and fishing areas. A curious reef at Taurikura and the lonely stretch of beach north of Bream Head invite exploration.

Tutukaka Coast. Northeast of Whangarei, a string of beautiful bays and beaches indents the Pacific shore. Known as the Tutukaka Coast, it extends from Ngunguru some 13 km/8 miles north to Sandy Bay. The small resorts of Ngunguru, Tutukaka, and Matapouri offer accommodations for vacationers.

Pohutukawa trees border sandy beaches, where families spread picnic lunches and children splash in the waves. Pleasure boats anchor in sheltered harbors. Along the shore, fishermen surfcast from rocky peninsulas or along the beach at Woolley Bay. Surfers head for Sandy Bay. To reach Whale Bay's delightful cove, you follow a short trail through the woods.

At Tutukaka's marina, parties can charter deep-sea fishing launches for the day (all equipment provided) or arrange for sightseeing or skin-diving trips to the Poor Knights Islands about 19 km/12 miles offshore.

On a leisurely 80-km/50-mile loop, you can return to Whangarei through the Waro Limestone Reserve, where bare outcrops have eroded into unusual shapes and patterns, and the small farming town of Hikurangi.

West to kauri country

Provincial highways loop west from Highway 1 to Kaipara Harbour, Dargaville, the kauri parks, and remote Hokianga Harbour.

A century ago, ships of the kauri timber trade sailed the intricate Kaipara and Hokianga waterways, and small port and mill settlements sprang up along their shores. Today, pleasure boats cruise these lonely waters, and vacationers enjoy quiet holidays along the banks. Between the harbors, two kauri parks preserve portions of the forest that once covered much of North Island.

Kaipara Harbour. Southwest of Whangarei, the fingers of Kaipara Harbour probe deeply into the dairy lands. From the main north-south route, take Highway 12 west toward Maungaturoto. On the northern inlets you can picnic, swim, or camp at several beaches, including Pahi and Tinopai, both south of Paparoa. Numerous boat launching ramps testify to good harbor fishing.

At Matakohe, west of Paparoa, the fascinating Otamatea Kauri and Pioneer Museum chronicles the kauri era. Photographs depict the hard life of the bush-

Northland—the essentials

Tourists head for the lovely Bay of Islands for boating, big-game fishing, and other outdoor activities. Whangarei, at the head of a large, deep-water harbor, is the region's industrial and commercial center; Dargaville, near the west coast, is gateway to the kauri reserves. The center for excursions to the Far North is Kaitaia.

Getting there. From Auckland, direct flights on Mount Cook Line serve the Bay of Islands airport at Kerikeri, with connecting motorcoach service to Paihia. Air New Zealand flights link Auckland with Whangarei, on the east coast, and with Kaitaia, in the north.

Railways Road Services provides scheduled motor-coach service from Auckland to Whangarei, Kawakawa, Bay of Islands tourist centers, and Kaitaia. Buses also connect Auckland with Maungaturoto and Dargaville. Guided tours depart from Auckland for the Bay of Islands and other Northland attractions.

Accommodations. Leading resort in the Bay of Islands is the THC Waitangi Hotel, facing the bay at Waitangi; motel units are also available. In Paihia, you can choose from numerous large motels, such as the Autolodge Motor Inn, Busby Manor Motor Inn, Beachcomber, and Edgewater, as well as many smaller ones catering to family groups. Russell accommodations include the Duke of Marlborough Hotel and Commodore's Lodge, both facing the waterfront, and several smaller motels. You'll also find lodging in Kerikeri.

Elsewhere in Northland, Whangarei has a range of hotel and motel accommodations. In Kaitaia, you'll find the Northerner, Orana Motor Inn, Sierra Court Motel, and Kaitaia Hotel; many small motels are located along Highway 1 and at nearby Ahipara. In game-fishing ports, hostelries such as Kingfish Lodge in Whangaroa cater to anglers.

Getting around. Railways Road Services motorcoaches connect the larger towns and tourist centers. From Dargaville and Kawakawa, there's local service to Rawene, on the south shore of Hokianga Harbour; here, a vehicular ferry provides daytime service between Rawene and the north shore. Rental cars are available in Whangarei, Paihia, Kerikeri, and Kaitaia.

In the Bay of Islands, a passenger ferry links Paihia and Russell; vehicular ferries shuttle automobiles between Opua and Okiato. Motorcoach excursions depart from Paihia and Kaitaia for Cape Reinga and Ninety Mile Beach; local sightseeing trips on land or in the air are also available. Boat excursions leave from Paihia, Russell, and Kerikeri.

Tourist information. Visitors can obtain facts on local attractions and sightseeing tours at tourism offices in Whangarei, Paihia, Russell, Kaitaia, and Dargaville.

man, and you'll see some of the heavy equipment and tools they used in felling and milling the trees. A typical 19th century dwelling, built of kauri, contains hand-crafted kauri furniture and other period articles. Panels show the grain of various native woods, and you can study an outstanding collection of kauri gum.

Birdwatchers can head for Pouto, south of Dargaville near the tip of North Head, where waterfowl nest in shallow fresh-water lagoons.

Dargaville. Bordering the Wairoa River, Dargaville was a thriving port during the heyday of the kauri timber and gum trade. Today, it's a prosperous dairy center and the touring base for Northland's west coast.

Dargaville's museum features articles associated with the kauri industry, as well as local maritime relics; the collection is temporarily housed in the municipal building just north of the post office.

Bayly's Beach, just west of Dargaville, is a favorite summer recreation site and, in winter, a target for toheroa (clam) diggers. It's situated about midway along Northland's longest ocean beach, stretching some 109 km/68 miles from the mouth of Kaipara Harbour north to Maunganui Bluff. Side roads from Highway 12 provide access to this majestic coast at several points.

Near Maropiu, the three Kai Iwi lakes in Taharoa Domain attract trout anglers, sailors, and water-skiers.

Kauri parks. An extensive stand of kauri is preserved in Waipoua Kauri Forest, near the coast about 52 km/32 miles north of Dargaville. As you follow Highway 12 through the forest, towering trees loom above dense undergrowth. Short signposted trails lead through the bush to several of the oldest and tallest trees. In a small cottage museum at forest headquarters, you can see tools and other articles used by early kauri bushmen.

For those who want to linger, Trounson Kauri Park, located about 17 km/10 miles southeast of Highway 12 on the Donnelley's Crossing Road, has a campground and well-defined trails leading into the kauri grove, where you'll see young "rickers" as well as aged giants.

Hokianga Harbour. Carving a ragged inlet in the north-western coast, Hokianga Harbour and its coastal tributaries jut deeply into sparsely populated farm lands. Omapere and Opononi, two small, unpretentious beach towns on the southern shore of the inlet, offer the quiet pleasures of boating, fishing, and exploring.

Two historic buildings on the southern shore are worth a detour. At Rawene is Clendon House, built in the late 1860s by James Clendon, the first United States consul in New Zealand; open daily, it contains many of his possessions. Farther east at Horeke is the 1838 Mangungu Mission House, the oldest Methodist mission building in the country; it's open Saturday through Wednesday. Hours at both buildings are 10 A.M. to noon and 2 to 4 P.M.

A vehicular ferry links Rawene with the Narrows, near Kohukohu on Hokianga Harbour's north coast; from Kohukohu, it's about an hour's drive to Kaitaia.

Highway 12 continues east through Kaikohe, a farming center and site of the outdoor Pioneer Village. Hot mineral baths await travelers at Ngawha Springs. You'll rejoin Highway 1 at Ohaeawai, north of Kawakawa.

The Bay of Islands

What makes the Bay of Islands special? For some visitors it's the scenery—broad vistas of sky and sea blended with wooded islands. For others it's the beaches, boating, and water sports. Some savor its historic sites. Yachters and anglers regard it as one of New Zealand's finest harbors and a top game-fishing area. Residents treasure its unhurried pace, its balmy climate, and its serenity.

Rich in legend and mystery, the Bay of Islands is a microcosm of early New Zealand history, with ties to the Maoris, whalers, missionaries, and early settlers. For decades this quiet pastoral district had few contacts with the outside world. Today, it's a popular holiday resort.

Tourist facilities and accommodations are concentrated at Paihia. Across the bay is Russell, one-time whaling port and now center of game-fishing activities, and headquarters for the Bay of Islands Maritime and Historic Park. Other historic sites include Waitangi (across the river from Paihia), Kerikeri, and Waimate North (pages 34–37). Farming and administrative center of the region is Kawakawa, south of the bay on Highway 1. Nearby is Waiomio Caves, a series of caverns with striking limestone formations and a glowworm gallery.

New Zealand's earliest settlements. The Bay of Islands has lured explorers for many centuries. According to Maori legend, the great Polynesian explorer Kupe visited the bay in the 10th century. Captain Cook, anchoring here in 1769, bestowed the simple name that captures its unpretentious charm. Three years later, the French explorer Marion du Fresne established a temporary base on Moturua Island.

In the early 1800s, sealers and whalers followed Cook's Pacific travels, anchoring in the harbor for ship repair and reprovisioning. An unruly settlement at Kororareka (now Russell) attracted assorted brigands and adventurers. Traders and colonists soon followed.

Next came the missionaries. Rev. Samuel Marsden and his party established an Anglican mission station at Rangihoua Bay in 1814; other missions followed at Kerikeri (1819), Paihia (1823), and Waimate North (1830). A Catholic mission was established at Kororareka in 1838.

By the early 1830s, most of New Zealand's white population had settled along the bay, and Britain appointed a British Resident, James Busby, to deal with problems caused by haphazard settlement. In 1840, Captain William Hobson arrived to negotiate with Maori chiefs. On February 6, 1840, British and Maori representatives signed the Treaty of Waitangi, proclaiming British sovereignty over New Zealand. Later that year the capital was moved south to Waitemata Harbour (Auckland), and the bay's era of influence was over.

The kauri: magnificent forest giant

Today, only a few pockets remain of the vast native kauri forests that once covered much of North Island. Now protected in reserves, these magnificent trees rival California's redwoods in age, height, and girth. Mature kauri trees (*Agathis australis*) can be as old as 2,000 years.

Kauri timber and kauri gum figure prominently in Northland's early settlement. Pioneer settlers cut the slow-growing trees at a rapid rate. The valuable timber became the country's first export—sought after for ships' masts and as a building material. Within a few decades, the vast forests were depleted.

As the timber trade declined, gumdiggers swarmed to Northland to "bleed" the remaining trees and dig the resinous kauri gum—used as a base in slow-drying hard varnishes—from the beds of buried prehistoric forests.

In the forest, the massive, ashen-trunked trees grow only in a few scattered groups, dwarfing smaller trees such as tawa, rimu, kahikatea, towai, and northern rata. They can reach 52 meters/170 feet in height with a maximum girth of 15 meters/50 feet. As the tree grows, its lower branches drop off naturally, yielding a tall, straight-grained, ash-colored trunk. In mature trees, the first branches appear high off the ground.

You can see kauri growing with other native trees in several forest reserves. Largest of these is Waipoua Kauri Forest, north of Dargaville on the west coast (page 32).

At Matakohe, west of Paparoa on Highway 12, the Otamatea Kauri and Pioneer Museum (page 31) focuses on the days when kauri was king. You'll also learn about the kauri timber and gumdigging industries at museums in Kaitaia, Dargaville, and Russell.

A maritime and historic park. Many island and mainland reserves and historic areas — extending from Whangaroa Harbour in the north to Whangaruru Harbour, south of Cape Brett—have been brought together in the Bay of Islands Maritime and Historic Park. Many historically significant sites, as well as scenic and recreational lands, are included within its boundaries. At the park visitor center on The Strand in Russell, you'll learn more about this delightful region and the feast of activities awaiting you: swimming, picnicking, fishing, boating, skin diving, camping, walks and hikes, scenic drives, charter boat trips, and visits to historical sites. Midsummer visitors can join in guided excursions.

Park information is available from the chief ranger in Russell (P.O. Box 134; phone Russell 685), from the ranger in Kerikeri (P.O. Box 128; phone Kerikeri 78-474), or from the information officer, Bay of Islands Maritime and Historic Park, P.O. Box 5249, Auckland (phone Auckland 771-899).

A fascinating water world. Sports enthusiasts from around the world come to fish these fabled waters, first popularized by American writer-fisherman Zane Grey in the 1920s. Other visitors skin-dive in the subtropical waters or cruise amidst the islands. The Bay of Islands is a favored port of call for large yachts and cruise ships.

More than a dozen game-fishing boats are available for charter, either for day or overnight trips. The main summer season extends from November through May and is climaxed by a major competition in early May.

Colorful subtropical fish glide through these clear seas, and corals and sponges thrive in the deeper water. Cape Brett is a favorite spot for divers; you can arrange for transportation and equipment in Paihia.

On the Paihia and Russell waterfronts, you can rent small boats by the day or week; charter boats are available at Opua and Russell (page 28).

Boat trips. To fully appreciate the beauty of this fabled, island-strewn bay, plan to cruise amid the wooded islets and explore the sparsely populated shore.

Best known of the boat excursions is the Cream Trip, named for a coastal launch route of the 1920s that collected cream and delivered mail and supplies to scattered dairy farms. You sail along the coast and among the islands; on some trips, you stop to deliver mail, newspapers, and freight to waiting islanders.

Another favorite is the launch or catamaran cruise to Cape Brett, where a lighthouse marks the bay entrance. You'll circle Piercy Island, cruise into Cathedral Cave, and pass through the Hole in the Rock. Schoolfish (which attract marlin) and dolphins abound in these waters.

During holiday periods, a replica of one of the early coastal steamers departs from Kerikeri for a trip on the Kerikeri Inlet (page 36).

Water taxi service links the resorts with the islands and more remote bays. You can arrange a trip to Moturua or Motukiekie Island, for example, and hike the trails that connect one beach to the next. After transporting your party to the site, the boat returns at a prearranged time. Take along a picnic and, if you like, fishing tackle or snorkeling equipment.

Paihia, busy harbor resort

Strung out along the waterfront, Paihia is the accommodations and excursion center for visitors to the Bay of Islands. The tourist information office is on Williams Road, across from the post office.

Busiest spot in town is the Paihia Pier, jutting into the bay at the end of Williams Road, where excursion launches, game-fishing boats, water taxis, and the passenger ferry jockey for position. In the nearby Maritime Building you can book tours and excursions, charter boats, and make other travel arrangements.

Motorcoach excursions depart daily from Paihia for Cape Reinga, the kauri forests, and other historic Northland destinations. You can arrange aerial sightseeing trips, also.

On the Paihia waterfront, a memorial church stands on the site of the original Paihia Mission Station. Nearby, a carved arch marks the entrance to the Ti Beach *marae*, where Maori chiefs and warriors camped before crossing the river to discuss and sign the Treaty of Waitangi.

Permanently moored near the Waitangi Bridge is the three-masted barque *Tui*. Now the Museum of Shipwrecks, it displays gold coins, jewelry, and other articles salvaged from Northland marine disasters.

Historic Waitangi

Across the river from Paihia, Waitangi National Reserve surrounds the historic Treaty House, symbol of New Zealand's birth as a nation. You can walk through the restored house and stroll beneath century-old trees on the spacious, well-kept grounds overlooking the Bay of Islands. The Treaty House is open daily from 9 A.M. to 5 P.M.

It was here, on the lawn in front of the house, that representatives of the British Government and Maori chiefs signed the Treaty of Waitangi on February 6, 1840. The Maori people voluntarily accepted British rule, New Zealand became part of the British Empire, and Maoris and Europeans were granted equal status as British subjects. Each year on February 6, an impressive evening ceremony commemorates the anniversary.

The Georgian-style Treaty House was built in 1833-34 by James Busby, after his appointment as British Resident. Wings were added to the original three-room dwelling in the 1870s. Inside, visitors find a small collection of Maori artifacts, paintings and photographs, and articles associated with the area's early settlement and the treaty signing. In front of the house, a tall flagstaff marks the signing site.

Nearby, the Waitangi *whare runanga* (meeting house) reflects traditional Maori craft skills. A gift to the nation from the Maori people during the 1940 centennial celebration, the building is unique in that its wall carvings are the work of many different North Island tribes.

Below the house, an open-air pavilion shelters a 36-meter/118-foot kauri war canoe. During the centennial festivities, 80 Maori warriors paddled the canoe from across the bay. A riverside trail begins here.

One of the country's finest 18-hole golf courses is nearby on Waitangi National Reserve, overlooking the bay.

Russell—whaling port to fishing center

Russell's tranquil waterfront belies the town's wild and bawdy origins as the whaling port of Kororareka. Beginning in the early 1800s, sealing and whaling ships anchored here. Despite the efforts of the missionaries, Kororareka was a lawless town, crowded with grog shops and Maori shipgirls who catered to the rough seafarers.

European traders and colonists soon followed, and by 1830 there was a sizable settlement. Soon after British control was established, conflict developed between British troops and disgruntled Maoris who resented white authority. Four times Chief Hone Heke chopped down the British flagstaff in an effort to rid his land of the newcomers. On the final attempt in 1845, his rampaging warriors also sacked the town.

Today, Russell is a peaceful retreat with an old-world charm—though it bustles in season with vacationers and sailors from the yachts and launches anchored offshore. Big-game fishing is the leading topic of conversation, and when word spreads of a major catch, crowds gather on the wharf for the weigh-in.

You can arrange for boat trips, water-skiing, big-game or line fishing, and charter boats here. A short sightseeing tour by mini-bus departs from the wharf.

Along The Strand. Buildings along The Strand — Russell's waterfront promenade—face the curve of a deep blue bay. At the Bay of Islands Maritime and Historic Park visitor center, you can get information about park activities.

Facing the wharf is the Duke of Marlborough Hotel, rebuilt for the fourth time in 1932. Nearby is the Police Station, originally the port's customs house, and at one time the courthouse and jail.

At the south end of The Strand is Pompallier House, built in 1841-42 to house the printing presses of the country's first Roman Catholic mission; the presses and other historic items are displayed inside. It's open daily from 10:30 A.M. to 12:30 P.M. and from 1:30 to 4:30 P.M.

At the end of the beach is a restored bungalow, built in 1853 by Captain James Reddy Clendon, the first American consul. Replicas of the Crown jewels of England are displayed in the Jewel House on The Strand.

Other attractions. New Zealand's oldest church is still in use at the corner of Church and Robertson streets. Built in 1835-36 by local settlers, Christ Church also served as courthouse and public hall. It still bears bullet holes and battle scars from the 1845 conflict; in the cemetery are the graves of those who died defending the settlement, as well as the remains of whalers, early settlers, and Maoris.

In Captain Cook Memorial Museum on York Street are relics of Kororareka and a seaworthy scale model (1/5 size) of Cook's barque H.M.S. *Endeavour*.

Overlooking the Bay of Islands, Waitangi Treaty House symbolizes New Zealand's birth as a nation. Maori and British officials signed an historic treaty here in 1840.

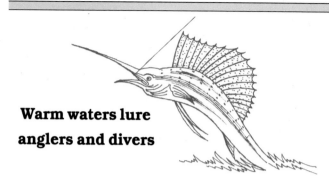

Warm waters lure anglers and divers

Anglers come from around the world to challenge the big, fighting game fish lurking in the warm Pacific coastal waters off North Island. Surf fishing is also popular here, as is snorkeling and scuba diving among the islands and reefs that border the long, irregular shore.

Big-game fishing. Along the coast from North Cape southeast to Cape Runaway, deep-sea anglers congregate in search of New Zealand's big-game fish: black and striped marlin, broadbill swordfish, shark (mako, thresher, hammerhead, and tiger), yellowtail (kingfish), and five species of tuna.

Activity centers in the Bay of Islands, but big-game fishing bases are also located at Whangaroa, Whangarei (Tutukaka), Whitianga (Mercury Bay), Tauranga (Mayor Island), and Whakatane (Whale and White islands). Though you can fish any time of year, you'll reel in the best catches from mid-January through April.

Since all the fishing bases are less than 200 miles from Auckland, anglers can enjoy a day of challenging fishing even if their time is limited. Charter boats, available in coastal resorts, provide equipment and tackle, and no license is required. For more information, contact the New Zealand Tourist Office.

Many visiting anglers join a local fishing club. A nominal membership fee entitles members to use club facilities, have their catches weighed and recorded, and partake of the general club conviviality.

Surf fishing. On weekends, you'll see surfcasters on just about every stretch of beach and rocky shoreline. Local camps and stores near the beach sell tackle and bait, and some rent equipment.

Surfcasting is popular during the summer, but some of the best fishing comes in the colder months of March to November. An annual contest on Ninety Mile Beach every January attracts hundreds of participants.

Underwater activities. Snorkelers and scuba divers also head for North Island's northeastern coast. Good diving areas lie offshore, from Three Kings Islands off the northernmost tip south to the Bay of Islands, Hauraki Gulf, Coromandel Peninsula, and Bay of Plenty.

The waters surrounding Poor Knights Islands, off the Tutukaka Coast east of Whangarei, are regarded as a marine sanctuary rich in exotic and colorful underwater life. Huge sponges and lacy corals cluster on vertical rock faces well below the surface. Reefs surrounding volcanic Mayor Island are also particularly lush.

Good South Island diving areas are located off the northern tip of the island, along stretches of the eastern and southwestern coasts, and around Stewart Island.

The best diving season is January to May, but many locals dive the year around. You'll need a wet suit in winter and for prolonged diving. Though winds sometimes make diving uncomfortable, divers don't need to worry about sharks.

Charter planes or boats transport divers from coastal towns to offshore islands and reefs. Some boats even provide gear, though you can rent or buy diving equipment in Auckland or in coastal towns. Paihia, in the Bay of Islands, has a thriving dive center.

Several dozen diving clubs are located throughout the country. All are affiliated with the New Zealand Underwater Association, P.O. Box 875, Auckland. Often club members serve as guides, though professional diving guides are also available. Some clubs organize excursions to popular diving areas.

For a splendid panorama, take the road to the summit of Maiki Hill (Flagstaff Hill). Swimmers can head for Long Beach, just across the peninsula facing Oneroa Bay.

Kerikeri for history, citrus, and crafts

Historic Kerikeri was founded as a mission station in 1819, second of the area's settlements established by the Church Missionary Society of London. Two of the country's oldest buildings, both open to visitors, overlook the head of Kerikeri Inlet. At high tide, pleasure boats sail up the inlet and anchor near the wharf.

Inland, tall hedgerows hide orchards of oranges and other citrus fruits. Other subtropical fruits grown here include kiwifruit, feijoas, passion fruit, and tamarillos.

In recent years, Kerikeri has attracted many artists and craftspeople, who display their work in local shops.

New Zealand's oldest surviving building is porticoed Kemp House, surrounded by an old-fashioned garden. Completed in 1822, it was part of the original settlement, and missionaries lived here until 1832, when it became the home of the Kemp family. Now operated by the New Zealand Historic Places Trust, it's open daily.

The two-story Stone Store, built in 1833, once housed Bishop Selwyn's library; now it contains a souvenir shop and a small museum of mission-related items.

The hillside across the river basin offers a fine view of the old buildings. You can also visit Rewa's Village, a replica of a pre-European unfortified Maori village.

During school holiday periods, you can explore Kerikeri Inlet aboard the M.V. *Ernest Kemp*, a replica of the shallow-draft steamers which operated along the coast in the early 1900s.

Several easy trails lead to destinations along the Kerikeri River. Ask for trail information and a map at the ranger station.

At Waimate North, a mission house

Inland from the Bay of Islands at Waimate North stands the Waimate Mission House, built in 1831-32 and the sole surviving building of a once-thriving mission farm. Of New Zealand's historic buildings, only Kemp House at Kerikeri is older.

Last of three similar late Georgian-style houses built in the mission's early years, the building is designed symmetrically around a central stairhall. In the 1870s, a gabled roof replaced the original hip roof and dormer windows. Period furniture and missionary items recall the early days. You can visit the house daily from 10 A.M. to 12:30 P.M. and from 1:30 to 4:30 P.M.

Nearby is the Church of St. John the Baptist, built in 1871. Its oak-shaded churchyard contains carved wooden grave markers unique to Northland.

Coastal route to the Far North

From the Bay of Islands, two roads head north to New Zealand's northern tip. Highway 1 follows a direct inland route to Kaitaia; Highway 10 skirts Whangaroa and Mangonui harbors and Doubtless Bay as it winds along the eastern coast. Narrow side roads branch off Highway 10 to coastal settlements and remote coves and beaches; mangrove trees grow in many tidal estuaries in this subtropical area.

Whangaroa Harbour. North of Kaeo, a road branches off to Whangaroa, where eroded volcanic pinnacles and steep timbered slopes enclose the calm harbor. Wooden houses with gabled roofs peek out from between the trees. Whangaroa attracts deep-water anglers who come here to fish the waters around the Cavalli Islands.

The only way to fully appreciate the inlet's scenic setting is by boat. From September through May, sightseeing cruises from Whangaroa follow the shoreline to the narrow-necked harbor entrance. Day trips and big-game fishing charters can be arranged.

A coastal road loops east from Whangaroa to fine ocean beaches at Wainui and Matauri bays.

Mangonui. Houses climb the rolling hills encircling attractive Mangonui Bay. In the early days, the harbor was the gateway to the Far North and served as a whaling base and mill port for ships engaged in the kauri trade.

Today, local fishing boats tie up at Mangonui's wharf. It also houses the Mangonui Sea Lab and Aquarium, which contains marine life found in local waters. Small boats anchor at Mill Bay. For a sweeping view over Mangonui and Doubtless Bay, take the road to the Rangikapiti *pa* site overlooking the harbor.

Doubtless Bay. According to Maori legend, the great Polynesian explorer Kupe landed at Taipa centuries before the "great migration" south from Hawaiki. In 1769, Captain Cook sailed past the entrance and named the bay; eight days later, French explorer de Surville anchored here and narrowly escaped being wrecked.

Splendid beaches along the shore attract families during holiday periods. Surfcasters and shell collectors enjoy Tokerau Beach; skin divers favor Matai Bay and Cape Karikari. Game fishing is excellent outside the entrance to the bay.

Kaitaia, hub of the "winterless north"

Shaped by decades of geographical and cultural isolation, the sparsely populated Far North retains an elusive quality that attracts an increasing number of visitors. Many residents are descendants of Dalmatian gumdiggers who stayed on to wrest a living from scrubby lands.

Tourist and commercial center of the Far North is Kaitaia, which was, in turn, a Maori village, an 1830s mission station, and a boom town for kauri gumdiggers. For today's visitors, it's the departure point for motorcoach trips to Cape Reinga and Ninety Mile Beach and for exciting safaris to remote beaches by expanded dune buggy. Scenic flights over the Northland countryside depart from Kaitaia Airport.

Stop first at the Far North Regional Museum on South Road (open daily) to obtain tourist information and learn more about the Far North.

Pride of the museum is its de Surville anchor, lost at the bottom of Doubtless Bay in 1769 and recovered for the museum in 1974. Photographs and artifacts recall pioneering days in the kauri forests, gumfields, and flax lands. You'll also see missionary relics, a large collection of kauri gum, and other excellent displays.

A 15-minute drive through dairy lands takes you to Ahipara, at the southern end of Ninety Mile Beach. From the hills sheltering the bay, you gaze northward along a magnificent sweep of sand.

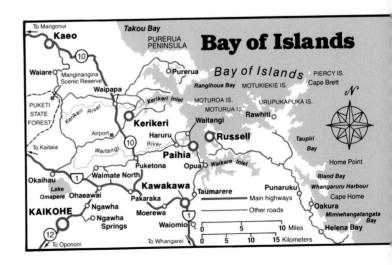

Neat houses on wooded slopes ring Mangonui Harbour, an inlet of Doubtless Bay. Mangonui began as a milling center and shipping port for the kauri timber trade.

For an adventurous day exploring windswept beaches and secluded coves, sign up for a trip by 38-seat dune buggy; it travels from Kaitaia to Wreck Bay, the gumfields, and wave-cut Reef Point.

North to Cape Reinga

From Kaitaia, a narrow road wends 116 km/72 miles north along the Aupouri Peninsula to Cape Reinga, popularly regarded as the country's northernmost point (cliffs on North Cape actually extend slightly farther north).

Motorcoach tours depart each morning from Kaitaia and Paihia for Cape Reinga, returning along the peninsula's Ninety Mile Beach. Depending on the time of high tide, the route may be reversed. Though the bus follows Te Paki Stream from the main road to the coast, quicksand in the stream bed makes this route unsafe for other vehicles.

At Houhora Heads, motorcoaches pause at the Wagener Museum, a collector's storehouse of exhibits ranging from natural history and Maori artifacts to old-time phonographs and washing machines in working order. Houhora, once the center of gumdigging activity, still boasts New Zealand's most northerly tavern.

Beach grasses and the young pine trees of Aupouri Forest are reclaiming some former gumfields and dunes. Near the peninsula's tip, the road winds through Te Paki Coastal Park before emerging at Cape Reinga.

Cape Reinga. A trail leads out to the cape's lonely lighthouse, perched 165 meters/541 feet above the waves. At night its light can be seen about 50 km/30 miles offshore. Below, two mighty bodies of water — the Pacific Ocean and Tasman Sea — collide in foamy combat. Views stretch west to Cape Maria van Diemen, first sighted by Tasman in 1642, and east across Spirits Bay toward North Cape.

Below the lighthouse, a twisted pohutukawa tree clings to the headland. According to Maori legend, the spirits of departing Maoris pass down its exposed roots into the sea on their underwater return voyage to legendary Hawaiki.

The northernmost of the New Zealand Walkways routes begins at Spirits Bay. It skirts the coastline around Cape Reinga and Cape Maria van Diemen; then for some 83 km/51 miles it follows the beach from Te Paki Stream south to Ahipara. Several camping and picnicking areas in the park are equipped with fireplaces, fresh water, and toilets; for information on park facilities, contact the ranger at Waitaki Landing, Private Bag, Kaitaia (phone Te Kao 521).

Ninety Mile Beach. The magnificent white sand stretches along the Tasman all the way to Ahipara. Surfcasters converge here during the New Year holiday to compete in a big surfcasting contest. As the bus speeds along the firm clean sand, it splashes through occasional streams and scatters flocks of skittish shore birds. Off season, you may have the entire coast to yourself.

The Waikato

Today, the lush green rolling hills south of Auckland bear few scars of the turbulent era over a century ago when this region was a battleground between land-hungry European settlers and Maori warriors seeking to protect their tribal grounds. The disputes began in the 1850s when settlers pushed southward seeking to buy — and later to confiscate — rich Maori lands in the Waikato. Misunderstandings arose between Maori and *pakeha*, and the Land Wars raged here for more than 20 years.

From Auckland, Highway 1 cuts southeast across the peaceful Waikato plains toward Hamilton. For much of the way, the route parallels the Waikato River, which gives its name to this broad area south of Auckland. The river, the country's longest, flows from Lake Taupo some 354 km/220 miles to meet the Tasman Sea south of Manukau Harbour. Main source of North Island's hydroelectric power, the Waikato is harnessed by a series of dams and power stations. Boaters and water-skiers enjoy the reservoir lakes behind the dams.

Busy Hamilton

Hamilton, hub of the Waikato plains and New Zealand's largest inland city, straddles the Waikato River about 138 km/85 miles south of Auckland. From its origin as a military settlement in 1864, Hamilton has grown into a busy farming, industrial, and agricultural research center.

Dubbed the fountain city, Hamilton is rich in parks and gardens. The main commercial and shopping district lies west of the river; Victoria Street is its principal thoroughfare. In the heart of the city is Garden Place, a landscaped pedestrian mall.

A 48-km/30-mile scenic drive begins at the Chief Post Office on Victoria Street. For information on city walks and local attractions, visit the Public Relations Office, in the Irvin & Stern Building on Barton Street.

Parks and gardens. Parks border both banks of the placid Waikato, which meanders through the city. On the western shore, strollers enjoy Ferrybank Park, where steamers and ferries docked in Hamilton's early years. Parana Park and Memorial Park rim the eastern bank.

Hamilton's largest and most popular park borders Lake Rotoroa (often called Hamilton Lake), an aquatic and recreational playground just southwest of the central district.

Floral displays take the spotlight in Rogers Rose Gardens and Hamilton Gardens. Jubilee Park preserves a remnant of the native forest that once covered this district.

Other attractions. The Waikato Art Museum, 150 London Street, features a Maori gallery dominated by a long war canoe and exhibits on the history of Hamilton and the Waikato district. It's open daily except Monday.

Centrally located in Boyes Park is the Founders' Theatre, opened in 1963. The Riverlea Performing Arts Centre is located southeast of Hamilton off Highway 1.

Northwest of the business district, Hilldale Zoo Park on Brymer Road has an extensive collection of animals and birds; you can visit daily from 9 A.M. to 5 P.M.

Swimmers will enjoy the impressive facilities of the indoor-outdoor Centennial Swimming Pool complex on Garnett Avenue. Nearby, racing fans watch some of New Zealand's best horses compete at the Te Rapa Racecourse. For trotting contests and greyhound racing, visit Claudelands Showgrounds, which also hosts the Waikato A & P Show and other annual events.

Touring the western Waikato

From Hamilton, you can venture north to a Maori village at Ngaruawahia and the Waingaro thermal baths, west to the coast at Raglan, south to an agricultural museum and the Waitomo Caves (page 40), and east to gracious Cambridge and horse-breeding country (page 41).

Ngaruawahia. The largest Maori *pa* in the country is at Ngaruawahia, 18 km/12 miles north of Hamilton at the junction of the Waikato and Waipa rivers. Home of the Maori king movement, Turangawaewae *marae* is the official residence of the present monarch, Queen Te Atairangikaahu. The best view of the buildings is from across the Waikato River. On Regatta Day in mid-March, Maori canoe races and other competitions take place here.

Waingaro. First known to the Maoris, this bubbling thermal spring 22 km/14 miles west of Ngaruawahia became a popular stagecoach stop on the Raglan road. Extensively developed in recent years, the baths offer sulphur-free waters in thermal pools, spa pools, and water slides.

Raglan. Normally quiet and peaceful, Raglan, situated 48 km/29 miles west of Hamilton, becomes a busy seaside resort during holiday periods. Anglers find excellent harbor and surf fishing here and, in season, whitebait in local streams. Surfers ride long, curling waves at Whale Bay.

Clydesdale Museum. Learn about New Zealand's agricultural pioneers at the country's largest agricultural museum, located at Mystery Creek, 16 km/10 miles south of Hamilton near the airport. You'll see implements used by pioneer farmers, examples of rooms in which they lived, and demonstrations of early farming methods. Historic buildings have been moved to the site, and the National Dairy Museum is located here.

Te Awamutu. Rose gardens bloom at the northern entrance to town. You can learn about regional history in the Te Awamutu Museum in the Civic Centre on Roche Street. Picnickers and boaters head for Lake Ngaroto north of town; trails in Pirongia Forest Park attract hikers.

Otorohanga. Farther south on Highway 3, Otorohanga is known for its bird park, where you can see kiwis and other native birds; it's open daily from 10 A.M. to 4 P.M.

Kawhia Harbour. Remote Kawhia, 60 km/37 miles west of Otorohanga on Highway 31, offers the timeless fascination of a remote settlement bypassed by main road and rail routes. Traders and missionaries arrived here in the 1830s. White settlers were ousted during the Land Wars, and the port never regained its early vigor.

In season, launches depart from Kawhia's wharf on harbor sightseeing trips. On Te Puia Beach, hot springs well up through the sands, and you can scoop out your own hot pool at low tide.

Exploring the Waitomo Caves

In the rugged hills south of Otorohanga, subterranean limestone outcroppings have been transformed into a series of spectacular caves. Three of these are open to visitors—the famous Waitomo Caves, renowned for their dramatic formations and a magical glowworm grotto.

You can visit the caves on a guided tour, conducted at regular intervals daily from 9 A.M. to 4:30 P.M.; wear walking shoes and bring a sweater.

Waitomo Cave. Highlight of the 45-minute tour is a boat ride, where you'll glide silently along an underground river in a flat-bottomed punt into a cavern spangled with the radiant blue green lights of thousands of tiny glowworms. You'll see some close up, their long, sticky "fishing lines" hanging to snare insects attracted by the lights.

Striking limestone formations include the famous Organ and the lofty chamber called the Cathedral.

Ruakuri and Aranui caves. Less frequently visited, these caves are about 3 km/2 miles beyond the Waitomo Cave entrance. They can be toured twice daily, in the morning or the afternoon; schedules are timed to coordinate with tours of the main cave.

Largest of the caves is Ruakuri, a fantastic complex of underground caverns resounding with the roar of a hidden waterfall. An underground river mysteriously appears and disappears in the cave.

Smallest and loveliest of the three caves is enchanting Aranui, noted for its delicate fluted limestone formations and unusual colorings.

Other attractions. Near the caves you can visit a replica Maori *pa* in Ohaki Maori village. Te Anga Road heads west to Mangapohue Natural Bridge, where a stream flows through a deep, narrow gorge and beneath a large limestone arch tunneled thousands of years ago by an underground river. At Marokopa Falls, the river plummets in a series of spectacular waterfalls. The road ends at the seaside fishing settlement of Marokopa, 48 km/29 miles from Waitomo.

Waikato—the essentials

Hamilton is the hub of the Waikato and the touring center for exploring the district. To the south are the famous Waitomo Caves and the rugged King Country.

Getting there. Air New Zealand offers direct flights to Hamilton from Wellington, and commuter airlines link the Waikato with Auckland. The Northerner and Silver Fern trains serve Hamilton, Te Awamutu, Te Kuiti, and Taumarunui on the main Auckland-Wellington line. Railways Road Services motorcoaches provide daily service to Hamilton and other Waikato towns from Auckland, Rotorua, Taumarunui, and other towns.

Accommodations. Visitors can choose from a wide selection of motor inns, small hotels, and motels in Hamilton. At Waitomo Caves, the THC Waitomo Hotel offers gracious hospitality in a relaxed country setting. Small motels are available in country towns.

Getting around. Main line rail service and Railways Road Services motorcoaches link the main towns. Round-trip excursions operate daily from Auckland and Rotorua to the Waitomo Caves. Rental cars are available in Hamilton.

Tourist information. Travelers can obtain maps and local sightseeing information at visitor information offices in Hamilton, Cambridge, Matamata, Otorohanga, Paeroa, Te Aroha, and Te Awamutu.

The rugged King Country

It was not until formal peace was made in 1881, ending the Land Wars, that the government could extend its North Island rail line south to open up new farm lands. Highways 3 and 4 link the farming centers of the King Country with major markets. Te Kuiti, just south of the Waitomo turnoff, is a farming, mining, and timber town with a rich Maori heritage. Of special interest is the carved meeting house built in 1878 (ask permission before visiting). South of Te Kuiti, Highway 3 bends southwest, cutting through the scenic Awakino Gorge to the coast.

At Eight Mile Junction, Highway 4 veers southeast through the heart of the King Country to Taumarunui, a farming and timber center at the confluence of the Ongarue and upper Wanganui rivers. For generations, Maori canoes plied these inland waterways; today, canoeing parties still take to the scenic Wanganui River. From Taumarunui, highways lead east to Lake Taupo and south to Tongariro National Park.

Traveling in the eastern Waikato

East of Hamilton, highways crossing the plains toward the Kaimai Range pass through lush pasture land. Stud farms, where thoroughbred race horses are bred and trained, cluster around Cambridge and Matamata. South Waikato's prosperity is based on timber.

Cambridge. Both its name and its tranquil setting lend an English flavor to Cambridge, a river town on the Waikato 23 km/15 miles southeast of Hamilton. Giant trees, stately churches, and a village green add to the town's gracious charm. The Public Relations Office is in the public library on Victoria Street.

Visit the Cambridge Cultural Centre, just north of the town clock tower; then stop in Te Koutu Domain, where trees border an attractive lake. Southeast of town is Lake Karapiro, farthest downstream of the Waikato reservoirs and a favorite for water sports.

Putaruru. On Highway 1 just south of Putaruru, a timber museum is being developed. Plans call for a restored sawmill complete with forest tramway, historic buildings, and exhibits on the district's old timber mills.

Matamata. In Matamata, a historic area preserves Firth Tower, built about 1880 as a lookout and retreat in the event of an invasion by hostile Maoris; it's now a museum and art gallery.

Te Aroha. The area's mineral springs have spawned several spas and resorts, the best known of which is Te Aroha, a fashionable Victorian spa complete with quaint buildings. Public and private thermal pools are open daily. Marked trails lead through the woods, and a bus transports visitors to the summit of Mount Te Aroha.

Paeroa. Once a river port, today Paeroa is a farm town well known for its mineral-rich drinking water. On the Waihou River north of town, the Paeroa Maritime Park society operates several old river boats.

Coromandel Peninsula

Southeast of Auckland, the clawlike Coromandel Peninsula separates the Hauraki Gulf from the Bay of Plenty. Along its coast, the surf crashes against rocky cliffs and gently laps sandy crescents. Remnants of gold mining and kauri milling days still survive in its rugged interior.

Coastal roads border much of the shoreline; elsewhere, side roads lead down to the sea. Several winding mountain routes across the forested Coromandel Range link the western and eastern coasts.

The peninsula's population has fluctuated as wildly as its fortunes. Prospectors flocked here in the late 1860s in search of gold. Later, timber traders and gumdiggers razed the kauri forests and plundered the land; museums in larger towns recall this colorful era. In recent years, many craftspeople have settled here to pursue their work.

The peninsula's isolation is part of its charm, but it limits touring options. Nearest airports are in Tauranga and Auckland. Railways Road Services coaches travel between Auckland and Thames, largest of the towns; from Thames, there's limited bus service to Coromandel and Whitianga. Rental cars are available in Thames.

Most accommodations are concentrated in Whitianga and in Whangamata, deep-sea fishing headquarters, but you'll find motels in Thames, Coromandel, and smaller towns as well. Tourist information offices are located in Thames and Tairua.

Along the western coast

Located about 120 km/75 miles southeast of Auckland, Thames is a convenient base for exploring the peninsula. Displays in the Thames Museum, at Brown and Cochrane streets, evoke the mining era.

Southeast of Thames, the Kauaeranga Valley road leads to pleasant riverside picnic sites and forest walks in Coromandel Forest Park. For trail information, stop at Forest Service headquarters, located alongside the river.

Farther north at Coromandel, memories linger of the 1867 gold rush that brought quick prosperity to the area. The road continues north to Long Bay, a popular picnicking and camping area; to Kennedy's Bay, a yachters' haven; and to secluded bays and beaches near the tip of the sparsely populated Colville Peninsula.

Slow but scenic Highway 25 winds from Coromandel high above Whangapoua Harbour and Mercury Bay to Whitianga. Narrow, winding Highway 309 is the direct route across the mountains; from it, a short, marked trail leads to a glade of giant kauri trees.

East coast attractions

The peaceful harbor town of Whitianga takes on a carnival atmosphere in summer as vacationers flock here for swimming and water-skiing, big-game fishing and surfcasting, gemstone hunting, and bush walking. A passenger ferry makes the short trip across the Narrows to Ferry Landing, where you can walk to several destinations.

From Whenuakite, side roads lead northeast to beautiful Hahei Beach and Hotwater Beach, where hot springs seep up through the sand. From Hahei, it's a 20-minute walk north over the bluff to Cathedral Cave, a magnificent sea-carved cavern between two coves.

Tairua and Pauanui are popular seaside resorts; diving and big-game fishing are favorite activities. You can also arrange guided hiking trips to learn more about the Coromandel's scenic attractions and birdlife. Busy Whangamata attracts surf swimmers and water-skiers. Offshore is Mayor Island, a major deep-sea fishing base.

Waihi, situated on the wooded southern slope of the Coromandel Range, flourished during the local gold rush. One of New Zealand's largest gold strikes was made here at the Martha Mine. Many of the town's buildings reflect an earlier era; you can learn about this period at the Waihi Museum, 50 Kenny Street.

Highway 2 swings inland toward Paeroa through the Karangahake Gorge, where mining settlements boomed —and subsequently vanished—in the late 19th century.

The Bay of Plenty

Gentle waves lap the golden sand beaches bordering the Bay of Plenty. The coastal towns of Tauranga, Mount Maunganui, and Whakatane are magnets for summer visitors who come here to relax on the beach, frolic in the surf, and go deep-sea fishing. Relaxing hot mineral springs and pools dot the area. Offshore is White Island, New Zealand's most active volcano.

Citrus and subtropical fruits thrive in the balmy climate. Timber from Kaingaroa State Forest is processed into paper and wood products in the mill town of Kawerau, at the foot of Mount Edgecumbe.

Tauranga: busy port and resort area

Sprawling along the shore of its harbor, Tauranga is a bustling agricultural and timber center, as well as a thriving summer resort. Across the water on the harbor's eastern shore is Mount Maunganui, a holiday town named for the peak rising above it.

Daytime passenger ferry service operates between Tauranga's Coronation Pier, at the east end of Wharf Street, and Mount Maunganui's Salisbury Wharf. You can arrange sightseeing and fishing excursions in both towns. The Tauranga tourist information office is located on The Strand, near Coronation Pier.

Missionaries established a station on the Te Papa Peninsula in 1835, but the settlement didn't begin to flourish until the 1860s when the military arrived. On a short walk you can visit Tauranga's mission house and walk around "The Camp," site of the military settlement on a cliff overlooking the harbor. An excellent open-air museum is located south of town.

Visitors and residents picnic and swim in Memorial Park, a waterfront beach bordering Devonport Road. City sports facilities are located in Tauranga Domain, west of Cameron Road.

Informal wine tasting is available daily except Sunday at Preston's Kiwifruit Winery on Belk Road, Tauranga. Unique to New Zealand, the fresh and fruity white wine available here is made from kiwifruit, grown in fields throughout the district.

Mission days. One of the country's oldest homes, the handsome old Te Papa mission house on Mission Street (now known as "The Elms") was built in the 1840s by Rev. Alfred N. Brown. Now filled with articles relating to the area's early history, the mission was a peaceful oasis during the troubled days of 1864-65, when Maoris and Government troops battled at Gate Pa and Te Ranga.

The elegant house faces a large garden shaded by spreading trees, including a pair of Norfolk pines that guided early sailors into port. The grounds are open Monday through Saturday, with guided tours at 2 P.M.

Robbins Park links two wooded knolls, one the site of the old mission burying ground and military cemetery off Mirrielees Road, and the other the location of the well-preserved earthworks of Monmouth Redoubt. Trees ring the old cemetery, with its monument and lichen-encrusted tombstones. At the southern end of the park, earthworks outline the redoubt, which housed soldiers and sheltered European women and children during the warfare.

Tauranga Historic Village. History comes alive at this open-air museum on 17th Avenue West. Open daily from 10 A.M. to 4 P.M., it portrays New Zealand town life around the turn of the century. Original and replica buildings typical of those used in early Bay of Plenty settlements have been erected here.

The small colonial town features shops, dwellings, a school, church, jail, post office, livery stable, and blacksmith shop. Other displays include a Maori village, and gold mining and sawmill exhibits. Visitors can ride in vintage vehicles or horse-drawn wagons. You'll also see the old steam tug *Taioma*.

Bay of Plenty—the essentials

Fine beaches, big-game fishing, thermal hot springs, and seaside resort activities draw vacationers to Tauranga, Whakatane, and neighboring coastal towns.

Getting there. Air New Zealand serves Tauranga and Whakatane from Auckland, Wellington, and other North Island towns. Railways Road Services motorcoaches link Auckland and Wellington with Tauranga and other Bay of Plenty towns.

Accommodations. Hotels and motels are concentrated in Tauranga and Mount Maunganui, but you can also stay in Whakatane, Ohope Beach, and Opotiki.

In Tauranga, accommodations include the Willow Park Motor Hotel, Tauranga Motel, Tauranga Motor Inn, and many small motels; in Mount Maunganui, the Westhaven Motor Lodge; in Te Puke, the Te Puke Country Lodge; and in Whakatane, the Motel Riviera.

Getting around. Limited bus service connects the resort towns, but you'll find a car handy for touring; rental cars are available in Tauranga and Whakatane.

Tourist information. For visitor information, check tourist offices in Tauranga (on The Strand) and in Whakatane (on Commerce Street).

Lawn bowlers, dressed in their "whites," compete on Rotorua's greens in front of handsome old Tudor Towers. Lawn bowling season lasts from October to Easter.

Day trips from Tauranga. Narrow-necked Tauranga Harbour, sheltered from the sea by Matakana Island, is marked by pleasant tidal beaches at Omokoroa and Pahoia and several developed hot mineral springs.

From October to March, you can join a short white-water rafting trip on the Wairoa River, about 15 km/9 miles from Tauranga.

East of Tauranga, Highway 2 veers inland to Te Puke, center of a thriving dairy and fruit-growing district. Farther east, a side road leads to the small coastal village of Maketu, where a cairn near the mouth of the Kaituna River marks the traditional landing site of the Arawa canoe, one of the ancestral canoes that transported Maoris to New Zealand in the 14th century.

Mount Maunganui's peak and beach

Across the harbor from Tauranga, Mount Maunganui's wooded peak rises 232 meters/761 feet above the bay. Allow about 1½ hours if you want to hike to the summit for a magnificent view along the coast.

A long, slim, sandy peninsula connects "The Mount" to the mainland. The resort of Mount Maunganui clusters at the base of the peak. A coastal road parallels the town's famous golden beach, which curves gently along the bay southeast to Papamoa Beach and beyond.

Two bay islands

From Tauranga and Mount Maunganui you can arrange excursions to Mayor Island, a big-game fishing center, and to White Island, an active volcano.

Big-game fishing. Mayor Island lies about 35 km/22 miles off the coast in waters teeming with yellowfin, mako shark, and other fish. Peak season extends from late December to early May. Charter fishing boats operate from Tauranga and Mount Maunganui.

Skin divers come here to view colorful marine life. The pohutukawa-bordered island has twin volcanic craters, each with a small lake. Hikers enjoy walks through the bush, where birdlife abounds.

An active volcano. New Zealand's most active volcano, White Island rises about 50 km/30 miles offshore at the northern end of the Taupo-Rotorua volcanic zone. The island regularly issues forth a billowing cloud of steam visible from the mainland.

Riddled with thermal activity, the volcanic island has boiling pools, steam and gas vents, and holes filled with sulphuric acid. The volcano erupts periodically, spewing lava and ash over the island. Flights offering a close look at the island from the air operate from Tauranga, Whakatane, Rotorua, and Taupo. The island is also accessible by launch from Tauranga.

Whakatane and the eastern bay

Located 100 km/62 miles southeast of Tauranga, the timber and farm town of Whakatane traces its origin to the landing of the Mataatua canoe, one of the ancestral canoes that brought Maoris to New Zealand in the 14th century. The town has its own waterfall, located behind the Commercial Hotel on Mataatua Street.

Big-game fishing trips depart from Whakatane, and scenic flights offer aerial views over White Island and the

Bay of Plenty district. Jet boat trips up the scenic Rangitaiki River depart from above Lake Matahina dam, south of Whakatane. A small museum, open daily, displays historic articles. Inquire at the Public Relations Office on Commerce Street about fishing, flightseeing, and jet boat excursions, as well as other attractions.

Ohope Beach. The long ocean beach of this seaside settlement east of Whakatane is lined with pohutukawa trees. A slim peninsula shelters Ohiwa Harbour, where anglers seek flounder and shellfish and water-skiers glide across the water. Skin divers cross the headland at the western end of the beach to Otarawairere Bay.

Rotorua—the essentials

In addition to luring visitors to its superb fishing lakes and thermal attractions, the resort of Rotorua also puts you in touch with Maori culture.

Getting there. Mount Cook Line, Air New Zealand, and Newmans Air link Rotorua with various North Island cities and tourist areas. All three also fly here from Christchurch and other South Island points. Railways Road Services motorcoaches serve Rotorua from many North Island cities and towns.

Accommodations. Large tourist hotels are located in town (Hyatt Kingsgate, Travelodge); near Whakarewarewa Thermal Reserve (THC Rotorua International, Sheraton); and along Fenton Street—Highway 5—connecting the two (Rotorua Hotel, Four Canoes Inn). Many smaller hotels and motels in the lake district also cater to visitors.

Travelers seeking a bit of luxury can try Muriaroha, on Old Taupo Road, where a few guests stay in a gracious home filled with antiques and art. Excellent fishing and a serene lakeside setting draw guests to Solitaire Lodge on Lake Tarawera; also popular with anglers are Lake Okataina Tourist Lodge and Lake Rotoiti Hotel.

Getting around. Half-day and full-day motorcoach excursions depart from the N.Z.R. Travel Centre on Amohau Street. The short tour covers city sights, the Agrodome, trout springs, and thermal attractions; longer trips travel to the Waitomo Caves and the Taupo district. Sightseeing flights over the lakes and thermal areas depart from Rotorua Airport, float plane trips from the Lake Rotorua waterfront. Other excursion choices include lake cruises and a four-wheel-drive trip up the slopes of Mount Tarawera.

Tourist information. For assistance with travel arrangements, tours, and accommodations throughout the country, stop at the Government Tourist Bureau at the corner of Fenton and Haupapa streets. Information on local tours is also available at the N.Z.R. Travel Centre. The Public Relations Office is on Haupapa Street.

Opotiki. Once a large Maori settlement, Opotiki is known for its martyr's church; it's also the starting point for a trip around the East Cape. Hukutaia Domain southwest of town offers pleasant walks in unspoiled forest. Rafting and jet boat trips on the Motu River depart from Opotiki.

Rotorua, a thermal resort

The resort of Rotorua curves along the southwestern shore of Lake Rotorua, largest of a cluster of tree-rimmed lakes at the northern end of North Island's volcanic plateau. To the east looms Mount Tarawera, split open by a violent volcanic eruption in 1886. For a view over the lake basin and plateau, drive northwest of town to the summit of Mount Ngongotaha.

Rotorua offers three exceptional attractions for visitors: an opportunity to learn about Maori culture, an intriguing variety of thermal activity, and some of the country's best trout fishing. A busy tourist area, Rotorua is the hub for numerous sightseeing excursions in every direction.

An important part of Rotorua's history and culture revolves around the Maoris who settled here. Ancestors of the present residents landed on the Bay of Plenty coast about 1340. Migrating inland, they established scattered villages on defensible hills, peninsulas, and islands. Violent battles between the warring Maori tribes were common.

After the Land Wars ended, the area's thermal attractions — including the famous Pink and White Terraces bordering Lake Rotomahana—began to draw an increasing number of visitors. And after Mount Tarawera's 1886 eruption, Rotorua flourished as a turn-of-the-century spa, highly regarded for the curative powers of its mineral waters.

Getting settled in Rotorua

Fenton Street is Rotorua's main north-south artery, linking the commercial district at the north end of town near the lakeshore with Whakarewarewa Thermal Reserve to the south. Stores and offices line both Fenton Street and perpendicular streets to the west.

East of the thoroughfare, on a peninsula jutting into Lake Rotorua, is Government Gardens, developed during the town's heyday as a Victorian thermal spa. Many of the city's sports facilities are concentrated here.

At the Government Tourist Bureau on Fenton Street, sports enthusiasts can obtain fishing and hunting information and hire a guide for a day of trout fishing. For big-game fishing, head for the Bay of Plenty, about an hour's drive north of Rotorua. Golfers can choose from several local courses. Watch out for a different kind of hazard at Arikikapakapa Golf Course—here, thermal vents dot the links with escaping steam. Horse racing events take place at Arawa Park.

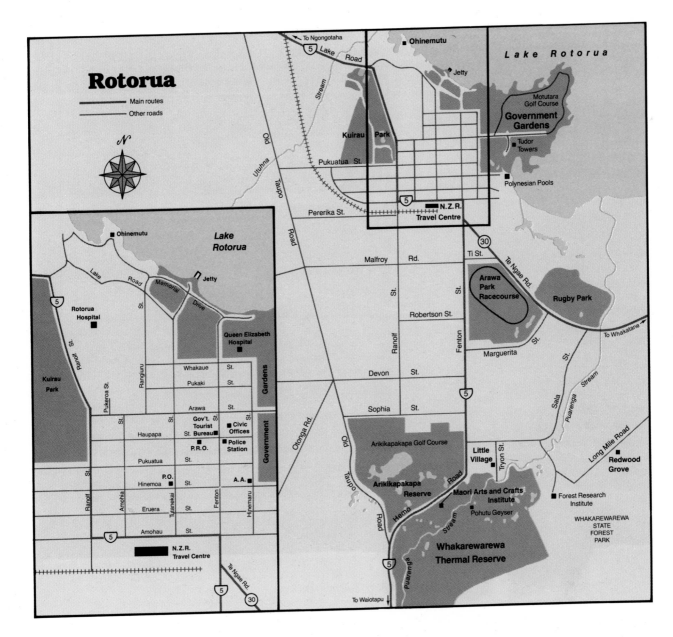

Walk through Government Gardens

Visitors to Government Gardens, a spacious peninsula park extending east from Hinemaru Street, are greeted by a distinctive Maori carving at the main Prince's Gate entrance on Arawa Street. Thermal attractions are interspersed amid the park's sports fields and flower beds.

From October to Easter, lawn bowlers, dressed in their proper "whites," compete in matches on the greens in front of the dignified old Tudor Towers building. Elsewhere, residents and visitors enjoy croquet, tennis, golf, roller-skating, or swimming. Indoor sports activities take place in the nearby sports and conference center.

One of New Zealand's most photographed buildings, the elegant Tudor Towers was built in 1906-07 as a bathhouse for people seeking the curative mineral and mud baths. Transferred to town ownership in 1963, the restored building now houses a museum, art gallery, licensed restaurant, and cabaret.

In the building's south wing, the Rotorua Museum features geological displays on the volcanic plateau, thermal activity, and the Tarawera eruption of 1886. Maori cultural exhibits contain family and tribal treasures contributed by local Maoris.

The city's art gallery, in the north wing, presents exhibits tracing the development of New Zealand painting and printmaking.

Relax in thermal waters

Developed as a spa, Rotorua for decades attracted visitors who came to "take the waters" to treat rheumatism and other ailments. Today's bathers enjoy these mineral-rich waters primarily for the feeling of well-being they bestow.

Many hotels and motels have pools for their guests, and there are large swimming pools in the Blue Baths in Government Gardens. At the Polynesian Pools, located at the east end of Hinemoa Street, you can relax in warm mineral waters or plunge into a thermal swimming pool. Private pools are available for those who prefer to soak *au naturel*. Pool hours are 9 A.M. to 10 P.M. daily.

Learning about the Maoris

Visitors who want to experience the Maori culture have many opportunities in Rotorua, including observing craftspeople at work, visiting Maori settlements, sampling Maori foods at a festive *hangi*, and enjoying programs of traditional songs and dances.

Maori Arts and Crafts Institute. Outside the main entrance to Whakarewarewa Thermal Reserve, at the south end of town, young Maori woodcarvers practice the skills taught to them by elder craftsmen. Women fashion skirts out of flax, make baskets, and demonstrate *taniko* weaving of bodices and headbands. Visitors are welcome on weekdays from 8:30 A.M. to 4:30 P.M.

Whakarewarewa Thermal Reserve. To take in one of Rotorua's top attractions, walk through the reserve with a Maori guide, or, if you prefer, stroll the paths at your own pace. The reserve is open daily from 8:30 A.M. to 4:30 P.M.

You'll see a model *pa* (Maori village), visit a kiwi house, then walk down through the thermal valley past bubbling mud pools, silica terraces, and vents of escaping steam. Periodically, Pohutu Geyser spurts high above the terraces.

At the lower end of the valley, you walk past Whakarewarewa village, where Maori residents use the hot pools for cooking, bathing, laundering, and heating.

Ohinemutu. Bordering Lake Rotorua northwest of town is the lakeside village of Ohinemutu. For generations, its residents have used the escaping steam and thermally heated water for daily activities.

Maori carvings and *tukutuku* panels decorate the interior of the Tudor-style St. Faith's Anglican Church, built in 1910. In the side chapel, a magnificent window depicts Christ wearing a chief's cloak of kiwi feathers. In the churchyard, tombs lie above ground because of thermal conditions.

Facing the church is a meeting house enhanced by traditional carvings. Some of the interior decoration dates from the early 1800s. Evening programs of Maori songs and dances are often presented here.

Maori food and entertainment. Rotorua's the place to attend a Maori *hangi*, a Polynesian feast traditionally steam-cooked in an underground pit. *Kai* (food) may include pork, lamb, chicken, seafood, marinated fish, venison, *kumara* (Maori sweet potato), salads, Maori bread, and fresh fruit.

After dinner, Maori entertainers serenade guests with traditional songs and perform Maori dances featuring twirling *poi* (balls on string) and the fierce *haka* (a posturing war dance).

The THC Rotorua International Hotel presents a traditional *hangi* every Sunday night throughout the year, and more often in summer. Food is cooked in an earthen

Excursion launch cruises past Lake Rotomahana's steaming cliffs. Fumaroles were created by the enormous volcanic eruption of nearby Mount Tarawera in 1886.

oven by natural steam. Hangi feasts and Maori entertainment are also presented at the Geyserland Motor Hotel, Sheraton-Rotorua Hotel, Travelodge Hotel, and Tudor Towers.

Programs of Maori songs and dances that chronicle events in tribal history and village life are presented at the Rotorua Maori Cultural Theatre, 18 Eruera Street, and at the Tamatekapua Meeting House in Ohinemutu.

Other city attractions

For a change of pace, take a walk through a grove of redwoods, shop for crafts, or visit Kuirau Park.

Whakarewarewa State Forest. Southeast of town, the tranquil trails of this forest park offer a relaxing break in sightseeing activity. Stop at the Forest Information Centre on Long Mile Road for a trail map.

A favorite destination is the Redwood Memorial Grove bordering Long Mile Road. Planted in 1901, the towering trees here are part of an experimental reforestation project begun after the Tarawera eruption devastated the area.

The large park extends from the Whakarewarewa Thermal Reserve and the Taupo highway east to the Blue and Green lakes. Other popular trails include the Blue Lake walk around the shoreline, a climb to the Tokorangi Pa site, and walks in the Green Lake Picnic Area.

Little Village. Near the exit from the Whakarewarewa Thermal Reserve, the Little Village on Tryon Street offers an intriguing collection of tourist and craft shops in a colonial village atmosphere. Often you'll see artisans at work on the premises.

Kuirau Park. Children will love Kuirau Park, located at Ranolf and Pukuatua streets; the park features the "Toot 'n' Whistle" miniature steam railway, a children's playground, an aquarium, sports fields, and an aquatic center. Walkways meander around the park's small lake, boiling mud pools, and large thermal fountain.

Excursions from Rotorua

Tourism is one of Rotorua's main industries, and a large number of excursions are available to visitors.

If thermal activity intrigues you, you can visit spouting geysers, steaming cliffs, boiling pools, and colorful silica terraces. Or cruise secluded lakes rimmed by native forest, walk down a thermal valley, explore a buried village, feed trout by hand, climb the side of a volcanic peak by four-wheel-drive vehicle, raft down a river, or take a flightseeing tour over lakes and valleys.

Aside from excursions to nearby attractions, one bus trip takes visitors south to Huka Falls, Wairakei, Lake Taupo, and Orakei Korako; another tour goes to Waitomo Caves. A 5-day hiking trek in Urewera National Park also departs from Rotorua (page 60).

Big fighting trout await the lure

Some of the world's best fresh-water fishing draws both casual and serious anglers to New Zealand's lakes and streams. In fact, if you want to eat trout here, you'll *have* to catch it yourself. Trout fishing is strictly a sport, with no trout grown or caught commercially. The hotel chef will cook your catch for you for breakfast or dinner.

Introduced late in the 19th century, rainbow and brown trout thrive in New Zealand's clear lakes and cold, fast-flowing rivers. Famed both for their size and tenacity, the trout can challenge the skills of even an expert angler. Yet each year, hundreds of visitors who have never fished before proudly display their catch.

You can fish throughout the year in the Rotorua and Taupo lake systems, but in most districts the season opens on the first Saturday in October and extends through April (in some districts through May or June). Most serious anglers try to avoid the January family vacation period.

On North Island lakes, trolling is popular during the warm summer months, but in autumn the action shifts to the mouths of lake tributaries as trout congregate prior to spawning runs. Most streams are for fly-fishing only.

Thousands of miles of uncrowded trout streams, along with excellent lake fishing in the Southern Lakes region, attract fly-fishing devotees to South Island. Brown trout predominate here, but rainbows and landlocked salmon also inhabit the lake systems. Salmon spawn in some of the east coast rivers, and South Westland has large runs of sea-run brown trout in spring and late summer. Whitebait migrate up many of the coastal rivers from September through November.

Your best insurance for a successful expedition is to hire a local professional fishing guide, available by the hour or day in all major fishing areas; the local tourist office can direct you to qualified guides and tell you where to obtain a fishing license. In addition to fishing know-how, guides usually supply the boat, all gear and tackle, and even transport to and from your hotel. Most guides charge a fixed price per party (up to three or four persons), depending on services and equipment required.

Dedicated anglers may want to spend a few days at a fishing lodge—or even plan an entire vacation around fishing. Several tour operators offer packaged itineraries that feature fishing; check with your travel agent or with international airlines flying to New Zealand. The New Zealand Tourist Office can provide general fishing information.

Maori legends and traditions reflect a unique culture

When European immigrants arrived in New Zealand in the early 19th century, they found the distinctive and well-established Maori culture. Hereditary warrior chiefs and powerful priests ruled the tribal society. History and traditions were passed down from father to son, mother to daughter, through legends, songs, and crafts.

Learning about the Maori culture is an integral part of the New Zealand experience. Many museums have fascinating exhibits of carved buildings, canoes, tools, ornaments, and garments.

At the Maori Arts and Crafts Institute in Rotorua, you can watch Maori woodcarvers at work; elsewhere in Rotorua, you can sample foods at a *hangi,* enjoy Maori entertainment, and learn about village life (page 46). In the Bay of Islands, the Waitangi meeting house (page 34) brings together carving styles of tribes from all parts of North Island. Maori communities are located throughout North Island, but visitors should ask permission before looking around a village.

To enrich your first-hand experiences, here is a description of some aspects of the Maori culture.

Myths and legends. Colorful, imaginative, and often touching legends, handed down from generation to generation, offer insights into how the early Maori viewed his world and accounted for the origin of the universe, the elements, and man.

Tales recount a time long ago when mountains fought and walked, their tears became streams and rivers, and men and gods spoke together. Many Maori legends explain distinctive landscape features. Other stories relate tales of heroism and endurance.

Before the arrival of the missionaries, Maoris had no written language. Oratory was regarded as an important art in passing on tribal history and culture.

Meeting house. Focal point of a Maori village is its open square *(marae)* and the traditional carved meeting house *(whare runanga)* facing it. Inside, symbolic carvings depict tribal ancestors and mythical figures.

The *poupou* (carved wall panels) record tribal history and legends. Woven *tukutuku* panels in geometric patterns usually separate the wooden carvings. Posts supporting the ridgepole are also carved. Patterned *kowhai-whai* designs painted in black, red, and white decorate the rafters.

Woodcarving. Intricately designed woodcarvings—stylized figures and grotesque birds, fish, and animals—depict stories of tribal events. Each tribe had its own distinct carving style.

Craftsmen preferred totara wood for carving. The distinctive color came from red ochre mixed with shark oil; iridescent paua shells were used for eyes. Distinctive motifs include curves and spiral designs, slanted eyes, and a three-fingered hand with backward-turned thumb. Figures were often depicted in warlike poses, eyes bulging and tongue outthrust in defiance.

Examples of the carver's art decorate not only meeting houses but also storehouses, gateways, and posts. In museums you'll see intricate carvings ornamenting articles used in daily life, such as war canoes, weapons, and musical instruments.

Greenstone. Valued by the Maoris for its hardness and beauty, greenstone (nephrite jade or bowenite) was carved into prized ornaments, tools, and weapons. Maori parties made difficult journeys through the mountains to certain West Coast valleys in search of the comparatively rare stone. New Zealand's good luck talisman is the *tiki,* a neck pendant carved in the form of a fetus. Several museums have fine greenstone collections.

Weaving. Women excelled in weaving flax and reeds into the *tukutuku* panels that decorate many meeting houses, dwellings, and churches. Among other women's crafts are basketry, *taniko* weaving of decorative bodices and headbands, and preparation of the flax *piupiu* kilts worn by both men and women.

Music and dance. Traditional Maori music includes a variety of chants and poetic songs expressing joy and sadness, welcome and farewell. Familiar melodies such as *Haere ra* ("Now is the hour") date from the 19th century. Simple nose and mouth flutes and trumpets of shell, bone, and wood sometimes accompany the singers; rhythm is supplied by stamping the feet, slapping the body, or tapping a piece of wood with a stick.

Most familiar of Maori dances is the spirited war dance *(haka pukana),* in which the performer engages in vigorous posture dancing as he grimaces, rolls his eyes, and thrusts out his tongue to frighten the enemy. New Zealand sports teams often perform it before international matches. Women entertain with the gentle *poi* dance, where they twirl raupo balls on string in time with music.

Tattooing. In traditional Maori society, tattooing was a form of adornment and status. A chief used his tattoo design *(moko)* as his signature. Males were liberally embellished with distinctive patterns on face and body as well as buttocks and thighs. Women were less heavily decorated, usually only on lips and chin. Tattooing was a long and painful process. A tiny bone chisel was used to make incisions according to a pattern, and soot was rubbed into the open wounds to provide coloring.

Most local sightseeing trips operate daily from December through April, less frequently the rest of the year. For information, inquire at the Government Tourist Bureau at the corner of Fenton and Haupapa streets.

Cruising on the lakes

Good roads provide access to most of the larger lakes. If you cruise their clear, tree-rimmed waters, you'll enjoy them even more.

Launch trips. Largest of the district's lakes is Rotorua, nearly circular in shape, with wooded Mokoia Island in its center. You board the launch at the jetty at the end of Tutanekai Street. After circling the island, the launch docks there and you have time for a short walk, and perhaps a quick swim in Hinemoa's Pool and a wish by the Arawa wishing rock. Trips leave Rotorua at 2 P.M. daily (additional trips in summer).

Renowned for its trout fishing, tree-bordered Lake Rotoiti is a favorite. Tourist facilities are concentrated at the western end of the lake. A launch trip on the lake departs from Okawa Bay Holiday Camp daily at 2 P.M.

You can also board a launch for a trip on Lake Tarawera, a tranquil retreat at the base of Mount Tarawera.

Fishing trips. Within a 16-km/10-mile radius of Rotorua are many good fishing lakes, and catches are legendary. At Lake Rotorua, for example, anglers catch rainbows weighing 2 to 4 pounds each. During the May to June spawning season, 9 to 10-pound rainbow trout are netted nearly every day at Lake Tarawera. A local guide can introduce you to some of the district's best fishing areas.

A circuit of Lake Rotorua

Trout springs, trained sheep, and redwood trees are only a few of the sights you'll see on a drive around the lake. Looming above the countryside northwest of Rotorua, Mount Ngongotaha looks out on a sweeping panorama toward the Bay of Plenty.

Trout springs. Clear, pure, cold water wells up from underground springs west of Rotorua. In several places, visitors can roam down fern-lined paths along clear trout streams and toss food to the fish. The springs are cool, woodsy retreats to visit on hot days.

You can stop at Paradise Valley Springs, west of Rotorua on the Valley Road; Rainbow and Fairy Springs, bordering Highway 5 west of the lake; or Taniwha Springs, near Awahou on the lake's northwestern shore. Rainbow and Fairy Springs has an animal park and nocturnal kiwi house. At Taniwha Springs there's a Maori *pa*.

The Agrodome. Nineteen trained champion rams, each representing a different New Zealand sheep breed, take the stage during a 1-hour pastoral show at the Agrodome, set in lush pasture land at Riverdale Park in Ngongotaha, west of Rotorua. Demonstrations of shearing and the maneuvers of sheep dogs help illustrate the story of wool,

one of New Zealand's most important products.

Shows are presented daily at 10:30 A.M. and 2:30 P.M., with extra performances during busy periods.

Hamurana Springs. A grove of lofty redwood trees shades Hamurana Springs, on the northern shore of the lake. You can rent a boat and paddle along the willow-bordered stream, watch trout in an upstream pool, feed tame deer, or golf on the nine-hole course.

Okere Falls. The clear green outflow of lakes Rotorua and Rotoiti surges and foams through a narrow rift, then plunges into a broad pool of the Kaituna River. Many an angler has caught a prize trout here. Rocky steps lead down the steep wooded slope to the foot of the falls and to caves where Maori women reportedly hid in time of war.

Spectacular views by land and air

Four-wheel-drive vehicles transport passengers on a half-day safari up the slope of Mount Tarawera, site of New Zealand's greatest volcanic eruption. From the brink of the crater, you peer into the deep, color-streaked chasm and gaze over an awesome panorama of lush forests and sparkling lakes.

One of the best views of the lakes and thermal attractions is from the air. Float planes lift off from Rotorua's lakefront jetty; helicopters and other aircraft leave from the Rotorua Airport on the eastern shore of the lake.

You can fly over the town of Rotorua and the lake district, Mount Tarawera's gaping volcanic chasm, and steaming geothermal areas. Longer flights circle volcanoes at White Island and Tongariro National Park.

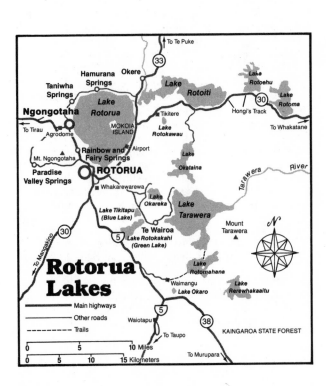

East to fishing lakes

Northeast of Rotorua, the Whakatane road (Highway 30) passes the thermal area of Tikitere and skirts the southern shore of three bush-rimmed fishing lakes — Rotoiti, Rotoehu, and Rotoma. A side road south of Rotoiti leads to unspoiled Lake Okataina.

The lakes figure prominently in local history as links in the Maori canoe route to Lake Rotorua. In 1823, Hongi

---

Volcanic plateau—the essentials

Trout fishing in Lake Taupo and its nearby rivers and streams, together with hiking and skiing in Tongariro National Park, are highlights for visitors to this region.

Getting there. Air New Zealand flights link Taupo with Auckland, Wellington, and other towns. New Zealand Railways' main line passes west of Lake Taupo and Tongariro National Park with stops in National Park and Ohakune. Railways Road Services motorcoaches travel from various North Island cities and towns to Taupo, Turangi, and Taihape.

Accommodations. Most visitors stay in or near Taupo or Tongariro National Park, though anglers range far afield. Among Taupo's many lakefront motels are the Ashley Court Motel, Lake Terrace Motel, Manuels Motor Inn, and Moana Reef Motel. North of Taupo at Wairakei is the comfortable THC Wairakei Hotel, noted for its excellent 18-hole golf course.

Several fishing lodges cater to trout anglers. These include the Waikato River Lodge near Reporoa; Huka Lodge, a historic fishing retreat on the Waikato River above Huka Falls; Wilderness Lodge, in the Kaimanawa wilderness southeast of Taupo; and Tongariro Lodge and small Bridge Fishing Lodge, both near the mouth of the Tongariro River at Turangi. Here you'll also find the DB Turangi Motor Hotel and several small motels.

Farther west at Tokaanu, the recently renovated THC Tokaanu offers an irresistible package for anglers—free accommodation if you don't catch a fish.

Tongariro National Park visitors can live in luxury at the renowned THC Chateau on Mount Ruapehu; nearby is the Ruapehu Skotel (skiers' hotel). Development of Turoa Skifield has brought many new accommodations west of the park, among them the Buttercup Alpine Resort and Drumlin Lodge Motel in National Park; and Sunbeam Ski Lodge and Venturelodge in Ohakune.

Getting around. Mount Cook Line motorcoaches travel between Wairakei and the Chateau, with stops at Taupo, Turangi, and Tokaanu. Rental cars are available in Taupo.

Tourist information. Visitor information centers are located at Taupo and Turangi. Park headquarters for Tongariro National Park is at Whakapapa Village on Mount Ruapehu (near the Chateau); ranger stations are situated in Ohakune and Turangi.

Hika and his warriors paddled across the lakes, portaging their heavy wooden canoes when necessary, on their way to attack the fortified Arawa settlement on Mokoia Island.

The district's most active thermal area, Tikitere is an inferno of sulphurous steam, boiling water, and bubbling mud. White pumice and golden sulphur combine to shape bizarre formations. Take the short bush walk through native trees and ferns to Kakahi Falls, where thermal waters cascade into an inviting pool.

A bush-bordered avenue south of Lake Rotoiti leads to lovely Lake Okataina. Totara trees and punga ferns shade the road, and *kotukutuku* (native fuchsia) brightens your way in late spring and early summer. Dense forest rims the lake. Okataina attracts people who enjoy peace and quiet — along with some of the area's best trout fishing.

Waimangu Valley—Lake Tarawera loop

Situated southeast of Rotorua are the steaming Waimangu Valley, lakes Rotomahana and Tarawera, and the buried village of Te Wairoa.

Half-day and full-day guided tours depart from the New Zealand Railways Travel Centre on Amohau Street. The shorter trip includes a tour of the valley, a launch cruise on Lake Rotomahana to the steaming cliffs, and transport back up the valley. Only travelers on the full-day tour make the entire loop.

Early on the morning of June 10, 1886, Mount Tarawera erupted in tremendous volcanic fury, awakening Aucklanders nearly 280 km/175 miles away. Splitting open from end to end, the volcano spewed forth a cubic mile of molten rock, boiling mud, and volcanic ash, which covered the countryside for miles around. Three villages were buried and more than 150 people died. The eruption destroyed Lake Rotomahana's famous Pink and White Terraces, fan-shaped silica staircases world-renowned for their beauty and shimmering colors. When the smoke cleared, Mount Tarawera was left with a gaping chasm and craters up to 210 meters/700 feet deep.

Evidence of the area's thermal activity abounds on the 4-km/2½-mile walk down the Waimangu Valley. Steam rises from the surface of the Waimangu Cauldron, a large thermal lake fed by subterranean boiling springs. Off the main path is Ruamoko's Throat, a turquoise lake rimmed by colorful cliffs. Your path down the valley follows a scalding stream. Near the lake, thermal waters fan over Warbrick Terrace, its silica deposits patterned with colorful algae.

At the bottom of the valley, you'll board a launch and cruise slowly past Lake Rotomahana's stratified cliffs, laced with steaming fumaroles.

Travelers on the full-day excursion disembark on the lake's northern shore and hike across the narrow saddle separating it from larger Lake Tarawera. Another launch waits at the Tarawera dock for a leisurely trip across the lake, where a bus picks up passengers and transports them on the final leg of the trip.

Before Mount Tarawera's eruption, Te Wairoa Village was the departure point for excursions to the terraces. Buried under 5 to 6 feet of volcanic mud, the village has been partially excavated. A self-guided walk links a museum and several structures. You can follow Te Wairoa Stream, Green Lake's outlet into Lake Tarawera, as it tumbles over Te Wairoa Falls.

On the way back to Rotorua you'll pass a pair of jewel-like lakes — Green Lake (Rotokakahi) and Blue Lake (Tikitapu). Off the main route is secluded Lake Okareka, a relaxing spot for a picnic, a swim, or a bit of fishing.

South to Waiotapu

Located 30 km/19 miles south of Rotorua near the Taupo road (Highway 5), Waiotapu is noted for the colorful silica surrounding its thermal attractions.

Lady Knox Geyser erupts daily at 10:15 A.M. Other attractions include the Artist's Palette silica terraces, tinged in delicate colors; lovely Bridal Veil Falls; and the shimmering Champagne Pool, which bubbles when sand is tossed into it.

Volcanic plateau

Dominating the center of North Island is a vast volcanic plateau, marked by Lake Taupo—North Island's largest lake—and a trio of active volcanoes in the heart of New Zealand's first national park.

Kiwis and visitors alike who love the outdoors come here for superb fishing, for water sports on Lake Taupo, and for hiking, climbing, and skiing in Tongariro National Park. Thermal energy is transformed into electricity at Wairakei's steaming geothermal bore field and at power stations along the Tongariro and Waikato rivers.

Silica terraces at Orakei Korako

Extensive silica deposits and a legendary cave draw visitors to Orakei Korako, 27 km/17 miles north of Wairakei. To reach the area, you board a jet boat and skim across the Waikato River where it flows into Lake Ohakuri.

Largest of New Zealand's silica terraces, the broad cascade called Great Golden Fleece extends along an ancient fault scarp. Above it is Artist's Palette, a large level basin riddled by dozens of small geysers and hot springs. Algae create color variations in the crusty silica deposits.

Tall tree ferns frame the entrance to Ruatapu (Aladdin's Cave) and filter sunlight to a small mirrorlike pool far below. For generations Maori women came here to bathe and beautify themselves.

Harnessing geothermal energy at Wairakei

Clouds of billowing steam greet travelers at Wairakei, located in the center of North Island's thermal belt. One of the world's foremost geothermal power projects,

Ranger-led group learns about Mount Ruapehu's rugged volcanic terrain on a summer nature walk in Tongariro National Park.

Winter fun on the slopes

When autumn weather turns chilly and snow begins to pile up on the high peaks, the thoughts of many Kiwis turn to winter sports. A great number take to the slopes—for alpine (downhill) skiing, for nordic (cross-country) ski touring, and in the Southern Alps, for glacier skiing, where ski-equipped planes and helicopters transport skiers to the high slopes.

Skiing. New Zealand's ski areas offer abundant powder snow, fine downhill runs, and uncrowded, timber-free slopes. Since seasons are reversed from those in the Northern Hemisphere, New Zealand's challenging slopes attract expert skiers from North America, Europe, and Japan. You'll find a relaxed, easy-going atmosphere and ample après-ski conviviality in the country's ski resorts. Though skiing can begin as early as May and extend into November, the season typically lasts from mid-July through October on North Island, and from early July through September on South Island. Several resorts feature ski package holidays, and major ski areas offer equipment rentals, ski schools, and public transport to the slopes.

Mount Ruapehu in Tongariro National Park is North Island's leading ski area. Well-established Whakapapa Skifield on the mountain's north-facing slopes is noted for spring skiing; the newly developed Turoa Skifield is on Ruapehu's southern slope.

Top resort sites on South Island are Coronet Peak, near Queenstown, and Mount Cook. South Island's most extensive skifield is Mount Hutt, located near Methven southwest of Christchurch.

Smaller areas include Rainbow Valley, in the St. Arnaud ranges near Nelson Lakes National Park; Porter Heights, off Arthur's Pass Road west of Christchurch; Mount Dobson, near Fairlie, and Tekapo, near Lake Tekapo, both in the vast Mackenzie Country; Lake Ohau, south of Mount Cook; and Treble Cone and Cardrona, both near Wanaka.

Mount Cook is the country's principal ski-touring and ski-mountaineering center. Ski-equipped planes and helicopters transport skiers to the high glaciers of the Southern Alps.

New Zealand has more than 60 ski clubs; just about every one operates huts in its particular area. Visitors can often arrange to stay in club bunk-style lodges and ski very economically. National administration of the ski clubs is handled by the New Zealand Ski Association, Inc. (P.O. Box 2213, Wellington 1).

Wairakei has attracted considerable attention since it began generating electricity in 1959. Visitors can learn about the project at the power plant's information office; guided tours are offered at the power stations.

Several thousand feet below the surface, hot volcanic rocks heat water to above-boiling temperatures. Deep bores intersecting this layer channel escaping steam to the surface, where hot water is extracted. "Dry" steam funnels through insulated mains to generating stations along the Waikato River. U-shaped loops in the pipes allow for expansion and contraction.

Inside the power stations, cold water pumped from the river condenses the steam; water is then returned to the river.

The upper Waikato River

Near Taupo, travelers satiated with thermal wonders can watch the powerful, yet placid Waikato River cascading over Huka Falls and Aratiatia Rapids.

About 5 km/3 miles north of Taupo, the Waikato suddenly funnels into a narrow chasm. Surging and foaming through the gorge, the roaring waters of Huka Falls catapult over a ledge into a wide, calm pool below. Though not high, Huka Falls is impressive in its raw power.

The Huka Falls loop road follows the river between Taupo and Wairakei. A trail parallels the river from Huka Falls downstream to Aratiatia Dam.

Aratiatia Rapids. Long regarded as one of the loveliest stretches of the Waikato Valley, Aratiatia represents a compromise between scenic beauty and the nation's power needs. At the head of the valley, a control dam holds back the Waikato, whose waters are channeled to a power station. Every afternoon from 2:30 to 4 the pent-up river is released to thunder down the deep, rocky ravine. To reach Aratiatia, turn east off Highway 5 north of Wairakei.

Huka Village. A North Island pioneer village has been re-created about 2 km/1 mile north of Taupo beside the Huka Falls Road. Pioneer buildings, moved here and restored, depict life during the era of the 1860s and '70s. Artisans demonstrate crafts of a bygone era. The village is open daily from 10 A.M. to 5 P.M.

Relaxing at Taupo

When you approach Taupo from the north on Highway 1, Lake Taupo's sparkling panorama spreads before you. Fed by dozens of streams, the lake fills a gigantic volcanic crater. Its only outlet is the Waikato River, which leaves the lake alongside the town of Taupo. In the distance rise the huddled peaks of Tongariro National Park.

The town dates from 1869, when an Armed Constabulary garrison was built here. Later, thermal activity attracted visitors. The town's growth spurted in the 1950s during construction of the Wairakei geothermal project.

At the Information Centre on Tongariro Street, you

can obtain maps and brochures, arrange local accommodations, and inquire about fishing and hunting trips, boat rentals, and flightseeing and coach excursions.

Fun on the lake. Pleasure boats and fishing launches anchor near the head of the river, upstream from the gates that control the lake's water level and regulate the flow of water downstream. You can rent small boats at the marina. Boat excursions leave from the wharf.

Though fishing is extremely popular, it's not the only activity on Lake Taupo. Water-skiers skim over lake waters along marked routes. Children splash in shallow water or paddle canoes just offshore. For a picnic by the lake, consider tree-bordered Acacia Bay, west of town.

Other diversions. You can soak away stiffness at thermal or heated fresh-water pools. If you'd rather swim in lake water, Waipahihi Hot Springs bubble from the lake bed along the northeastern shore (access off Lake Terrace).

South of the Napier turnoff, Waipahihi Botanical Reserve overlooks the lake at the end of Shepherd Road.

Back-country adventure. White-water rafting trips on the Tongariro and Mohaka rivers and hiking excursions in the Kaimanawa Mountains are organized by Kaimanawa Tours & Treks Ltd. (P.O. Box 321, Taupo). Trips depart from Taupo from mid-December through March.

Fabled lake and stream fishing

As Highway 5 skirts the eastern shore of Lake Taupo, it crosses a number of sparkling tributary streams flowing swiftly down from the Kaimanawa Mountains. Many anglers cast their lines near the mouths of these tributaries. Others prefer the waters of Lake Taupo or the famed trout pools of the snow-fed Tongariro River.

Just how good is the fishing? Wildlife authorities estimate that about 700 tons of trout are caught annually in Lake Taupo. Here, rainbows weigh in at 3½ to 6 pounds, and brown trout average more than 5 pounds.

Most of the main fishing streams, including the Tongariro River, enter the lake near its southern tip. River fishing is best here from April to August during the spawning runs. Streams flowing into the lake from the west can be reached only by boat.

The lake's southern shore

The town of Turangi owes its growth to construction of the nearby Tongariro hydroelectric power project and expansion of the district's farming and forest industries. Learn about local recreation, the power plant, and area history and geology at the Power Project Information Office, alongside Highway 41 at Turangi.

Nearby Tokaanu has a small thermal reserve with hot pools, boiling mud, geysers, and a small bathhouse. St. Paul's Anglican Church, decorated in Maori style with *tukutuku* panels and painted rafters, memorializes early missionaries.

A side road off Highway 41 leads to Waihi, a picturesque Maori village backed by a steep wooded cliff.

West of Turangi, the scenic Pihanga Saddle Road climbs to a viewpoint overlooking Lake Taupo and winds through luxuriant forest. About 10 km/6 miles southwest of Tokaanu, a signposted trail leads south from the road to Lake Rotopounamu, a small green lake nestled in a greenery-rimmed crater. A naturalist's delight, the 25-minute walk winds through forest abundant with ferns.

Just south of the road's intersection with Highway 47 stand the fortifications of Te Porere *pa*, site of the last major engagement of the Land Wars in 1869.

Volcanoes shape Tongariro National Park

South of Lake Taupo, three volcanic peaks loom above the plateau in a terrain unique in New Zealand. For generations, Maoris regarded these high mountains with awe, weaving legends about them. New Zealand's first national park, Tongariro is an unspoiled region shaped by eruption, glaciation, and erosion.

The park takes its name from the northernmost and lowest of the peaks, 1,968-meter/6,458-foot Tongariro, whose truncated crest is a maze of craters—some mildly active. A docile plume of smoke drifts from Ngauruhoe's symmetrical cone; every few years the 2,291-meter/7,515-foot volcano erupts spectacularly, belching lava and ash over its slopes. Highest of the three is 2,797-meter/9,175-foot Ruapehu, North Island's highest peak and foremost ski area. Snow-capped the year around, it has a simmering acid crater lake and small glaciers on its high slopes.

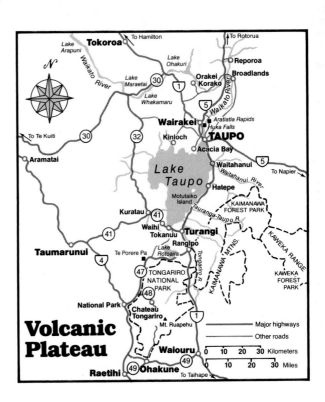

Mount Egmont's snowy cone, partially shrouded by clouds, looms above Taranaki's dairy pastures. Hikers, climbers, and skiers enjoy the peak's wooded slopes.

Among the park's most fascinating aspects are its varied terrain, vegetation, and birdlife. Wet lowland forests, lush with ferns and orchids, on Ruapehu's southwestern slope contrast dramatically with tussock grasslands, wildflower-sprinkled alpine rock gardens, and stark volcanic formations at higher elevations. More than 500 native plant species have been identified in the park.

Year-round fun at Tongariro

Center of park activity is Whakapapa Village on Mount Ruapehu. Skiers flock here in winter, hikers and climbers in summer.

At park headquarters, open daily from 8 A.M. to 5 P.M., you learn about the park's geology and volcanic activity, history, plants, and birdlife. You can also obtain trail information and check the weather forecast. In summer, rangers conduct nature walks, climbing excursions, and illustrated programs. They also arrange for climbing guides, hunting permits, and use of mountain huts.

You can also obtain park information by contacting the chief ranger (Park Headquarters, Mount Ruapehu; phone Ruapehu 814). Ranger stations are located at Ohakune, on the Mountain Road (phone Ohakune 578), and at Turangi (phone Turangi 8520).

Skiing on Mount Ruapehu. Whakapapa Skifield, on Ruapehu's north slope, is one of New Zealand's oldest established ski areas. From Whakapapa Village, the Bruce Road climbs about 7 km/4 miles to the ski area. Rental equipment and ski holiday packages are available.

Recently developed on Ruapehu's southwestern flank is Turoa Skifield, which boasts the highest vertical lift in Australasia (720 meters/2,360 feet). You can obtain information on Turoa skiing in Ohakune; ski buses transport skiers from town to Turoa. At the skifield, T-bars and triple chair lifts offer access to uncluttered, challenging slopes where skiing lasts until November.

Walks and hikes. Summer visitors venturing forth on foot to explore the park can follow any of several short walks beginning near Whakapapa Village. Trails cut through varied terrain—beech and fern forests, golden tussock, boggy areas, and alpine meadows. From Highway 47 it's a steep, uphill tramp to Ketetahi Hot Springs, but a soak in the warm waters below the springs rejuvenates tired muscles.

Several fine walks begin along the Ohakune Road; consider the Mangawhero Forest Walk through a pocket of lush subtropical rain forest or the bush walk to Waitonga Falls, the park's highest waterfall.

Longer hikes lead to the Tongariro Craters and to Mount Ruapehu's hot acid lake, surrounded by ice and snow. A round-the-mountain tramp curves from the Chateau to the Ohakune Mountain Road.

The Mount Ruapehu Alpine Walk, a 5-day guided trek above the timberline with accommodations in mountain huts, explores this fascinating country. Hikers make a high traverse around the mountain, with side trips to small glaciers and to Ruapehu's crater lake. Groups depart from Ohakune weekly from mid-December to early February, weather permitting. Information is available from Venturetreks Ltd., P.O. Box 3839, Auckland.

Ohakune Mountain Road. Motorists can drive up Ohakune Mountain Road, which climbs from the town of Ohakune straight up Ruapehu's southwestern flank.

Ascending, you traverse a cross section of the park's varying climate and vegetation zones—from lowland rimu forest through silver and mountain beech into high tussock shrublands to the alpine gravel fields at road's end. You can picnic beside the Mangawhero River as it falls over the edge of old lava flows. Ask at park headquarters for a descriptive leaflet of the road.

Across the Rangipo Desert

One of North Island's most unusual drives crosses the desolate, windswept Rangipo Desert just east of the park. From Turangi 63 km/39 miles south to Waiouru, Highway 1 is known as Desert Road. Generations of Maori travelers hurried across the forbidding plains, not daring to stop or look at the sacred mountains for fear of antagonizing the gods, who might punish them with storms of snow and ice.

Dry, cold winds sweep down from snowy Mount Ruapehu, and only sparse and stunted plants survive in the harsh climate. Sculptured by wind and frost, road cuttings expose the region's layered volcanic deposits.

On Highway 1 south of Waiouru, the Queen Elizabeth II Army Memorial Museum chronicles New Zealand's military history—from the Maori Land Wars to the present—with exhibits of weapons, uniforms, photographs, paintings, and personal memorabilia. The museum is open daily from 9 A.M. to 4:30 P.M.

Continuing south, Highway 1 passes through the railway town of Taihape and follows the Rangitikei River southwest through white-walled gorges. Several forest reserves are located near Hunterville, in the heart of the district's farm lands. Highway 1 meets the west coast road (Highway 3) at Bulls, another agricultural center.

Exploring the western coast

From the King Country, Highway 3 veers southwest through the wooded Awakino River gorge to the coast. A trio of small fishing settlements—Awakino, Mokau, and Tongaporutu—marks the mouths of coastal rivers.

New Plymouth, the hub of rich Taranaki farm lands, is a city of splendid parks and gardens, and the gateway to mountain recreation in Egmont National Park.

The coastal highway continues southeast to Wanganui, at the mouth of the Wanganui River, and through the Rangitikei and Manawatu farming districts to Wellington.

Taranaki—land of dairy farms

Renowned for its lush pastures, Taranaki is often called the "garden of New Zealand." Solitary Mount Egmont, its snowy cone looming above the surrounding green fields and dairy farms, dominates the province.

Western coast—the essentials

Taranaki's largest town, New Plymouth, is the starting point for visiting Egmont National Park and exploring the Taranaki countryside. Farther south is Wanganui, where travelers embark on trips up the Wanganui River.

Getting there. Air New Zealand flights serve both New Plymouth and Wanganui. Newmans Coach Lines travels from Auckland, via Waitomo and Hamilton, to New Plymouth. Railways Road Services provides service from Wellington north to Wanganui and New Plymouth.

Accommodations. On the west coast, hotels and motels are concentrated in New Plymouth and Wanganui, though you'll also find accommodations in smaller towns.

Largest of New Plymouth's many hostelries is the Plymouth Hotel; others include the Autolodge, Devon Motor Lodge, and Westown Motor Hotel, all centrally located, and DB Bell Block Hotel, near the airport.

Mountain guest houses offer simple but friendly family-style accommodation for Egmont National Park visitors. Dawson Falls Tourist Lodge perches on Mount Egmont's southeast slope, and Stratford Mountain House occupies a site on the east flank. At North Egmont, visitors can stay at a camp house with bunks and stove, or at huts on some of the hiking trails (contact the chief ranger for information). Motels are located in towns along Highway 3 east of Egmont.

Among Wanganui's leading hotels and motels are Avenue Motor Inn and Bryvern Motor Inn, both a few blocks north of the business district, and Hurley's Grand Hotel, in the center of town.

Getting around. Railways Road Services motorcoaches travel between New Plymouth and Wellington, with stops at Stratford, Hawera, Patea, Wanganui, and other towns. Rental cars are available in New Plymouth and Wanganui. Wanganui River trips depart from Wanganui, Pipiriki, and Taumarunui.

Tourist information. Visitor information centers are located in New Plymouth, Hawera, and Wanganui. The main Egmont National Park visitor center is at North Egmont, near Egmont Village.

Exploring the countryside by car

One of the best ways to see new Zealand is to rent a car and head for the country, where you can explore out-of-the-way places at your leisure. Outside the metropolitan areas, traffic is usually light; in rural districts, you'll occasionally run into a flock of sheep or herd of cattle being prodded along the road to pasture.

Rental cars are available in cities and larger towns. Visitors from the United States, Canada, Australia, and the United Kingdom may hire a car by presenting a current driver's license. A variety of fly-drive touring programs are available for travelers, or you can plan your own itinerary or weekend excursion.

The New Zealand Automobile Association offers reciprocal membership privileges to members of other national automobile touring clubs; bring your membership card. At A.A. offices in the major cities, you can obtain maps, comprehensive motoring information, and accommodation and camping guides. District A.A. offices are located in many large towns.

You'll drive on the left side of the road in New Zealand. The speed limit is 80 kph/50 mph on the open road, 50 kph/30 mph (or as posted) in built-up areas. As you travel, yellow A.A. signposts direct you to points of interest.

Roads are sealed (bitumen surfaced) or metalled (graded gravel, usually all-weather). Country roads have improved considerably in recent years, but city drivers may find some unfamiliar conditions.

Use care and common sense on narrow roads, keeping left and driving at country speeds. Resist the impulse to brake suddenly on graveled roads, since it's easy to skid. Corrugations form in sandy road surfaces despite regular grading, so drive slowly and learn to spot ridges in advance. On narrow bridges, traffic in one direction has the right-of-way; oncoming traffic yields.

In rural areas, you may meet stock on the roads, particularly in early morning and late afternoon. Usually, the farmer will direct his dogs to make a path through the group for you. Move slowly but steadily; don't toot your horn or rev your engine unnecessarily. If the herd is moving toward you, it's simplest just to stop and let them move past. When you're driving after dark, stay alert; animals occasionally wander onto the roads.

New Zealand observes the right-hand rule: unless otherwise controlled by traffic signs or lights, you give way to all traffic on your right (unless you're on a main highway). When turning, you give way to *all* traffic. Use of seat belts is compulsory.

The A.A. booklet *Motoring in New Zealand*, available from the New Zealand Tourist Office or A.A. offices, contains helpful information for motorists.

A historic Maori battleground, Taranaki was invaded many times by fierce tribes from the north and was the scene of the first major battles in the Land Wars. Hostilities spread through the central part of North Island and lasted until 1881. In Waitara, the meeting house at Manukorihi Pa contains outstanding examples of characteristic Taranaki carvings and *tukutuku* work.

In the early 1960s, natural gas was discovered at Kapuni, south of Mount Egmont, and in 1969, offshore drilling rigs began tapping the vast Maui natural gas field off the coast. Natural gas from Taranaki fields now supplies most of North Island and a number of petrochemical industries.

Lush parks enhance New Plymouth

Located about midway between Auckland and Wellington, New Plymouth is Taranaki's only large town. Famous for its outstanding parks and gardens, the town is an important agricultural center, as well as the mainland point for development of the offshore natural gas deposits. The Port Taranaki complex serves coastal and overseas shipping.

Settlers from the British counties of Devon and Cornwall laid out the New Zealand Company's colonizing settlement in 1841. Devon Street (Highway 3) marks the town's main commercial area, and superb parks and gardens lie only minutes away from the central district.

Stop at the Public Relations Office, 81 Liardet Street, for information on city and regional attractions, scenic drives, and other excursions.

City parks. The city's jewel is Pukekura Park, often called the country's most outstanding city park. Just a 10-minute walk up Liardet Street from downtown, it has footpaths winding around two manmade lakes and through the wooded reserve. Azaleas, rhododendrons, and other spring flowering plants put on a spectacular show here from September through November. Rare ferns flourish in the Fernery, and begonias, orchids, and fuchsias bloom in the Begonia House. From the tea kiosk, visitors can enjoy a fine view of Mount Egmont. During summer and holiday periods, rowboats crowd the upper lake.

Adjoining Pukekura Park is Brooklands, a park occupying the wooded site of a pioneer homestead. Native pines ring the Bowl of Brooklands, a natural amphitheater that accommodates up to 19,000 people. During the annual Festival of the Pines in January and February, spectators sit on the grass to enjoy music, dance, and drama under the stars.

Taranaki Museum. Noted for its Maori and colonial collections, the Taranaki Museum, at the corner of Brougham and King streets, is open afternoons only. It has an excellent Maori collection and an Early Colonists' exhibition portraying living conditions in Taranaki's early days.

Other city attractions. Several buildings recall the town's early years. Near Brooklands Park on Brooklands Drive stands The Gables, last of four cottage hospitals built in New Plymouth in the 1840s. Small and simple Hurworth, built in 1856, has been restored by the New Zealand Historic Places Trust; located at 548 Carrington Road, it contains mementos of the family of Sir Harry Atkinson, four times Prime Minister of New Zealand.

Govett-Brewster Art Gallery on Queen Street has a collection of contemporary art from New Zealand and other Pacific countries; it also presents changing exhibits.

For a view over the city and port, follow the scenic drive west to Moturoa Lookout. Inland, Mount Egmont's snowy peak juts above Taranaki pasture lands.

Taranaki excursions

For a different look at Taranaki's abundance, explore some of the region's natural attractions. On two easy side trips from New Plymouth, visitors can hike through remote areas of central North Island and savor the outdoors in Egmont National Park.

Lake Mangamahoe. Located 10 km/7 miles south of New Plymouth off Highway 3, Lake Mangamahoe is famed for its magnificent view — the snow-capped cone of Mount Egmont mirrored in the greenery-framed lake. For the best reflections, come in early morning and drive to the far end of the lake.

Pukeiti Rhododendron Trust. Some 800 varieties of rhododendrons, along with many alpine, bog, and woodland plants, thrive in this large, internationally known private garden about 24 km/15 miles south of New Plymouth. Reached by Upper Carrington Road, the reserve is open the year around, but peak blooming season is from September to November. Grassy paths and forest trails wind through the valley.

A look at Egmont National Park

Loneliest and loveliest of North Island's peaks, Mount Egmont was sighted and named by Captain James Cook in 1770. An almost perfect cone, it dominates the Taranaki Peninsula. Egmont National Park encompasses the mountaintop and its densely wooded slopes, popular with climbers and hikers in summer and with skiers in winter. Mountain guest houses offer simple but cozy family-style accommodations for visitors.

Learn about the park and its activities at the excellent North Egmont Visitor Centre, near Egmont Village, open daily from 9 A.M. to 5 P.M. More park exhibits are located in the Dawson Falls Display Centre on the southeast slope. You can also get park information from the Public Relations offices in New Plymouth and Hawera, or by contacting the park's chief ranger (P.O. Box 43, New Plymouth; phone 80-829).

Mount Egmont's tranquil appearance masks a dormant volcano that last erupted over 200 years ago. Great variations in rainfall and altitude (from sea level to 2,518 meters/8,260 feet), coupled with the mountain's isolation from other high peaks, have endowed it with an unusually varied flora, including a number of plants unique to Egmont.

Nature walks and picnic areas are located near facility areas at North Egmont, East Egmont, and Dawson Falls. In good weather, the climb to the summit isn't difficult, but weather conditions can change rapidly. In summer, you can join a guided excursion. On clear days, hikers gaze inland to the peaks of Tongariro National Park and over undulating dairy lands to the sea.

To reach the park, take Highway 3 southeast from New Plymouth toward Hawera. Roads penetrate the park from Egmont Village in the north, from Stratford in the east, and from Kaponga in the southeast.

Friendly Wanganui

Beyond Egmont, Highway 3 continues southeast through a belt of farming communities — bordering the south Taranaki coast. You'll pass the remains of several historic Maori fortifications.

At the mouth of the Wanganui River is the large town of Wanganui, nestled in a broad curve along the river's west bank. Attractive parks, a well-planned central district, and an outstanding regional museum make Wanganui an inviting stop for travelers. It's also a departure point for boat trips up the Wanganui River.

Wanganui's cultural center is attractive Queen's Park, occupying the site of an early stockade east of Victoria Avenue. Here you'll find the Wanganui Regional Museum, the Sarjeant Art Gallery, a memorial hall complex and conference center, and the public library. Nearby is Cooks Gardens, the town's sports center.

For information about city sightseeing, boat trips, walking tours, and other activities, stop at the Information Centre (Hospitality Wanganui Inc.) beside the City Council Chambers at Guyton and St. Hill streets.

Wanganui Regional Museum. A Maori-style entry invites visitors into the country's largest regional museum. Its outstanding Maori collection is displayed around a 22-meter/72-foot war canoe once paddled by Maori tribesmen on the Wanganui River. You can also see natural history exhibits and a replica settler's cottage.

Jet boats skim the wild rivers

Jet boats were developed in New Zealand for navigating the country's shallow rivers. Fast, versatile, and highly maneuverable, they add a thrilling dimension to New Zealand sightseeing and provide convenient transportation to remote recreation areas.

The jet-propulsion motor that powers the boat was designed by the late Bill Hamilton, a New Zealand farmer with an engineering background and an ability to improvise. His North Canterbury sheep station covered wild and desolate high country, much of it accessible only by traveling up the fast, rock-strewn rivers that raced down from the icy Southern Alps. He wanted access to this remote country, not only to muster his stock but also to open up the magnificent, untamed hunting and fishing country that otherwise took days to reach on foot or horseback.

The powerful jet boat engine Hamilton devised sucks up water beneath the hull of the craft and spits it out behind; this gives the boat the required thrust, as well as enables it to perform at full speed in as little as 10 centimeters/4 inches of water.

Today, on many of the world's wild rivers, Hamilton jet boats skim through white-water rapids, avoiding midstream boulders and sheer canyon walls often by just a deft turn of the wheel.

Located at the entrance to Queen's Park at Watt Street and Maria Place, the museum is open on weekdays from 9:30 A.M. to 4:30 P.M., and on weekends and holidays from 1 to 5 P.M.

Sarjeant Art Gallery. Visitors enjoy changing exhibitions and displays from the gallery's permanent collection of 19th and 20th century British and New Zealand paintings. The gallery's domed building is located in Queen's Park above the Veterans' Steps. Hours are Monday from noon to 4:30 P.M., Tuesday through Friday from 10 A.M. to 4:30 P.M., and weekends and holidays from 1 to 4:30 P.M.

Durie Hill lookout. For a splendid view of the town and surrounding countryside, cross the river on the City Bridge, at the end of Victoria Avenue. From Anzac Parade at the bridge, pedestrians walk through a tunnel to the hill elevator, a commuter service for hilltop residents. For the best views, climb the spiral stairway to the top of the elevator building or ascend the nearby Durie Hill Memorial Tower, a city landmark. Motorists drive up Portal Street to reach the summit.

Parks. Wanganui's floral showplace and favorite picnic spot is serene and lovely Virginia Lake, surrounded by attractive residential areas north of the city on St. John's Hill. Highway 3 skirts the lake's southern shore. You can walk around the lake or through the woods, feed the waterfowl, visit the walk-through aviary, or enjoy flower displays in the Winter Gardens.

An imaginative children's playground and several picnic areas attract families to Kowhai Park, beside the river on Anzac Parade by the Dublin Street Bridge.

Other attractions. At Holly Lodge Estate, a colonial homestead, visitors can sample local wines, browse in a craft shop, and view displays in a small museum. From the lodge jetty, jet boat trips depart daily at 10 A.M. and 2 P.M. up the Wanganui River to Hipango Park. To reach the estate, take Somme Parade along the river.

Southeast of the Wanganui River in Putiki, St. Paul's Memorial Church is an outstanding example of Maori craftsmanship. Carvings, *tukutuku* panels, and painted rafters decorate the interior. From Wanganui, cross the river on the Cobham Bridge (Highway 3); turn left at the first street (Wikitoria Road) and left again on Anaua Street.

The beach at Castlecliff, west of town, attracts swimmers. Walkers can explore Bushy Park Homestead and bush reserve at Kai-Iwi, northwest of Wanganui.

Up the Wanganui River

Maori canoes and flat-bottomed river steamers once plied this historic waterway, which links the rugged interior of North Island with the west coast. Flowing down from Mount Tongariro, the Wanganui is one of New Zealand's longest and most beautiful waterways.

The most scenic stretch of the river is above Pipiriki; this section is accessible only by jet boat, canoe, and trail. For much of the way, the upper river winds between steep, fern-draped banks and tumbles over some 240 rapids. Below Pipiriki, the lower river is generally placid and bordered by willows.

Wanganui River Road. Close by the river is Wanganui River Road, which follows a winding route above the river northwest to Pipiriki, then turns east to meet Highway 4 at Raetihi, southwest of Tongariro National Park.

Several of the riverside settlements began as mission stations, their original names transliterated into Maori equivalents. Most travelers stop at Matahiwi to see the historic water-powered Kawana Flour Mill, built in 1854. At Pipiriki, the Colonial House Information Centre and Museum is open daily in summer from 10 A.M. to 5 P.M., at other times on request at the ranger's house.

Excursions. Jet boat operators in Pipiriki and Taumarunui transport sightseers and hikers deep into the Wanganui country, and several canoe operators offer guided trips during the summer. Information on the Wanganui River reserves is available from the senior ranger (Pipiriki, RD 6, Wanganui; phone Raetihi 4631).

On the East Cape Road *between Te Kaha and Waihau Bay, a tiny Anglican church overlooks the reef at Raukokore. Norfolk pines tower above the burial ground.*

From Wanganui, jet boat excursions explore the lower river some 32 km/20 miles upstream to Hipango Park. In summer, the riverboat M.V. *Waireka* also operates on the lower river. Mini-bus tours take sightseers from Wanganui to Pipiriki on weekdays during the tourist season. Information on excursions is available from the Information Centre in Wanganui.

The Wanganui River Walk, operated by Venturetreks Ltd. (P.O. Box 3839, Auckland), is a 4-day escorted hiking trek into this country. Departing from Ohakune from December through February, the excursion includes transportation and all camping equipment. Camps are set up each night, and hikers carry only personal gear.

Along the eastern coast

From Opotiki on the Bay of Plenty, motorists can follow Highway 35 as it twists around the rugged, heavily forested East Cape or take Highway 2, which runs southeast across the base of the cape. The routes meet again at Poverty Bay, and Highway 2 continues south along the coast.

Two mountain highways cut inland to central tourist areas. From Wairoa, Highway 38 heads northwest through Urewera National Park and Kaingaroa State Forest to Rotorua. Highway 5 follows a historic Maori track and stagecoach route northwest from Napier to Taupo.

Around the East Cape

Cut off by wooded mountains from the rest of North Island, sparsely populated East Cape clings to the leisurely pace of an earlier era. Pohutukawa trees border curving bays and deserted, log-strewn beaches.

To explore the cape, follow the coastal road (Highway 35) from Opotiki. The route closely borders the Bay of Plenty northeast to Cape Runaway, then loops around past New Zealand's most easterly point and continues south, briefly touching the shore at Tokomaru and Tolaga bays before reaching Gisborne.

Captain Cook sailed along the East Cape shore in 1769 and anchored at Tolaga Bay to take on water and wood. In the 1830s, whalers operated along this scenic coast, but the cape's isolated location discouraged European settlement. East Cape traditionally has had a sizable Maori population; you can see excellent examples of Maori carving and art decoration in churches and meeting houses in Te Kaha, Hicks Bay, Tikitiki, and Ruatoria.

Along the coast road, you'll pass Te Kaha, set in an attractive cove, and Hicks Bay, a popular campground. Te Araroa is known as New Zealand's most easterly village. Hot mineral springs are located at Te Puia. South of Tokomaru Bay, a short side road leads travelers to a magnificent stretch of beach and a coastal trail through Anaura Bay Scenic Reserve. Attractive Tolaga Bay offers good swimming and fishing; it's an easy walk to Cook's Cove, with its lookout points over the sheltered bay.

Eastern coast—the essentials

The winding shoreline road (Highway 35) skirts the East Cape shore between Opotiki and Gisborne. The more direct route is Highway 2, which cuts across the base of the cape and continues south past Poverty Bay and Hawke Bay. Tourist towns along the route are Gisborne, on Poverty Bay; the busy seaside resort of Napier; and Hastings, a fruit-growing and winemaking center.

Getting there. Air New Zealand flights serve Gisborne and Napier from Auckland and Wellington. New Zealand Railways provides daily train service between Wellington and Gisborne, with stops at larger towns. Motorcoach service by Mount Cook Line and Railways Road Services links the east coast centers with Auckland, Hamilton, Rotorua, and other towns; Newmans Coach Lines operates on the Wellington-Napier route.

Accommodations. Simple accommodations are available in some of the scattered East Cape settlements, among them Waihau Bay, Hicks Bay, Te Araroa, Ruatoria, Te Puia, and Tolaga Bay. Gisborne accommodations include the Sandown Park Motor Hotel, DB Gisborne Hotel, Teal Motor Lodge, Blue Pacific Beachfront Motel, and Orange Grove Motel. Urewera National Park visitors stay in motel, cabin, and camping facilities at Waikaremoana and Ruatahuna.

In Napier, centrally located accommodations include Napier Travel Inn, Tennyson Motor Inn, and the refurbished Masonic Establishment Hotel. Modern motels are clustered along Kennedy Road in the suburb of Pirimai and along Highway 2 north of town. In Hastings, there's a wide choice, including the Angus Inn, Mayfair Hotel, and Elmore Lodge Motel. In Havelock North, the DB Te Mata Hotel and several small motels serve travelers.

Getting around. Railways Road Services motorcoaches provide scheduled service from Gisborne around East Cape to Opotiki (Bay of Plenty), and stop at Napier and Hastings on longer runs. Mount Cook Line coaches operate local service between Gisborne and Napier. Rental cars are available in Gisborne, Napier, and Hastings.

Tourist information. Obtain sightseeing suggestions at Public Relations Offices in Gisborne (209 Grey Street), Napier (on Marine Parade near the Colonnade), and Hastings (on Russell Street North). In Urewera National Park, tourist information is available at Aniwaniwa.

Gisborne—Captain Cook's landing site

Bordering the shore of Poverty Bay, prosperous Gisborne belies the name bestowed by Captain Cook. His party came ashore at Kaiti Beach, near the mouth of the Turanganui River, on October 9, 1769, the first Europeans to land on New Zealand soil. A monument on Kaiti Beach Road marks Cook's landing site.

From a lookout atop Kaiti Hill, you have a splendid view over the city, harbor, and surrounding river valleys. Nearby is Cook Memorial Observatory.

For information on local activities, visit the Public Relations Office at 209 Grey Street. A regional museum and arts center is located on Stout Street. In summer, bathers enjoy Waikanae Beach, near the center of town at the end of Grey Street. Other good swimming beaches extend north of Gisborne from Wainui to Whangara.

Urewera National Park

Dense virgin forests cover the rugged Urewera ranges west of Gisborne. Following an old Maori route, Highway 38 branches inland from Highway 2 at Wairoa; it proceeds northwest through mountains and valleys to remote Urewera National Park and its sparkling gem, Lake Waikaremoana.

You can enjoy the park's scenery from the highway, but if possible, allow time for at least a short walk through the dense forest. At park headquarters at Aniwaniwa, visitors can obtain trail information, see exhibits, and purchase fishing licenses and shooting permits. In summer, rangers conduct field trips and nature programs. Park information is also available from the chief ranger (Waikaremoana, Private Bag, Wairoa; phone Tuai 803) or from rangers in Murupara (west of the park on Highway 38) or Taneatua (north of the park on Highway 2).

Walks range from a few minutes' stroll to nearby waterfalls to a 5-day tramp around the lake. Near the park visitor center, short trails lead to lovely Bridal Veil, Aniwaniwa, and Papakorito falls. A half-day excursion traverses beech forest and ferny glades to Lake Waikareiti. Huts are maintained on longer trails.

Many trout anglers cast near Mokau Landing, an inlet on Lake Waikaremoana's north shore. Water-sports enthusiasts come here for swimming, boating, and water-skiing. Picnickers enjoy Rosie Bay, south of park headquarters.

From November through March, Te Rehuwai Safaris (Ruatahuna, Private Bag, Rotorua) operates a 5-day Urewera adventure trek through Maori lands and the national park. Led by Maori guides well versed in local history and forest lore, the group departs from Ruatahuna (on Highway 38) and hikes about 30 km/19 miles down the Whakatane River Valley. Groups sleep in tents and cook meals over an open fire. All equipment is provided; trekkers carry only their personal effects.

Napier, lively seaside resort

One of North Island's prettiest towns, Napier is the main holiday and commercial center of the Hawke's Bay district, a region of sheep farms, fruit orchards, and vineyards. Along Napier's rocky beach runs a long esplanade bordered with tall Norfolk pines and an array of recreation facilities and activities.

Above the Marine Parade, white houses dot the slope of Bluff Hill above the blue waters of the bay. Most of

Napier's buildings were rebuilt after a 1931 earthquake and fire destroyed the town.

The Public Relations Office, on Marine Parade just south of the Colonnade, provides information on activities and a street map outlining the city's scenic drive.

Marine Parade. Most of Napier's attractions face this pine-bordered oceanfront avenue. Thousands of tiny lights festoon the trees during the summer holidays.

At the south end of the Parade is the handsome Hawke's Bay Aquarium, housing an 86,000-gallon salt-water oceanarium filled with an impressive display of marine life, a wave-action tank and tidal pool, New Zealand fish swimming in a fresh-water stream, and tanks displaying many kinds of marine life and imported fresh-water tropical fish. On the top floor you can see large turtles and native tuatara lizards.

Performing daily at Marineland of New Zealand, also on Marine Parade, are trained marine animals — dolphins, leopard seals, penguins, and sea lions.

You can see New Zealand's famous kiwis, wekas, opossums, and other night-roaming birds and animals at the Nocturnal Wildlife Centre; feeding time is 2:30 P.M.

Other seaside attractions include the Sunken Gardens, built on rubble from the 1931 earthquake; a boating lake; midget racing cars; outdoor roller-skating rink; putt-putt golf; outdoor salt-water pool (open in summer only); floral clock; and children's play areas. The Pania statue stands near the fountain. On alternate summer Saturdays, craftspeople set up stalls near the sound shell.

Bluff Hill. For viewpoints over Hawke's Bay, follow the city's scenic drive to a pair of overlooks atop Bluff Hill. At the top of Lighthouse Road, you look down on the harbor, where cranes load cargo onto freighters bound for overseas ports. A streetside platform beside Clyde Road offers another view over the town and tree-lined waterfront south to Cape Kidnappers.

Other attractions. Across Marine Parade opposite the Colonnade, you'll find the Lilliput Village and Railway. Miniature trains circle a model village populated by tiny animated figures engaged in daily chores and play.

The Hawke's Bay Museum and Art Gallery on Herschell Street features exhibits on the 1931 earthquake, Maori displays dating from the moa hunter era, artifacts of the region, and changing art exhibitions.

Napier's Botanical Gardens spill down the slopes of Hospital Hill. Trees give way to formal gardens, an aviary, and an outdoor amphitheater where open-air concerts are staged. Roses bloom in Kennedy Park.

Small boats anchor in the Iron Pot, an Ahuriri district inlet named by early whalers. Acres of lowlands, upthrust here during the earthquake, have been reclaimed.

Local sightseeing tours take in many Hawke's Bay attractions; on specialized tours, visitors can see rural homesteads, watch craftspeople at work, or spend a day fishing.

Rugby — a way of life

In New Zealand, rugby is not merely the national sport—it's a way of life. From May through September, rugby (officially, Rugby Union football) is played in every province and hamlet throughout the country. Good seats for important interprovincial and international games— such as New Zealand vs. South Africa, Australia, Britain, or France—are highly prized and difficult to obtain.

To be a team player on the champion All Blacks (so-called because of the color of their uniforms) is the ambition of every boy from the first time he handles the oval ball. Boys begin playing rugby, a completely amateur sport, at the age of seven and often continue into adult life.

Rugby has much in common with American football. Each side attempts to carry a blown-up pigskin over the goal line or kick it through the goal posts with more consistency than the opposition. Unlike football, though, rugby players don't wear heavy padding, and action is continuous. Play does not halt until someone scores, the ball goes out of bounds, or a rule is broken. Each side has eight forwards and seven backs, and every man on the field can run, pass (laterally or backward), and kick. When tackled, the man with the ball must let go once he is pulled down.

You can learn more about the history of the sport of Rugby Union at the National Rugby Museum, located at Grey and Carroll streets in Palmerston North. Open afternoons only, the museum exhibits clothing, photographs, badges, programs, and other memorabilia from the game's early years.

Safari trip to a gannet sanctuary

Getting there is half the fun when you travel to the world's only mainland gannet colony at the tip of Cape Kidnappers. Usually, the birds breed only on isolated islands.

The large sea birds, white with a golden crown and black-tipped feathers, return here in late July. Chicks hatch in late November and December. The best period to visit is from November to March, when migration begins.

Gannet Safaris operates four-wheel-drive vehicles from Summerlee Station on an overland route through gorges, along river beds, and atop cliffs to reach the remote sanctuary. Burden's Beach Safaris features a trip by tractor-drawn trailer from Te Awanga along beach and cliffs. At low tide, you can also reach the colony by a beach route.

Behind the commercial district, tidy houses climb the green hills surrounding Wellington's harbor. Numerous city walks offer splendid views.

Tread the Hawke's Bay wine trail

Vineyards thrive in the sunny Mediterranean climate of Hawke's Bay, second largest of the country's wine-producing areas. Wineries welcome visitors Monday through Saturday for informal tasting; a leaflet with map showing the locations of the wineries is available at tourist offices in Napier and Hastings.

After a mission station was established here in 1851, the French missionaries planted vineyards and soon began producing wine for church and table use. About 1,400 acres of vineyards now cover the sunny slopes and plains around Napier, Hastings, and Havelock North.

Commercial production began here in 1896; New Zealand's oldest winery is Te Mata Estate Winery on Te Mata Road, Havelock North, where visitors see historic buildings and displays on early winemaking in the region. Vidal Wine Producers in Hastings features a vineyard wine bar and wine museum. Some wineries offer guided or self-conducted tours.

Hastings—the country's fruit basket

Orchards and market gardens surround Hastings, a city of parks and gardens on the Heretaunga Plains. Often called "the fruit bowl of New Zealand," it is renowned for its productive orchards—apple, peach, pear, plum, nectarine, and other fruits. Though food-processing factories can and freeze most of the harvest, farmers still sell produce directly to the public at roadside stalls.

The tourist information office faces Russell Street North a half-block from the post office. Ask for a scenic drive folder routing motorists to the area's highlights.

Bagpipes herald the Highland Games in Hastings on Easter weekend. National and provincial champions meet here to compete in piping, drumming, dancing, and athletic events.

Parks. The city's best-known landmark is Fantasyland, a community playground for the young at heart in Windsor Park, east of the business district. Built around a fanciful storybook castle, the imaginative play equipment depicts children's storybook characters. A train chugs around the playground, and rental boats bob on the lake.

Cornwall Park is noted for its trees, superb formal flower gardens, and small aviary. In Frimley Park, you can picnic beneath rare trees, enjoy the rose gardens, and swim in the nearby aquatic center. A mile-long canopy of oak trees, especially lovely in autumn, graces Oak Avenue, northwest of the city off Omahu Road.

Havelock North. This choice residential area spreads along hilly slopes southeast of Hastings.

For the finest view of the Hawke's Bay district, follow Te Mata Peak Road 6 km/4 miles up to the mountain's summit. Your view extends over the region's orchards, gardens, vineyards, rivers, towns, and coast. Before leaving the peak, amble down one of the wooded nature trails in Te Mata Park.

Through the Wairarapa farm lands

South of Hastings, Highway 2 veers inland through rolling pastures and small farm towns toward Wellington. In the 1870s, Scandinavian settlers carved Norsewood, Dannevirke, and Eketahuna out of the vast totara forest then covering the region.

At Woodville, Highway 3 branches west through the magnificent Manawatu Gorge and the town of Palmerston North, noted for its agricultural research and as the home of Massey University. Several parks border the river.

From its headwaters in the Ruahine Range, the Manawatu slices westward through the mountainous spine of North Island and into the Tasman Sea. Built in the 1870s, the road through the scenic Manawatu Gorge was a difficult construction feat; at times, workers were suspended from the clifftops by ropes.

Pahiatua, on Highway 2 south of Woodville, marks the northern end of the rugged Tararua Range.

Rare native birds breed in captivity at the Mount Bruce Native Bird Reserve, 24 km/15 miles north of Masterton. Visitors can watch takahe, kakapo, kiwi, pukeko, and other birds daily from 10 A.M. to 4 P.M., except during the October to mid-December breeding period.

Heart of the Wairarapa farming district is Masterton, about 100 km/62 miles north of Wellington. The world's fastest shearers compete here each March at the Golden Shears International Sheep Shearing Contest.

The highway continues south through dairy and sheep-fattening farms and market gardens to Carterton, Greytown, and Featherston. Roads lead west from the highway to the edge of Tararua Forest Park.

Wellington, the capital city

Wooded hills curve like a green amphitheater around Wellington's sparkling harbor, giving New Zealand's capital city its character and charm. From atop Mount Victoria and other lofty viewpoints, your gaze sweeps over a magnificent vista with ever-changing moods.

Located at the southwestern tip of North Island, Wellington is the country's second largest city. Forested peninsulas and shipping wharves jut into the harbor. In the heart of the city, commercial and government buildings rim the waterfront; the curving thoroughfares of Lambton and Thorndon quays mark the city's original shoreline. Nostalgic Victorian buildings mingle pleasantly with more modern structures. Above the business district, dwellings cling precariously to the steep slopes.

Wellington was the first settlement organized by the London-based New Zealand Company. In 1840, shiploads of settlers sailed into Port Nicholson's sheltered waters. When the seat of government was transferred from Auckland to Wellington in 1865, the permanent character of the young town was determined.

Wellington's changeable marine climate is generally free from extremes of heat and cold. Bracing winds that funnel through Cook Strait clear the air and add zest to daily life. A nearby geologic fault subjects the city to occasional earthquakes.

Getting settled in Wellington

Heart of Wellington's shopping district is Lambton Quay, which winds through the middle of the commercial district. Featherston Street is the city's financial center. Transportation facilities are located north of the business center: the railway station borders Thorndon Quay; interisland ferries tie up at the terminal on Aotea Quay.

Shopping. Shops, boutiques, and department stores flank a mile-long thoroughfare extending from Lambton Quay south along Willis and Manners streets to Courtenay Place. Another lively district is The Oaks complex, a pedestrian shopping mall on Cuba and Manners streets. Downtown stores are generally open on weekdays from 9 A.M. to 5:30 P.M. and on Friday evening until 9 P.M.

Entertainment and the arts. Wellington is the home of both the New Zealand Symphony and the national ballet company; in addition, it supports numerous amateur drama and music groups. Much of Wellington's after-dark musical entertainment centers around the city's hotels and drinking establishments. Current attractions are listed in Wellington tourist publications and the daily newspapers.

New Zealand and overseas artists perform at the Town Hall. Plays are presented by the Downstage Theatre repertory group, the Circa Theatre, and the Wellington Repertory Theatre. The Wellington Operatic Society offers musical productions. In summer, the symphony plays a series of promenade concerts, and music groups perform in the Botanic Gardens sound shell.

The art scene is also flourishing, with many galleries and several craft markets showcasing the work of the country's artists and craftspeople.

Sports. Horse racing fans head north of the city to Trentham Racecourse in Upper Hutt; trotting events take place at Hutt Park Raceway in Petone. Rugby Union games are held at Athletic Park, Rugby League at Rugby League Park, soccer and cricket matches at Basin Reserve. Championship tennis matches are played at Central Park, and you can watch bowls and croquet at Kelburn Park. Golfers find several fine courses in and near the city; the seaside links at Paraparaumu, a 45-minute drive north of the city, rank among the country's top courses.

Oriental Bay's boat harbor is the center of yachting activities; in summer, you often see yachting and rowing races on the harbor. Swimmers can choose salt or fresh water, beach or pool, surf or calm harbor waters. No matter what the weather, swimmers enjoy Freyberg Pool off Oriental Parade. On warm, sunny days, crowds flock to the beach fronting Oriental Parade, near the heart of the city. Surfers head for the Miramar Peninsula.

Wellington—the essentials

New Zealand's capital city, Wellington curves around a scenic harbor at the southwestern tip of North Island. Nearby towns and beaches along the Tasman coast are favorite weekend destinations.

Getting there. Air New Zealand flights serve Wellington Airport, about 8 km/5 miles southeast of the city, from cities and larger towns on both islands. Wellington Railway Station on Waterloo Quay is the southern terminus for North Island rail service. Motorcoaches of Railways Road Services, Mount Cook Line, and Newmans Coach Lines also converge on the capital. Interisland ferries travel several times daily between Picton, on South Island, and Wellington's Aotea Quay terminal. Cruise liners moor at the Overseas Passenger Terminal during Wellington stopovers.

Accommodations. Largest of Wellington's downtown hotels is the James Cook, towering above the business district from its hillside site on The Terrace. New hotels commanding fine views over the city and harbor are the luxurious Parkroyal, at the eastern end of Oriental Parade, and the Terrace Regency, tucked away in a quiet part of The Terrace. Older downtown hotels include the St. George, De Brett, and Waterloo.

Among other modern, centrally located hotels are the Abel Tasman Courtesy Inn at Willis and Dixon streets, and the Wellington Travelodge and Town House Motor Inn, both near the Overseas Passenger Terminal.

Travelers who prefer to stay outside the central district can lodge at the Sharella Motor Inn, on Glenmore Street near the entrance to the Botanic Gardens, or the Shaw Savill Lodge, in suburban Kilbirnie near the airport.

Food and drink. Wellington offers a pleasant choice of elegant or informal restaurants. Reservations are recommended, especially on weekends. Several of the capital's best-known restaurants specialize in French cuisine; others feature Italian dishes or New Zealand specialties, such as seafood and game. For special atmosphere, consider Plimmer House, an elegant restaurant in a lovely old Victorian house, and Windows on Wellington, noted for its panoramic views over the city and harbor.

Getting around. Taxi stands are located at all terminals and at several downtown locations. Airport buses provide 20-minute shuttle service between the central district and the airport. Trolley and diesel buses of the Wellington City Transport Department fan out to the city's residential areas; for information, phone 856-579. Most bus lines begin at the railway station (platform 9) or on Courtenay Place and run along Lambton Quay at some point. The Kelburn cable car travels between Lambton Quay and Kelburn at 10-minute intervals.

Electrified suburban trains depart from the railway station for Hutt Valley towns and west coast settlements as far north as Paekakariki. Rental cars are available in downtown Wellington, at the airport and ferry terminal, and in Lower Hutt.

A city sightseeing tour departs daily at 2 P.M. from the Public Relations Office on Mercer Street. Weekend full-day excursions take visitors to Otaki and west coast beaches along the Golden Coast, and to Palliser Bay and the south Wairarapa coast.

Tourist information. Sightseeing suggestions and information on local walking tours and scenic drives are available at the Public Relations Office at Mercer and Victoria streets (phone 735-063). Travel accommodations and arrangements throughout the country are handled by the Government Tourist Bureau, a block away at 27-31 Mercer Street. Automobile club members can obtain motoring information and maps at the Automobile Association office at 166 Willis Street.

Savor harbor views

Arterial roads and suburban streets wind up, down, and around the city's hills, and spectacular views are only minutes away from downtown.

For the best view, make your way to the top of Mount Victoria. Below you, the city and its hills encircle the sparkling harbor. Your panorama extends north to the Hutt Valley, to the eastern bays backed by the Rimutaka Range, and south across the harbor and Cook Strait.

The quickest and easiest route to a magnificent view is aboard one of the bright red cable cars that climb from Lambton Quay to Kelburn. Board at the lower terminal on Cable Car Lane, off Lambton Quay opposite Grey Street. In 3½ minutes, the electrically operated cars ascend high above city traffic. Several interesting walks begin near the upper terminal and wind down through the Botanic Gardens and interesting neighborhoods to Lambton Quay.

The best water-level viewpoint of the harbor is from the Massey Memorial on the top of Point Halswell, about 11 km/7 miles from the city center. It's a favorite stop on the City Marine Drive that skirts the harbor.

On foot in Wellington

Despite its steep hills, you can explore much of the city on foot. Stairways and footpaths climb Wellington's slopes. Buses and the Kelburn cable car take you to more distant destinations.

Along the waterfront. As you walk along Wellington's waterfront, you may see ships docking at downtown wharves and Cook Strait ferries steaming across the harbor. From the Wellington Boat Harbour, look up at the pastel wooden houses clinging to the hills above Oriental Bay.

At Queens Wharf on Jervois Quay, tour the Maritime Museum in the fine old Wellington Harbour Board building. You'll see models and relics of ships that have sailed these waters, as well as historic charts, journals, photographs, and other articles chronicling the port's history. Visitors are welcome on weekdays from 10 A.M. to 4 P.M. and on Saturday from 2 to 5 P.M.

The commercial center. In Wellington's early years, Lambton and Thorndon quays bordered the waterfront. A series of sidewalk plaques mark the original shoreline. Settlers began reclaiming land as early as 1852, and today, much of the business district is built on reclaimed land.

You'll enjoy exploring Lambton Quay, the city's shopping thoroughfare, and its side streets. Higher on the hills, new office buildings and apartment towers indicate a building boom along The Terrace.

Few streets link Lambton Quay with the upper level commercial and residential areas. One shortcut is the Plimmer Steps, a pedestrian stairway connecting Lambton Quay (near Hunter Street) with Boulcott Street. An elevator runs between The Terrace, just north of the James Cook Hotel, and Lambton Quay.

Civic center. South of the shopping district is Wellington's Town Hall and the new Michael Fowler Centre, a multipurpose concert and conference center completed in 1983; its main entrance is on Wakefield Street. Across Mercer Street, the Rotary Garden Court with its handsome conservatory is a popular picnic spot for nearby office workers.

The Wellington Public Library, 8-18 Mercer Street, has a New Zealand room and a newspaper reading room where you can find domestic and international papers. The Golden Bay Planetarium, behind the library on Harris Street, offers programs on weekend afternoons.

Hillside walks. Several enjoyable walking routes begin near the upper terminal of the Kelburn cable car (page 64). Map brochures, available at the Public Relations Office, Mercer and Victoria streets, guide your way.

It's a pleasant downhill stroll through the Wellington Botanic Gardens, a large hillside reserve. In spring, azaleas, camellias, rhododendrons, and bulbs blossom forth in a spectacular display. Roses bloom from November to April in formal plantings in the Lady Norwood Rose Garden. Indoor flowering plants and ferns are on view daily in the Begonia House. On Sunday and on summer evenings band concerts are presented in the sound shell. Near the Rose Garden, you can board bus number 12 to return to downtown.

Just below the Botanic Gardens is historic Thorndon, one of Wellington's most charming districts. Though many of the city's older wooden dwellings have fallen victim to the motorway that cuts a broad swath along the hills, you'll still find delightful cottages and other buildings dating from the 1870s along Ascot Street, Tinakori Road, and terraces branching off it. The *Thorndon Walk* leaflet guides you along the way.

Weekend wanderings for city visitors

New Zealanders treasure their weekends. Most shops, offices, and services operate on a limited schedule or close completely on Saturday and Sunday, and city streets empty as Kiwis head for home, country, or shore.

The savvy traveler plans ahead. To learn about special events and other activities, check local newspapers and tourist officials. If you want to rent a car, reserve ahead (the earlier the better) and arrange a pick-up time. Travelers planning a weekend excursion using public transportation should confirm the time schedule in advance.

Explore on foot. If you've just arrived, get acquainted with the downtown district, walk along the waterfront, or follow paths through hillside forest parks. Join local families in admiring the flowers or listening to a band concert in the botanic gardens.

Take a boat ride. In most cities and tourist areas, you can board a harbor launch, ferry, jet boat, lake cruiser, or other boat for an afternoon on the water.

Visit a museum. Learn about New Zealand natural history, Maori culture, and the colonial days. Inspect vintage vehicles and even take a ride in one at a transportation museum.

Head for the beach. Soak up the sun, watch boats, swim, or surf in the waves. Take along a picnic and spread it out on the sand.

Watch a sports event. Saturday is sports day in New Zealand. Go to the races or attend a rugby match.

Join the animals. Visit the zoo. See a kiwi bird and other native—and introduced—birds and animals.

Visit the library. If the weather is gloomy, catch up on home news in the library's newspaper reading room or browse through the New Zealand book collection.

Another route is the *Town and Gown Walk,* which starts near the upper Kelburn terminal and cuts down through the hillside campus of Victoria University along Salamanca Road.

Government Centre—heart of the nation

One part of Wellington belongs to all New Zealanders: the country's political center. It crowns a knoll near the north end of Lambton Quay, where it intersects with Bowen and Molesworth streets.

Horse racing— a popular spectator sport

Some of the world's top thoroughbred horses are raised in New Zealand, where the breeding and racing of horses is big business. Spectators flock to racetracks throughout the country, and a Saturday or holiday spent at the races will bring you in close contact with a crowd of enthusiastic Kiwis.

Most of the important gallop racing meets take place at North Island tracks, including Ellerslie and Avondale (Auckland), Te Rapa (Hamilton), Trentham (Wellington), Awapuni (Palmerston North), and Hastings (Hastings). Among main South Island tracks are Riccarton in Christchurch and Wingatui in Dunedin.

Major harness racing tracks include Alexandra Park and Epsom in Auckland, Hutt Park in Wellington, Addington in Christchurch, and Forbury Park in Dunedin. Many races take place at night under floodlights.

Admission prices vary, depending on whether you buy an inside or outside enclosure. Inside is similar to reserved grandstand seating; outside is comparable to general admission.

Parliament Buildings. Dignified Parliament House, completed in 1922, and the lighter Gothic architecture of the 1897 General Assembly Library contrast dramatically with the new circular Executive Wing (commonly called "the Beehive"), opened by Queen Elizabeth in 1977. New Zealand materials, especially native woods and Takaka marble, were used liberally in their construction.

The buildings are not open to casual sightseers, but you can join a conducted tour of the public areas. Tours depart from the main reception desk at regular intervals; information is available from the Chief Messenger's Office (phone 749-199). Parliamentary procedures, modeled after those of Britain's Parliament, are explained. If Parliament is in session (usually from May through October), you can watch the proceedings from the visitors' gallery.

Other buildings. At Museum and Bowen streets behind the Parliament Buildings is Broadcasting House, center of the Broadcasting Corporation of New Zealand.

Facing Lambton Quay opposite the Cenotaph are the Government Buildings, a marvelous example of Wellington's early architecture. Constructed on reclaimed land in 1876, the 152-room wooden building converts traditional 19th century stone architecture into timbered Italianate style.

Open on weekdays, the buildings of the Law Courts on Ballance Street house three levels of New Zealand's legal hierarchy — the Magistrate's Court, the Supreme Court, and the Court of Appeals.

Reminders of the Victorian era

In older sections of the city, Victorian dwellings and other historic buildings provide nostalgic contrast to more modern structures. Gabled houses climb the hills, their brass doorknockers and tall bay windows adding touches of 19th century elegance.

Old St. Paul's Church. Just a short walk from the Parliament Buildings, Wellington's renowned old Anglican church is a Mulgrave Street landmark. Built in 1866, it adapted traditional Victorian Gothic architecture to colonial conditions and native woods. Inside, stained glass windows and brass plates provide a valuable century-long record of its parishioners.

Supplanted by a new cathedral in 1966, the church has been restored as a tranquil setting for cultural events. It's open to the public Monday through Saturday from 10 A.M. to 4:30 P.M. and on Sunday from 1:30 to 4:30 P.M.

Early houses. Among former dwellings still in use are the Plimmer House, an 1870s gem on Boulcott Street, now a fashionable restaurant; and the stately, turreted Williams residence at 53 Hobson Street, incorporated into Queen Margaret College. Antrim House, an ornate Edwardian town house at 63 Boulcott Street, is headquarters for the New Zealand Historic Places Trust.

Colonial Cottage Museum, 68 Nairn Street, is housed in a cottage built in the 1850s. Restored and furnished with period articles, it recalls the life of the city's pioneers. Museum hours are 10 A.M. to 4 P.M. Wednesday through Friday and noon to 4 P.M. on Saturday and Sunday.

National Museum and Art Gallery

Overlooking the city and harbor, the National Museum and National Art Gallery share a handsome building on Buckle Street. A large tower in front of the museum contains a carillon and the Hall of Memories, the national war memorial. To reach the site, take bus number 1 or 3 from the railway station to Basin Reserve and walk 2 blocks west.

The museum is noted for its fascinating Maori collection, which concentrates on articles from Taranaki and central North Island. Highlight of the colonial section is an early Wellington dwelling furnished in 1840s style. Relics from Captain Cook's voyages are also on display.

The National Art Gallery shows works by New Zealand and overseas artists and puts on special exhibitions.

Something for everyone

Depending on your interests, attractions ranging from historic manuscripts to collections of native plants and flowers invite your perusal.

Domed "Beehive," housing executive offices of Parliament, is a new Wellington landmark. Its modern lines contrast with older Parliament House.

Alexander Turnbull Library. Visitors as well as scholars come here to see the original signed parchment sheets of the Treaty of Waitangi, as well as changing displays from the library's fascinating collections. The library is celebrated for its valuable books and manuscripts, as well as its historic maps, charts, and pictures relating to New Zealand history and Pacific exploration. Located at 44 The Terrace (2nd floor), the library is open on weekdays from 10:30 A.M. to 5 P.M. and on Saturday from 9 A.M. to noon.

City Art Gallery. Located at 65 Victoria Street, the gallery sponsors a series of stimulating exhibitions. It's open on weekdays and on Saturday and Sunday afternoons.

Katherine Mansfield Memorial Park. This shaded garden on Fitzherbert Street, off Hobson Street just east of the motorway, honors New Zealand's most acclaimed writer of short stories (her real name was Kathleen Beauchamp). Many of her best-known works are set in Wellington. Her birthplace still stands at 25 Tinakori Road.

Native plant garden. New Zealand's most complete collection of native flora has been assembled at the Otari Open-Air Plant Museum in the northwest suburb of Wilton. Paths through formal areas lead into a sheltered, wooded valley where visitors can picnic. To reach the garden, located off Wilton Road, take bus 14 from the city.

Castle Collection of Musical Instruments. Also located in the Newtown district, this private working collection contains several hundred early and unusual instruments from all over the world. Tours are by prior arrangement only (at least a week in advance). The collection is housed at 27 Colombo Street (phone 898-296).

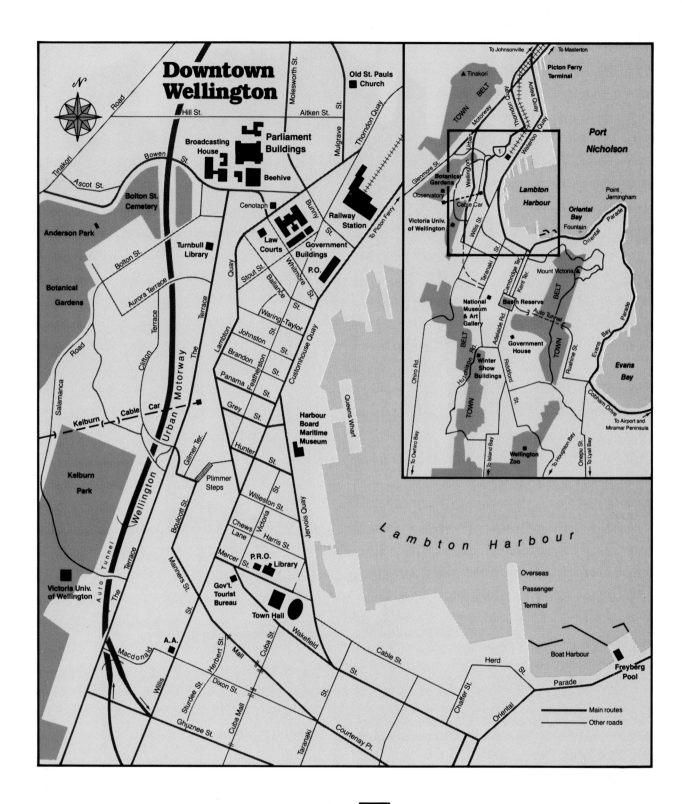

Wellington Zoo. Located about 4 km/2½ miles south of the city center, the zoo is open daily from 8:30 A.M. to 5 P.M. (Hours at the kiwi house are 10 A.M. to 4 P.M.) Leopards and tigers are fed in midafternoon. On weekend and holiday afternoons, you can board a miniature train for a ride around the zoo's pond. To reach the zoo, take bus 11 from the railway station to Newtown Park.

Excursions from Wellington

City sightseeing tours depart daily at 2 P.M. from the Public Relations Office on Mercer Street. You can take a scenic flight or a harbor cruise, or, if the day is pleasant, board a ferry for a trip across Cook Strait to Picton.

The City Marine Drive offers a look at suburban beaches east and south of the city. To the north, you can explore the Hutt Valley, the Golden Coast, or the Eastern Bays. On weekends, motorcoach tours travel to beach towns along the Tasman, and to rugged Cape Palliser.

Discover suburban beaches

From the city center, the 39-km/24-mile City Marine Drive follows the harbor shore to nearby beaches. The route skirts Oriental and Evans bays on the inner harbor, then loops around the Miramar Peninsula past a series of attractive bays. Along the way you'll pass moored pleasure boats, fine swimming beaches, and surfing areas.

On the northern tip of Miramar Peninsula, the Massey Memorial offers picnic tables and a fine view of the harbor. Along the peninsula's eastern shore, the road curves past a series of inviting beaches at Scorching, Karaka, and Worser bays. Outer harbor beaches at Lyall and Island bays attract hardy swimmers and surfers. Island Bay is home for a small fishing fleet.

The Hutt Valley and beyond

Hemmed in between hills, the Hutt Valley towns sprawl along Highway 2 over alluvial plains bordering the Hutt River. In Petone, the Settlers' Museum on the Esplanade commemorates the first landing of settlers in Port Nicholson. Lower Hutt is a center of scientific and industrial research. Railroad fans flock to the Silverstream Railway on Sunday afternoon. Farther north in Upper Hutt is Trentham Racecourse.

Hikers enjoy the rugged hills of Tararua Forest Park, an hour's drive north of the capital, where trails wind through the bush and along streams. Access routes to the vast reserve are signposted off the main highways.

Along the Golden Coast

North of Wellington, Highway 1 connects coastal towns along the Tasman shore from Plimmerton north to Otaki. Suburban trains link the capital with the larger beach towns, and Saturday shopping draws many weekend visitors to this region, dubbed the "Golden Coast." Many Wellingtonians have built beach cottages or retirement homes here.

If you're a fan of vintage vehicles, three museums await you here. At Paekakariki, the Engine Shed museum recalls the era of steam locomotives; the collection is open to visitors on Saturday. Trams, trolley buses, and an old-time fire engine await you in the Wellington Tramway Museum in Paekakariki's Queen Elizabeth Park, open on weekends and holidays; you can also picnic and swim in the park. Classic cars take the spotlight at the Southward Car Museum, open daily in Otaihanga, just northwest of Paraparaumu.

Otaki, 74 km/46 miles north of Wellington, has one of the country's finest Maori churches. Its plain exterior gives little hint of the outstanding interior.

The Eastern Bays

A pleasant excursion follows the harbor northeast through Petone to prime residential suburbs bordering the Eastern Bays. By bus, it's a 40-minute ride from the Wellington railway station to Eastbourne.

The road passes a series of sheltered beaches bordering Lowry, York, Mahina, and Days bays before reaching Eastbourne. Houses spill down the steep wooded slopes, and some hill dwellers have installed private cable cars to transport them between street and home. From Kowhai Street in Eastbourne, a signposted trail climbs over a hilly ridge with good harbor views and down to a peaceful valley at Butterfly Creek.

Rugged Cape Palliser

Cape Palliser, the rocky, storm-wracked southern tip of North Island, has been the scene of many shipwrecks. Crowning a hill is the Cape Palliser Lighthouse, linked by a long flight of steps with the keeper's dwelling below. Visitors can enjoy surfcasting here and can view seals at a nearby seal colony.

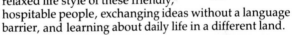

Home hospitality

New Zealanders enjoy meeting overseas visitors, and they believe hospitality begins at home. You'll enjoy sharing the relaxed life style of these friendly, hospitable people, exchanging ideas without a language barrier, and learning about daily life in a different land.

In some areas, residents who want to meet visitors join voluntary hospitality programs; they may extend an invitation for tea and an hour or two of conversation, or they may offer to guide you around their town. Learn about these programs through local tourist offices.

Throughout the country, families in towns and on farms open their homes to visitors on a paying guest basis. Several organizations can arrange host family accommodations; for information, contact the New Zealand Tourist Office or local tourist offices. Though many host families are located near major cities, there are host families scattered all over both islands.

If you have a special interest or hobby, you may be able to meet Kiwis with similar interests. Visitors who belong to international service organizations can often link up with members of local chapters in New Zealand's larger towns. If trout fishing is your idea of a perfect vacation, you can stay with a New Zealand angler host and fish the lakes and streams of Rotorua, Taupo, or South Island; for information, write to Club Pacific, 790 27th Avenue, San Francisco, CA 94121.

SOUTH ISLAND

The icy Southern Alps tower above rain forest, sea, and glacial lakes

Nelson
Blenheim

Greymouth

Christchurch

Mount Cook ▲
Timaru

Oamaru

Queenstown

Invercargill
Dunedin

On sparsely populated South Island, lofty mountains flanked by icy glaciers set the scenic tone. Adding to the visual drama are subtropical rain forests, coastal fiords of awesome beauty, vast grazing lands, deep alpine lakes bordered by thick forests, windswept headlands, and sunny beaches. The island proudly carries the imprint of the hardworking 19th century colonists, sheepmen, and prospectors who scouted and tamed this splendid and diverse land.

South Island's variety of natural scenery, climate, and vegetation is matched by seasonal changes more distinct than those on North Island. Springtime fruit blossoms give way to the ripe fields of summer. Colorful foliage brightens the autumn landscape. In winter, snow blankets much of the interior.

About 28 percent of New Zealand's 3.1 million people live on South Island. With a population of about 850,000, the entire island supports a population barely larger than that of Auckland, the country's largest city. Most settlements border the eastern coast.

An island overview

Separated from its sister island by narrow Cook Strait, elongated South Island stretches southwest some 800 km/500 miles. A diagonal geologic fault, rising abruptly from the western coast to create the magnificent mountain chain called the Southern Alps, divides the island for most of its length.

Thousands of years ago massive glaciers covered much of the island. Grinding down the valleys, they sculpted the mountains, sheared rocky cliffs, carved deep

Glowing autumn color brightens roads and river valleys north of Queenstown in late April; early snow already dusts the summit of Coronet Peak.

grooves in the southwestern coast, and gouged out long, slim lakes.

Immigrants transformed the land

Captain James Cook circumnavigated the islands and mapped the coast in 1769-70. Sealers and whalers established shore stations in the early decades of the 19th century. Finally, European colonists, who began arriving in earnest during the 1840s, founded settlements at Akaroa in 1840, Nelson in 1841, Dunedin in 1848, and, finally, Christchurch in 1850.

The English and Scottish colonists, transforming the virgin landscape, plotted neat townsites and planted thousands of trees. They erected sturdy buildings to house their churches, schools, and governmental bodies and reserved parklands for the enjoyment of succeeding generations.

While the Maori land wars raged across North Island, Australian sheepmen opened up South Island's hilly interior. Discoveries of gold in Central Otago in 1861 were followed shortly by rich new finds on the West Coast, accelerating the exploration and settlement of these remote regions.

That pioneer spirit never quite died—a strong streak of hardy individualism persists today.

Sparsely settled South Island is still the home of many proud descendants of pioneer stock, hospitable hard-working farm families who share the conviviality of country gatherings, as well as the problems of flood, drought, snow, stock losses, and isolation.

Lush forest and grassy plains

Luxuriant greenery descends to the blue Tasman Sea along the wet and wild western coast. Moisture-laden clouds drop more than 200 inches of rain annually as they sweep in from the sea and strike the steep barrier of the Southern Alps.

Along the northwest coast, the towns of Westport, Greymouth, and Hokitika were born during gold rush days. Farther south is Westland National Park, where Franz Josef and Fox glaciers descend steeply toward the sea, and the virtually untouched, fiord-indented southwest coast.

On the drier east side of the mountains, a vast network of waterways drains the alpine snowfields, hilly grasslands, broad plains, and coastal valleys. More than half of the island's population is concentrated along the Pacific coast near Christchurch and Dunedin and in the smaller towns of Timaru and Oamaru.

Other sizable towns are Invercargill, on the south coast, and Nelson and Blenheim, near the island's northern tip. South Island's leading resort is Queenstown, hub of the southern lakes district.

Scenic highways follow historic routes

Modern highways hug the coastline and cut across the mountains to link the island's eastern and western settlements. Highway 1, bordering the east coast from Picton to Bluff, passes through major cities and towns. Highway 6 cuts from Blenheim through Nelson and the Buller Gorge to Westport and down the western coast.

Centuries ago, Maoris seeking West Coast greenstone discovered riverside routes through the mountains. Today, scenic transalpine highways follow these traditional routes. The Lewis Pass Road (Highway 7) links Waipara and Greymouth. Arthur's Pass Road (Highway 73) winds through the high country from Christchurch to Kumara Junction, north of Hokitika. Highway 6, which cuts across Haast Pass from Wanaka, provides a southern route to Westland National Park.

Other main highways thrust deeply into the provinces of Canterbury and Otago and cut through the valleys of Fiordland to Milford Sound.

South Island's highlights

Beyond the cities, travelers find attractions in rich variety. Seven national parks and a maritime park preserve outstanding scenic areas of South Island for public enjoyment. On the north coast are historic Abel Tasman National Park and the delightful waterways of Marlborough Sounds Maritime Park. Nelson Lakes National Park contains a pair of slender, beech-fringed glacial lakes.

Straddling the snowy crest of the Southern Alps are four national parks—Arthur's Pass, Mount Cook, Westland, and Mount Aspiring—attracting climbers, hikers, and others who love the alpine country. Vast and varied Fiordland National Park offers awesome mountains, dense forests, tranquil lakes, and majestic fiords.

Many travelers enjoy the Queenstown district and the southern lakes, Nelson's sunny beaches, unspoiled Stewart Island, and the sleepy old mining towns of Central Otago.

Activities include fishing for trout and salmon; visiting coal mines, historic museums, or bird sanctuaries; walking on a glacier or through fern-filled rain forest; staying overnight with a farm family; dining on local scallops, crayfish, oysters, or venison; and exploring the island's remote districts on foot or horseback or by jet boat, sightseeing plane, or four-wheel-drive vehicle.

Christchurch on the Avon

Nestled at the base of the hilly Banks Peninsula, New Zealand's third largest city faces inland toward a broad panorama—the flat Canterbury Plains backed by the snowy Southern Alps. South Island's largest city, Christchurch is the busy yet relaxed capital of the province of Canterbury.

Though known for its peaceful ambience and unhurried pace, Christchurch is a city that gets things done. It has one of the country's busiest and most modern airports, a handsome town hall bordering the Avon River, and an outstanding sports complex developed for the 1974 Commonwealth Games. A new shopping mall on Cashel and High streets attracts downtown shoppers.

The Canterbury settlement was the last and most successful of the mid-19th century colonizing ventures. Four shiploads of hand-picked English colonists arrived at Lyttelton in 1850 and made a historic trek across the Port Hills to found Christchurch. Surveyors laid out the town in a grid pattern, its dignified order broken only by the serpentine course of the Avon River.

Enjoying Christchurch

Occupying a spacious square in the heart of the city is Christchurch Cathedral, a reminder of the important role the Church of England played in the settlement of Canterbury. Major arteries radiate from Cathedral Square.

Often called "New Zealand's most English city," Christchurch retains many features established by its Anglican settlers. Shaded by overhanging trees, the Avon River meanders through the city, adding a note of gracious, old-world charm. Still in daily use are many stately Gothic buildings, constructed by early civic leaders to house the settlement's religious, educational, governmental, and cultural institutions.

Parks soften the city's rectangular layout, and home gardens blaze with color from spring through autumn. You'll probably see uniformed students cycling along city streets or waiting for city buses. A special Christchurch touch: baby strollers hook a ride on the front of the buses, a convenience reflecting the city's relaxed pace.

Shopping. Christchurch's main shopping district clusters around Cathedral Square. Nearby shopping arcades such as Chancery Lane and New Regent Street offer shops and a relaxed atmosphere. A two-story shopping center links Hereford and Cashel streets near High Street, and a pedestrian mall—the Triangle Centre—connects High and Cashel streets.

Shops are generally open from 9 A.M. to 5:30 P.M. on weekdays and until 9 on Friday evening. The city mall and most suburban malls are also open on Saturday morning but closed on Sunday. In Riccarton, stores stay open late on Thursday night. New Brighton shops are closed on Monday; on Saturday they're open until 9 P.M.

Entertainment. Most ballet and theater performances, concerts, and touring shows take place at the city's handsome Town Hall. Plays are presented in the Court Theatre at the Arts Centre of Christchurch.

Major hotels and many restaurants offer live entertainment and dancing in the evening, particularly on Friday and Saturday. If you'd like to meet a local family, you can make arrangements through the Information Centre or the Government Tourist Bureau.

Sports and special events. In the Christchurch area, you can play golf, go river or surf fishing, and ski from May through November at Mount Hutt.

You can see some of the country's top horses in action here at two of the country's finest tracks. Light-harness racing (trotting) takes place at Addington Raceway; racing and steeplechase events are held at Riccarton Racecourse. Racing events highlight November's Carnival Week celebration. Premier classic on the racing calendar is the New Zealand Cup; the companion New Zealand Trotting Cup race takes place at Addington. The Canterbury Agricultural & Pastoral Show is also held during Carnival Week.

Other annual events include the New Zealand Grand National in August and the Easter Cup Carnival meetings in autumn. From late February to mid-March, the annual Christchurch Festival offers a program of floral displays, art shows, sporting events, and other activities.

Christchurch—the essentials

Christchurch, South Island's largest city, is also the hub of the island's transportation system. Air, rail, and motorcoach lines link Canterbury's capital with all parts of the island, as well as with more distant destinations.

Getting there. Passengers arriving by plane disembark at Christchurch International Airport, only 10 km/7 miles northwest of Cathedral Square.

Travelers who have made the interisland ferry crossing from Wellington to Picton continue by rail south to Christchurch. Other trains link Dunedin and Invercargill in the south and Greymouth on the west coast with Christchurch. The railway station is on Moorhouse Avenue.

Long-distance buses of Railways Road Services, Mount Cook Line, Newmans Coach Lines, and H & H Travel Lines connect all areas of South Island with Christchurch. Cruise liners anchor at Lyttelton, south of Christchurch.

Accommodations. Christchurch has dozens of hotels and motels, located in the central business district, in the suburbs, and near the airport.

Major downtown hotels include the high-rise Noah's Hotel and the older Clarendon Hotel (both overlooking the Avon River a block from Cathedral Square), and the Hyatt Kingsgate, on Colombo Street facing Victoria Square. Among the smaller downtown hotels are the refurbished 1884 United Service Hotel, facing Cathedral Square, and Coker's Hotel on Manchester Street. For a centrally located motor hotel, try the Avon Motor Lodge, Latimer Motor Lodge, or Avon Park Hotel, among others.

Accommodations near the airport include the Christchurch Travelodge, Commodore Motor Inn, and Hotel Russley. Among other leading hotels are the Chateau Regency on Deans Avenue, Shirley Lodge Motor Hotel on Marshland Road, Canterbury Inn in Riccarton, DB Redwood Court Hotel on Main North Road, Autolodge on Papanui Road, and Gainsborough Motor Lodge on Bealey Avenue.

Restaurants. In Christchurch and its surroundings, you can choose from restaurants offering continental dining, ethnic specialties, home-style cooking, or grilled meat and seafood specialties. Dinner reservations are advisable at leading restaurants, especially on weekends.

Getting around. Taxis are available at Cathedral Square and at all transportation terminals. Bright red city buses depart from Cathedral Square for city and suburban points; for route information, inquire at the kiosk in front of the cathedral.

Several companies operate half-day and full-day sightseeing tours. Some depart daily the year around; others are scheduled only on certain days or during the main October-to-April tourist period. Tours feature Christchurch attractions, the Port Hills and Lyttelton (page 78), Akaroa and the Banks Peninsula (page 79), Erewhon Park (page 101), and other destinations.

Tourist information. For city maps, local sightseeing tours, and information on points of interest in the Christchurch area, stop at the Canterbury Information Centre, 75 Worcester Street (corner of Oxford Terrace).

Travel arrangements, tour information, and accommodation reservations are handled by the Government Tourist Bureau, located in the Government Life Building facing Cathedral Square. For motoring information, visit the Automobile Association office, 210 Hereford Street.

On foot in Christchurch

Christchurch is a walker's city—compact, level, and varied. Begin your stroll at Cathedral Square, the city's bustling center. Along your route you'll get a close look at distinctive old and new buildings. You can linger along the Avon, sample outstanding parks and gardens, and visit some of the city's stimulating cultural centers.

Cathedral Square. Heart of the city is Cathedral Square, now a tiled pedestrian plaza softened by trees and flower-filled containers. Shoppers pause to rest on benches, office workers purchase fruit and flowers from pushcart vendors, and noontime entertainers amuse the lunch crowd.

Buildings around the perimeter of the square include not only sleek, high-rise office buildings but also elegant older structures—the main post office (built 1877-79), the *Press* newspaper building, and several vintage hotels. A statue honors John Robert Godley, called "the founder of Canterbury."

Christchurch Cathedral is the finest Gothic-style church in the Dominion and the spiritual center of this essentially Anglican city. Built of stone quarried in the Port Hills, it reflects the courage, vision, and dedication of the early settlers who began construction in 1864, only a few years after they arrived. Inside, memorial tablets and

windows record the origins of the town and Canterbury province. If you feel energetic, you can climb the 133 steps up through the bell tower to observation balconies overlooking the city. The cathedral spire towers more than 63 meters/207 feet above the square.

Victoria Square. Two blocks north of the cathedral is Victoria Square, departure point for some sightseeing tours. The Bowker Fountain provides a graceful backdrop for a sturdy statue of Captain Cook, and a replica of Queen Victoria keeps an eye on passing traffic.

Town Hall. A block beyond Victoria Square and bordered by the Avon River is Christchurch's striking glass and marble Town Hall. Opened in 1972, it's the center for civic and cultural activities, performing arts events, and meetings and conferences. Events are presented in the main auditorium or in the smaller 1,000-seat theater.

Guided tours leave the main lobby at frequent intervals on weekdays and on Saturday and Sunday afternoons. Tickets for theater and ballet performances, concerts, and other attractions are handled by the Town Hall booking office. A restaurant overlooks the placid river, Victoria Square, and the Ferrier Fountain.

Provincial Government Buildings. Follow the Avon upstream along Oxford Terrace. Near the river at Armagh and Durham streets, you'll see the stone tower and wooden extensions of the Canterbury Provincial Government Buildings, one of the most intriguing structures in the country. Seat of Canterbury's government from 1859 to 1876, the Provincial Council Chamber is open on weekdays from 9 A.M. to 4 P.M.; guided tours are available on Sunday afternoon at 2 and 3 P.M.

The chamber, on the Durham Street side near the river, was built in 1865 of local stone and native timber. Almost churchlike in appearance, the neo-Gothic chamber has a magnificent gilded and painted barrel-vaulted ceiling, mosaic wall panels, and stained glass windows. Balcony seats once accommodated the public.

During Canterbury's early years, the chamber was the scene of many lively debates and historic decisions. Provincial architect Benjamin Mountfort designed the complex, as well as many of Canterbury's other historic public buildings.

Along the river. Rimmed by grassy, tree-shaded banks and spanned by graceful stone bridges, the winding Avon provides a tranquil corridor skirting the center of the city. Couples stroll the riverside walkways, office workers eat their lunches on the lawn, and children feed the ducks. For a leaflet describing points of interest along the river, stop at the Information Centre, 75 Worcester Street.

Across Worcester Street is a statue of Captain Robert Falcon Scott, the famous Antarctic explorer. At Cashel Street you pass the Bridge of Remembrance, a war memorial. Continuing along Oxford Terrace, you see the distinctive wooden St. Michael's and All Angels Anglican Church, built in 1872.

Looking south to Antarctica

No city has stronger or more enduring ties with the icy southern continent of Antarctica than Christchurch. During the early days of exploration, Lyttelton was the port of departure for Antarctic expeditions. Beside the Avon River, a statue of Captain Robert Falcon Scott, the English explorer who lost his life returning from the South Pole in 1912, is a daily reminder of these hazardous explorations.

You can view an outstanding collection of relics, records, and equipment from both early and recent explorations in the Hall of Antarctic Discovery in the Canterbury Museum (page 76).

Today, a dozen countries are engaged in scientific research on the southern continent. Christchurch International Airport is the supply base and communications center for Operation Deep Freeze, the nonmilitary U.S. scientific study at McMurdo Sound.

Shaded by overhanging trees, the Avon River flows languidly through Christchurch's Botanic Gardens. Water lures boaters; grassy slopes beckon picnickers.

Boating on the Avon

It's pleasant to walk along the river, but the best way to enjoy the Avon's charm is by boat. You can hire a canoe, pedal boat, or rowboat any day at Antigua Boatsheds, facing the shallow river on Cambridge Terrace near Rolleston Avenue.

You step off the sloping wooden dock and lower yourself into your craft, then leisurely venture upstream under drooping willows past the Botanic Gardens and Hagley Park. In spring, you glide beneath blossoming trees; in autumn, golden leaves cast reflections in the water. Your fellow paddlers range from preteens to grandparents. On sunny weekends, picnicking families relax along the grassy bank and watch the passing parade.

A city of parks and gardens

The English colonists who settled Christchurch transformed the "flat, treeless, featureless" site of the 1850s by landscaping their young town with European trees and grasslands and by setting aside vast areas as public parkland. Today, pocket parks dot residential areas, and city gardeners groom their plots in competition for annual best-garden and best-street awards.

Botanic Gardens. A few minutes' walk from Cathedral Square takes you to the Botanic Gardens, a 75-acre reserve encircled by a deep bend of the Avon. Here you'll find mature trees gathered from all parts of the world (many are labeled), a rose garden, water gardens, and splendid seasonal flower displays. In late spring, the woodlands are bright with daffodils, azaleas, and rhododendrons. Tropical and flowering plants are displayed under glass.

On fine afternoons from noon to 4 P.M., you can climb aboard an electric cart—called the "Toast Rack"—for a tour of the gardens. Snacks and a smorgasbord lunch are available in the tea kiosk.

Hagley Park. Across the Avon from the Botanic Gardens is Hagley Park, a 450-acre playground for the city's cyclists, dog walkers, golfers, joggers, horseback riders, and model yachting enthusiasts. Often, there's a game of cricket, soccer, or rugby in progress, or you may see competitors engaged in croquet, lawn bowling, tennis, or other sports. A fitness course is located in North Hagley Park.

North of Harper Avenue is Millbrook Reserve, noted for its azalea and rhododendron displays.

Deans Bush (Riccarton House). Situated west of Hagley Park and north of Riccarton Road, this modest reserve contains the only remaining stand of native swamp forest originally found on these treeless plains. On the property are Riccarton House, the Deans family homestead for some 90 years (now used for receptions), and Deans Cottage, a tiny plains homestead built in 1843 and preserved as a small museum.

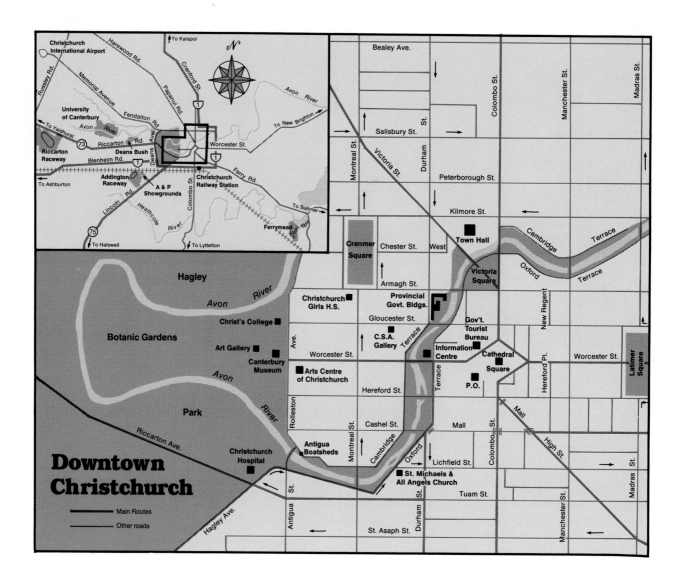

Downtown Christchurch

Fascinating Canterbury Museum

For many visitors, the city's most absorbing attraction is Canterbury Museum, a treasure house of Canterbury and New Zealand lore. One of the finest museums in the Southern Hemisphere, the museum is located on Rolleston Avenue. Hours are Monday through Saturday from 10 A.M. to 4:30 P.M. and Sunday from 2 to 4:30 P.M.

The museum's Hall of Antarctic Discovery contains a fascinating collection of articles used by Antarctic explorers. Personal effects, clothing, survival equipment, and diaries from the heroic era of exploration (1900 to 1917) give insights into Antarctic hardship, exhilaration, and tragedy. Modern thermal clothing and mechanized equipment contrast vividly with the historic artifacts. Additional exhibits offer information on Antarctic geology, fossils, and penguins, and on life beneath the sea.

In the Pacific Hall, you'll learn about the three voyages of Captain James Cook and see mementos collected during his travels. A 14-meter/47-foot-long war canoe dominates the exhibits on the Maori culture.

A replica Christchurch street typical of colonial days (1850s to mid-1870s) shows well-stocked shops patterned after actual businesses of the era. Other colonial displays include a three-room cob house containing costumed figures and a Cobb & Co. stagecoach.

A lively interest in arts and crafts

The activities of Christchurch's artistic community focus around the busy Arts Centre and excellent art galleries.

Arts Centre of Christchurch. When the University of Canterbury moved to a new campus in 1975, its historic townsite was presented to the people of Christchurch. The handsome stone buildings at Rolleston Avenue and Worcester Street have gained a new lease on life serving as the home of more than 60 local artistic, cultural, educational, and community organizations.

Visitors are welcome to stroll through the center's spacious quadrangles and cloisters. On weekdays from 8:30 A.M. to 5 P.M., you can stop at the Arts Centre Information Office in the Clock Tower for a descriptive leaflet and information on special events.

Artists, craftspeople, musicians, and dancers maintain studios and rehearsal space in the old neo-Gothic buildings. Cultural clubs and community service organizations meet here. A resident company performs plays in the 230-seat Court Theatre and in the more intimate 70-seat Studio Theatre. Ballet programs are presented by the Southern Ballet, and the former gymnasium has become a movie theater. Students learn new techniques in a theater workshop, and a youth orchestra rehearses here on Saturday mornings.

Visitors can watch skilled artisans at work and purchase their crafts at the Cornerstone Pottery and the Craft Workshop. Original prints and drawings by New Zealand artists are displayed in the Gingko Gallery. On Saturdays from October to March, artists and craftspeople offer their wares at an outdoor market under the trees.

You can visit the small basement laboratory, now a museum, where famed nuclear physicist Ernest Rutherford conducted his first scientific experiments in 1893-94 (apply at the reception office in the Clock Tower).

Robert McDougall Art Gallery. Located behind the Canterbury Museum facing the Botanic Gardens, this gallery houses the city's collection of early and contemporary Australasian and European paintings, sculpture, pottery, and weaving. Special exhibitions are presented throughout the year. The gallery is open daily (closed on Saturday and Sunday mornings).

Canterbury Society of Arts. You can view changing exhibitions of contemporary New Zealand art, as well as art from other countries, at the C.S.A. Gallery at 66 Gloucester Street. Other events include musical recitals, films, and photographic evening programs. Open daily, the gallery is closed on Saturday and Sunday mornings.

Other points of interest

If time permits, you may want to visit a pair of transport museums, some of the province's educational institutions, or Christchurch's seaside suburbs.

Transport museums. Still in the development stages, Ferrymead Historic Park and Transport Museum strives to recapture the pioneering atmosphere of early Christchurch. Volunteers have restored many early vehicles to working order; visitors can enjoy rides through the site on weekends. Replicas of colonial shops and houses recreate a community of the Edwardian era. Located on Bridle Path Road south of the Heathcote River, Ferrymead is open daily from 10 A.M. to 4 P.M.

At Yaldhurst, 12 km/7 miles from Christchurch on the Main West Road, the Yaldhurst Transport Museum features horse-drawn vehicles, dating from 1810, and other historic transport. The museum is open from 10 A.M. to 5 P.M. daily from September through May, weekends and holidays only during the winter.

Educational institutions. Reminiscent of an English public school, the gray stone buildings of Christ's College are grouped around a grassy quadrangle north of the Canterbury Museum bordering Rolleston Avenue.

You'll often see uniformed schoolboys cycling along city streets or competing in sports in nearby Hagley Park.

In 1975 the University of Canterbury, noted for its School of Engineering, moved from its town site to a spacious new campus in the western suburb of Ilam. Visitors are welcome to stroll the landscaped grounds.

Lincoln College (Canterbury Agricultural College) lies 21 km/13 miles southwest of the city near the village of Lincoln. Surrounded by acres of model farmland, it trains young farmers and supervises research in agriculture and animal husbandry. Founded in 1873, the college was one of the world's first schools of agriculture. It has been an important factor in Canterbury's agricultural growth and prosperity.

Bicycling around Christchurch

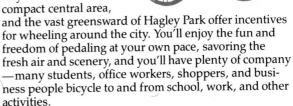

You'll see Christchurch in fresh perspective if you explore the city by bicycle. Level streets, a compact central area, and the vast greensward of Hagley Park offer incentives for wheeling around the city. You'll enjoy the fun and freedom of pedaling at your own pace, savoring the fresh air and scenery, and you'll have plenty of company —many students, office workers, shoppers, and business people bicycle to and from school, work, and other activities.

You can rent leisure bikes, 10-speed touring bikes, or tandems by the hour, day, or week. Two shops rent bikes: Rent-A-Bike, N.Z. Ltd., in the Avon Carpark Building, 82 Worcester Street; and Penny Farthing Cycle Shop, 17 Victoria Street. A refundable deposit is required; damage and theft insurance is optional and available at extra charge. Ask for city and touring maps.

You can explore the city easily in a few hours. Many roads have bicycle lanes. A favorite destination of cyclists is Hagley Park, where paved paths wind across green parklands and along the Avon. If country touring is your hobby, rent a 10-speed touring bike, equipped with carrier bags, and pedal off to the Banks Peninsula, Canterbury Plains, or other destinations.

Cyclists keep to the left of traffic, even on bicycle paths in the park. You're not permitted to ride on sidewalks or footpaths along the Avon River in the downtown area.

Gothic-style cathedral, begun by Canterbury settlers in 1864, dominates Cathedral Square. Lofty observation balconies offer a fine city view.

Seaside suburbs. Christchurch has its own coastal suburbs. New Brighton, traditionally known for its Saturday shopping, has a long beach bordering the Pacific. The Queen Elizabeth II Park complex, site of the 1974 Commonwealth Games, contains swimming pools, water slides, squash courts, and an all-weather athletic track.

South of the Avon-Heathcote Estuary is Sumner. Its esplanade curves past Cave Rock and along Sumner Bay. You can take the steep road over the bluff and descend to Taylor's Mistake, a pleasant sheltered beach, or climb to Evans Pass and the Summit Road.

Orana Wildlife Park. New Zealand's first drive-through wild animal park, open daily, is located near the airport on McLeans Island Road. Lions are a big attraction, but the park also includes tigers, camels, water buffaloes, Barbary sheep, kangaroos, and many exotic birds.

Canterbury excursions

If you prefer to see Christchurch and its surrounding area on a guided excursion, you'll find several tour companies ready to show you the sights. Since not all tours operate the year around, be sure to check at the Canterbury Information Centre, the Government Tourist Bureau, or other travel agencies for information on available excursions.

Visitors who want to explore the area on their own can head southeast across the Port Hills to Lyttelton or make a loop around the Banks Peninsula. To the north you'll find the scenic Kaikoura Coast and Hanmer Springs, a spa in the forest. Routes take motorists west across the Southern Alps or south over the Canterbury Plains.

Walkers will want to ask about the Christchurch area's excellent network of trails, many of them part of the N.Z. Walkways system. Trails winding through the Port Hills offer hikers spectacular views of the city, harbor, plains, and mountains.

Superb views from the Summit Road

Winding high above the city along the crest of the Port Hills, the Summit Road offers magnificent vistas northward over Christchurch and checkered plains to the snow-capped Southern Alps, eastward over Lyttelton and its harbor encased in the crater of an extinct volcano.

From the seaside community of Sumner, you climb to Evans Pass to meet the Summit Road as it snakes for 26 km/16 miles along the hills overlooking Lyttelton Harbour some 300 meters/1,000 feet below. A southern section continues from Dyers Pass Road (at the Sign of the Kiwi teahouse) along the western side of the harbor to Gebbies Pass.

Lyttelton. South Island's leading port, Lyttelton is connected with Christchurch by road and rail tunnels. Wooden houses cling to the steep streets above the harbor. Along the waterfront, cargo handlers service docked freighters, and weekend yachtsmen ready their boats for sailing the sheltered bays. Commuter launch service links Lyttelton and Diamond Harbour on weekdays, and launch cruises leave Lyttelton every afternoon.

A quartet of 19th century churches adds historic interest. On Saturday and Sunday afternoons you can see displays on the historic port and its ships at Lyttelton's museum, centrally located on Gladstone Quay.

The Canterbury Pilgrims who came ashore at Lyttelton in 1850 followed a zigzag bridle path across the Port Hills to found their colony on the plains. Today, walkers still enjoy the old Bridle Path trail, and hundreds make a nostalgic trek between Lyttelton and Christchurch annually on the Sunday nearest December 16.

Roadhouses. Along the route are three old stone roadhouses offering shelter to travelers. Best known is the Sign of the Takahe, overlooking the city from the Cashmere Hills. Modeled after a medieval baronial manor, this showplace has richly ornamented ceilings, wood carvings, intricate stonework, and colorful murals. You can stop for a meal or tea here.

Light refreshments are also available at the Sign of the Kiwi, located on Coronation Hill at the junction of Summit and Dyers Pass roads. The third roadhouse—the Sign of the Bellbird—serves no refreshments.

Akaroa and the Banks Peninsula

Set apart both geographically and geologically from the rest of Canterbury, the Banks Peninsula offers a relaxing retreat about 1½ hours southeast of Christchurch. Contrasting dramatically with the placid Canterbury Plains, the peninsula was formed by two extinct volcanoes whose collapsed craters now hold the splendid natural harbors of Lyttelton and Akaroa.

The road to Akaroa. From Christchurch, Highway 75 heads south through farming country to the peninsula. Lake Ellesmere, a shallow coastal lagoon, supports great flocks of waterfowl. The narrow, winding road snakes through the peninsula's green and golden hills past farmhouses and cottages tucked into folded valleys.

Cutting deeply into the eroded old volcanic cones are narrow bays, some of them used in the 1830s by whaling parties. From the main route, steep side roads lead down to these unpeopled inlets—Port Levy's protected harbor, Pigeon Bay and its campground, and Little Akaloa with its unusual church embellished with Maori-style carvings. At Barry's Bay, visitors can watch the traditional cheesemaking process at Settlers Farmhouse Cheese Factory.

Other roads lead to Okains Bay, known for its beach and museum; Le Bons Bay and its sports ground; and Peraki's historic whaling site.

Akaroa—village with a French flavor. New Zealand's first French settlers landed at Akaroa in 1840—nearly a

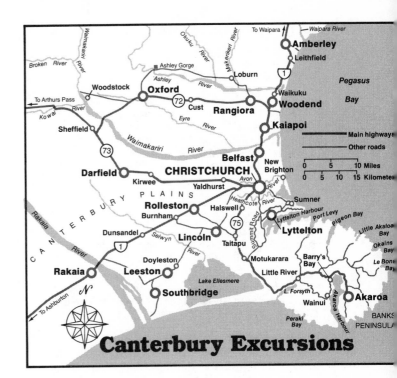

Canterbury Excursions

decade before the colonial settlements at Dunedin and Christchurch—and the village keeps alive its Gallic heritage. Located 84 km/52 miles from Christchurch, New Zealand's most English city, Akaroa is a popular spot for midsummer and weekend holidays. Accommodations are available at Akaroa Village Resort and at several small motels and hotels. You'll enjoy the village's unique charm more if you visit on a weekday or out of season.

Along the waterfront you'll see whalers' pots and the early customs house, but to sample Akaroa's real charm, stroll along the side streets above the harbor. Spreading trees shade wooden Victorian cottages, and decorative fences enclose flourishing gardens of subtropical flowers. Attractive small churches invite worshippers. One of the settlement's earliest buildings is the Langlois-Eteveneaux House and Museum; the two-room cottage is furnished in 1840s style. Open from 1:30 to 5 P.M. daily, it also houses the town's information center.

From the waterfront, you can walk up wooded glades to the surrounding hills for views over the town and harbor.

Exploring North Canterbury

From Christchurch, Highway 1 curves north, paralleling the coast and cutting across the rolling hills and lush river valleys of North Canterbury. Side roads lead to coastal beaches bordering Pegasus Bay.

An all-day loop from Christchurch takes you through farmlands to the dramatic gorges of the Ashley and Waimakariri rivers. You'll find pleasant picnic and swimming areas along both rivers. In season, there's good salmon and trout fishing. If you're interested in a raft trip

Marlborough—the essentials

Located on South Island's northeastern tip, the province of Marlborough is a favorite destination of boaters, thanks to the web of waterways—called "the sounds"— dotting its northern end. Picton, at the head of Queen Charlotte Sound, is Marlborough's main port and the hub of vacation activity in the area. The administrative center is Blenheim, 29 km/18 miles inland.

Getting there. From North Island, you can take a 30-minute flight from Wellington across Cook Strait to Blenheim, but the most satisfying approach is by ship. Interisland ferries make the 3½-hour crossing between Wellington and Picton several times daily.

Newmans Coach Lines link Marlborough's main towns with Nelson and Christchurch. Rail service connects Picton with Christchurch and intermediate towns daily except Sunday.

Accommodations. Most vacationers headquarter near the water. Prime holiday season in this sunny region extends from November through April; make peak season reservations well in advance.

In Picton, the Picton Motor Inn, Harbour View Motel, and several smaller motels overlook marine activity; the DB Terminus Hotel is near the waterfront. Other motels are situated near the central district or along Waikawa Road, east of the harbor. Blenheim's leading downtown hotels are the Autolodge Motor Inn and the DB Criterion; the town also has a number of good motels. Simple motel units are available at Havelock.

Rustic lodges and guest houses are nestled along secluded bays throughout the Sounds; some are accessible only by boat or float plane (inquire about access when you're making reservations). Among these waterside accommodations are Gem Resort and Punga Cove Holiday Resort, both bordering Queen Charlotte Sound; Furneaux Lodge Holiday Resort on Endeavour Inlet; and the Portage Hotel on Kenepuru Sound. There's a campground at Momorangi Bay and numerous informal camping areas at various bays throughout the Sounds.

Getting around. Motorcoaches link the region's larger towns. Rental cars are available at Picton Ferry Terminal and in Blenheim. On Picton's London Quay, several operators offer launch sightseeing excursions on Queen Charlotte Sound. You can also arrange for water taxi service and fishing expeditions. Mail boat trips depart from both Picton and Havelock (page 82).

In Picton you can arrange for scenic flights over the Sounds and for sightseeing trips by minicoach.

Tourist information. For ideas on what to see and do in Marlborough, inquire at the Public Relations Office, facing Market Square, in Blenheim. For information on Marlborough Sounds Maritime Park, contact the chief ranger in Blenheim or stop at the ranger station in Havelock.

or jet boat excursion up the Waimakariri River, inquire at one of the tourist information offices in Christchurch.

At Waipara, Highway 7 branches inland toward Hanmer Springs. Anglers find good fishing in the Hurunui and Waiau rivers. Highway 7 continues across Lewis Pass (page 96) to the West Coast (page 87).

Forest walks at Hanmer Springs

South Island's principal thermal resort, Hanmer blossomed as a spa in the late 19th century. Today visitors come not only to bathe in the hot springs but also to enjoy crisp mountain air and forest walks. An easy 1½ to 2-hour drive north of Christchurch, Hanmer sits on a high plateau ringed by mountain spurs of the Southern Alps. Forestry workers here tend one of the country's largest and most varied tree plantations.

In town, the thermal pools of Queen Mary Hospital are open daily; bring your bathing suit and a towel.

Walkers and hikers can take Jollie's Pass Road from the center of town to Hanmer Forest Park. At the trail information center, ask for a descriptive leaflet with a map of the trails, which vary from easy nature walks to strenuous day-long treks. In autumn, the woods are bright with color. For views over the forest and Waiau Plain, take the zigzag trail from Conical Hill Road to the summit.

Recreation opportunities abound in the Hanmer district. Tennis courts, a golf course, and a putting green are within walking distance of town. From Hanmer, you can arrange for horseback trips through the countryside and for expeditions into the rugged hill country by four-wheel-drive vehicle. Anglers find good fishing in nearby rivers, boaters enjoy Tennyson and Horseshoe lakes, and skiers head for nearby Amuri Skifield.

The Kaikoura coast

Scenery ranging from verdant farmlands to spectacular panoramas awaits travelers following the coastal road— Highway 1—between Christchurch and Picton.

South of Cheviot you can visit and picnic at Cheviot Hills domain, now a scenic reserve. You'll see the homestead and some buildings of the vast Cheviot Hills run, one of the earliest Canterbury sheep stations. At Hundalee you cross the Conway River, marking the Canterbury-Marlborough boundary, then descend through the hills to meet the sea at Oaro.

For nearly 100 km/60 miles north of Oaro, Highway 1 hugs the rock-strewn Pacific shore. Ever-changing seascapes, impressive views of rugged inland mountains, and the small resort town of Kaikoura are highlights. Seaside camping and picnicking areas are busy in summer.

Take the time to drive to the tip of Kaikoura Peninsula for a memorable panorama of village and sea backed by the snow-draped Seaward Kaikoura Range. A fishing fleet operates out of Kaikoura, where local crayfish are packed for export. The coastal town draws many surf-fishing enthusiasts and skin divers.

Marlborough Sounds

Narrow, watery fingers deeply indent the lush green Marlborough coastline at the northeastern tip of South Island. Called "the Sounds," these drowned coastal river valleys create more than 1,000 km/600 miles of shoreline, a delightful maze of sheltered waterways, inviting bays and coves, and wooded peninsulas sloping steeply to the sea. Pleasure craft now sail the waters first explored by Captain James Cook more than 200 years ago.

For a perfect introduction to Marlborough's water-side attractions and leisurely pace, plan to arrive aboard one of the interisland ferries that link Wellington and Picton. After crossing Cook Strait, you'll cruise majestically up Tory Channel into Queen Charlotte Sound, past densely forested hills and scattered settlements, to the vacation center of Picton.

Picton, the busy deep-water port

Recreational activity in the Sounds focuses on Picton, the small but bustling ferry port at the head of Queen Charlotte Sound. Pleasure boats and sightseeing launches cluster along the waterfront, and interisland ferries steam in and out of port.

Bordering Picton's foreshore is London Quay, where you can arrange for sightseeing trips or water taxi service, inspect local crafts, and observe waterfront activity. A small museum recalls the whaling era with displays of equipment and artifacts.

Vacationing families come to Picton to play in the sun—swim, fish, water-ski, hike—or to explore the endless waterways by boat. For a pleasant stroll, cross the humpbacked bridge arching above the marina and follow the path along the harbor shore to Bob's Bay, a sheltered cove where you can swim and picnic.

Sightseeing excursions. Tour operators along London Quay offer a wide variety of trips by boat, plane, or minicoach.

On a launch trip of Queen Charlotte Sound you'll be treated to spectacular scenery, close-up views of isolated vacation houses, and commentary on the region's fascinating history and unusual way of life. Many tours pause at the site of the shipwrecked *Edwin Fox* and at Double Cove, where tame fish swim to the surface when food is thrown to them.

On a longer trip you can picnic at Kumutoto Bay or Ship Cove, near the mouth of the sound, where Captain Cook's ships anchored in the 1770s. Queen Charlotte Sound was one of his favorite Pacific anchorages—he paused here on five separate occasions during his explorations.

You can also arrange for sightseeing trips by minicoach to Nelson and Port Underwood and along Queen Charlotte Drive. Flights departing from Picton offer grand, bird's-eye views of the Sounds.

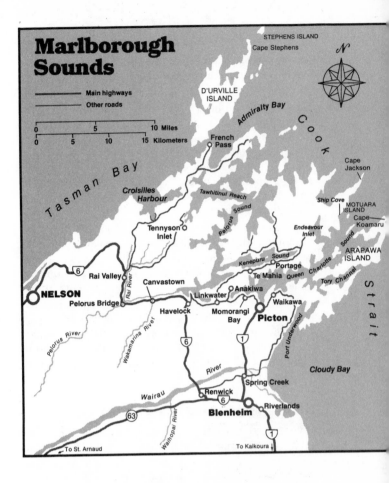

Beautiful drives. From Picton, scenic roads branch west along Queen Charlotte Sound and northeast to Waikawa and Port Underwood.

Closely following the shore of Grove Arm, Queen Charlotte Drive climbs to headland viewpoints, then dips to waterside to meet bays and coves. Side roads lead to the Cobham Outward Bound School at Anakiwa and to settlements bordering Kenepuru Sound. Allow about an hour for the leisurely drive through Moenui to Havelock.

Waikawa Road passes Picton's marina, then continues northeast toward Waikawa. Take the marked side road to Victoria Domain for a lovely view. Anchored boats bob on the sheltered waters of Waikawa Bay. A winding road continues across the saddle between Queen Charlotte Sound and Port Underwood, the center of feverish whaling activity in the late 1820s. Whaling ships from many countries operated in these waters.

Marlborough Sounds Maritime Park

A watery playground for vacationing Kiwis and other visitors, the park features sheltered tidal waters and myriad bays and coves backed by native bush. More than 100 separate reserves, interspersed with farmland and private vacation homes, make up the park.

Rich in history as well as scenery, some reserves recall Maori or pre-Maori occupation; others are linked with early European explorers, such as James Cook and Dumont d'Urville, or 19th century whalers. Still other reserves—particularly islands in the Sounds and Cook Strait—are breeding grounds for birds and animals.

Picton, facing Queen Charlotte Sound, and Havelock, at the head of Pelorus Sound, are departure points for launch trips to shore and island reserves. Though the park is best explored by water, roads lead to some recreational areas, and a float-plane service operates out of Picton. In addition to sightseeing cruises, you can arrange charter excursions and fishing trips in Picton; you can also hire small boats with outboard motors for exploring on your own.

Some reserves in the park offer good picnicking and camping sites, as well as trails for bush walking (some are accessible only by boat). Largest of the reserves is Tennyson Inlet, reached from Highway 6 by road from Rai Valley; here you'll find dense forests and varied birdlife.

Permits are required for camping, shooting, and visiting protected wildlife reserves. For information on permits, hiking trails, or other features of the park, contact the chief ranger in Blenheim (P.O. Box 97; phone Blenheim 86079) or the ranger station in Havelock (phone Havelock 159).

Sailing and fishing in Marlborough

If you're a sailing enthusiast, consider chartering a boat for a few days' cruising on the Sounds (page 28). You can explore the unspoiled shore, anchoring in secluded bays and coves for picnicking, swimming, and hiking on nearby trails. A popular destination of many sailors is beautiful Kenepuru Sound, a landlocked waterway branching off Pelorus Sound.

Anglers are attracted to the Sounds' sheltered waters, which abound with cod, terakihi, snapper, garfish, grouper, and kahawai. Along Marlborough's east coast, surfcasters concentrate in the area between Kaikoura and Cape Koamaru.

For fly-fishing, head inland for the Rai and Pelorus rivers. Brown trout are also abundant in the Wairau and Opawa rivers and in Spring Creek. In summer, salmon migrate up the lower reaches of the Wairau River.

Blenheim, the business center

A tidy town of parks and gardens surrounded by vineyards and farmlands, Blenheim lies 29 km/18 miles inland. With a population of 18,000, it's Marlborough's largest town, as well as its administrative and agricultural center. Focal point of the business district is triangular Market Place, featuring a filigreed band rotunda. Tourist information is available at the nearby Public Relations Office.

A walk through town. From Market Place, walk a block west on High Street to Seymour Square, colorful with seasonal flower displays. In the park you'll see the town's

Hitch a ride aboard the mail boat

For a unique view of life in the Sounds, take a trip aboard one of the boats that delivers mail and supplies to remote waterside settlements and that provides transportation for residents in those outlying areas.

You'll clamber aboard a launch piled high with mailbags, newspapers, boxes and bags of foodstuffs, hardware, and farm equipment—rolls of fencing wire, perhaps, or a shiny shovel tagged for its new owner. If rain threatens, a tarpaulin is tied over the cargo.

Your fellow passengers may be residents returning to their homes, campers stopping for a few days at one of the scenic reserves, anglers who will be dropped off at a remote site and picked up on the return journey, or student travelers stopping at the Havelock youth hostel.

The launch cruises mile after mile of unspoiled waterways, past countless coves and bays where lush greenery slopes down to the waterline. Occasionally, the boat may nose up to the bank to deposit or reclaim a party of campers or fishing enthusiasts. You'll pass scenic and wildlife reserves; if you have binoculars, bring them along to watch native birds.

Since many families living on outlying homesteads get "out" infrequently, the mail boat is their major link with the outside world. As you approach each destination, you'll see at least one person—often an entire family and a dog or two—eagerly awaiting your arrival. If no dock is available or the tide is low, a couple of children or an adult will row out to meet the boat, exchange greetings with the crew, and collect groceries and mail.

On most weekday mornings, you can board a mail boat in Havelock for a day-long trip on Pelorus or Kenepuru sounds. Trips on Queen Charlotte Sound depart from Picton. The Marlborough Public Relations Office in Blenheim has information on mail boat trips. Telephone the day before—Havelock 42-276 or Picton 175—to check departure time and reserve space. You can also enjoy a mail boat trip in the Bay of Islands (page 33).

Plan to arrive at the wharf early in the morning and bring your lunch. Dress warmly; you may want to carry rain gear if the weather is changeable.

memorial fountain and stone clock tower. Just across the street are the public library and the modern circular council chambers.

Other pleasant places to explore include Riverside Park, with its footbridges spanning a stream, and Pollard Park, a favorite for its rose gardens, sports grounds, and flower-bordered walkways along a creek.

Nearby attractions. Southwest of town on New Renwick Road, Brayshaw Museum Park contains a miniature railway, vintage machinery and vehicles, and other displays.

Riverlands cob cottage, a restored, mud-walled pioneer house built around 1860, is located about 5 km/3 miles southeast of Blenheim on Highway 1. A cobblestone path leads to the small cottage-museum, now refurbished with period household articles and costumed figures in colonial dress.

West of Blenheim you'll pass vast vineyards; Montana Vineyards opened its Riverlands Winery here in 1977.

Marlborough has its own skifield at Rainbow Valley, southwest of Blenheim; the ski season extends from June through late October.

Over the mountains to Nelson

West of Havelock, Highway 6 winds through the dairy country of the Pelorus and Rai valleys, across forested mountains, and down the Whangamoa Valley into Nelson province.

Along the highway at Havelock, an old bush logging engine outside a former church marks the local museum. Mussels are grown commercially in Pelorus Sound near Havelock; a small fishing fleet moors at the head of the sound. At Canvastown, a roadside display of 1860s mining equipment from the gold fields up the Wakamarina River evokes the mining activity that was concentrated upstream at Deep Creek.

Allow time to wander through a pocket of virgin bush at Pelorus Bridge Scenic Reserve. A short, self-guided nature trail called the Totara Walk identifies many of the native ferns and trees—rimu, miro, tawa, kamahi, a giant totara—and leads down to a swimming hole in the Pelorus River.

You can pick up picnic supplies in Rai Valley.

Nelson and the Sunshine Coast

One of the earliest settlements of the colonizing New Zealand Company, Nelson has its roots deep in the soil. Apples, kiwifruit, hops, and tobacco dominate the broad agricultural patchwork of the Waimea Plains and Motueka Valley.

Both Nelson province and its largest city — also named Nelson — honor Britain's great naval hero, and you'll see additional reminders of the region's links with

Vacation homes *at Moenui overlook sheltered coves of Pelorus Sound. Scenic Marlborough waterways and wooded reserves attract boaters and hikers.*

sailors of various periods and nations. Other sizable provincial towns include Motueka, Takaka, and—on the West Coast—Westport. Two national parks, Abel Tasman and Nelson Lakes, preserve areas of scenic beauty.

Sunny, relaxing Nelson

Facing a sheltered harbor and encircled by wooded mountains at the head of Tasman Bay, Nelson is one of the country's oldest cities; colonists settled here in 1841. The city's lively interest in the arts indicates that more than agriculture thrives in the delightful climate here.

Dominating the town's skyline on Church Hill is the towering Christ Church Cathedral, built of local Takaka marble. Open daily, the Anglican church contains many historic relics of the area.

Nelson—the essentials

Its sunny weather and sheltered coastline lure many visitors to Nelson. Two national parks—Abel Tasman and Nelson Lakes—preserve dramatic areas of rugged seacoast and glacial lakes.

Getting there. Air service links Nelson with Christchurch, Wellington, and Auckland. Newmans Coach Lines connect Nelson with Christchurch (via Blenheim or Lewis Pass), Picton, and Greymouth.

Accommodations. The province's only large city is Nelson; its main downtown hotels are the DB Rutherford and the DB Nelson. Numerous motels near Tahunanui Beach cater to vacationing families. Lodging is difficult to find during warm weather periods; many Kiwis book a year ahead for the school holidays in late December and January.

Modest accommodations (primarily small motels) are located in Motueka, Takaka, and Collingwood; along the coast you'll find beach campgrounds. At Nelson Lakes, simple accommodations, as well as camping areas, are available at St. Arnaud and Rotoroa.

Getting around. You can hire taxis in Nelson. Newmans Coach Lines has service to Picton, Blenheim, and Takaka. If you prefer exploring on your own, rental cars are available in Nelson.

Half-day tours take in Nelson's major attractions or head north through farmland to Motueka and Kaiteriteri.

Tourist information. Stop at the Nelson Public Relations Office, corner of Trafalgar and Halifax streets, for information on the city and province. To learn about activities in Abel Tasman National Park, visit the information office in Takaka (open only during the summer holidays) or contact the ranger in Motueka. Headquarters for Nelson Lakes National Park is in St. Arnaud; a ranger station is located at Lake Rotoroa.

Popular viewpoints for enjoying the panorama of city and bay are Cleveland Terrace and Princes Drive, two features of the city tour. Industrial and recreational waterfront activity is concentrated around Port Nelson, north of the business center near the entrance to Nelson Haven. Farther south is the magnificent white sweep of Tahunanui Beach.

A downtown stroll. For a look at Nelson's central district, begin your walk at the city's traditional meeting place, the church steps leading down to Trafalgar Street. The city's main downtown artery, Trafalgar bisects the business district and crosses the tree-lined Maitai River.

Queens Gardens offers a sylvan oasis about a 10-minute walk east of Trafalgar Street (on either Hardy or Bridge Street). Nearby, in an 1898 building on Bridge Street, the Suter Art Gallery contains one of the country's best small collections (open daily except Monday from 10:30 A.M. to 4:30 P.M.; open daily during school holiday periods).

Spreading trees shade the close-in sports grounds of the Botanical Reserve at the east end of Hardy Street. One of the favorite city walks is the 30-minute climb up 147-meter/483-foot Botanical Hill, where you're rewarded with a panoramic view of the city, port, and Maitai Valley.

Glimpses of the past. Nelson's early residents left a rich legacy of opulent houses and horticultural treasures. Many of the European trees they brought and planted have now grown to impressive maturity.

Just a few minutes south of Church Hill, the city-owned Melrose mansion reflects the Victorian architecture of the 1880s. Located in spacious grounds at Brougham and Trafalgar streets, it's used for a wide range of community activities.

Bishop's School, located on Nile Street East (next door to Marsden House), was established in 1844 and served as a school for almost 90 years. Now restored by the New Zealand Historic Places Trust, it's open daily from 10:30 A.M. to noon and 1 to 4 P.M.

At 108 Collingwood Street, you can savor the serenity of an old-world herb garden surrounding a century-old home. Lavender Hill Herb Garden is open on weekdays and Saturday morning.

Isel Park, 3 km/2 miles south of town, is the setting for Isel House and the Nelson Provincial Museum. Thomas Marsden, one of the original settlers of the New Zealand Company, built his two-story stone and timbered homestead in 1886 and surrounded it with a 12-acre garden planted with trees from around the world. The antique-filled house, located off Main Road in Stoke, is open on weekend afternoons (also Tuesday and Thursday in January).

Behind Isel House, the Nelson Provincial Museum contains exhibits depicting local maritime history and the early days of the colony. Museum hours are 10 A.M. to 4 P.M. Tuesday through Friday (also Monday in January), 2 to 4 P.M. on weekends.

Not far away—on Nayland Road in Stoke—is Broadgreen, a restored 1855 cob house flanked by tree-shaded lawns and a large rose garden. Modeled after a Devonshire farmhouse, the two-story house has thick walls made of packed earth originally dug from the cellar. Refurnished with period furniture, Broadgreen is open to visitors on weekends from 2 to 4:30 P.M. (also on Tuesday and Thursday during school holiday periods) or by appointment.

Walking trails. If you'd enjoy exploring the area on foot, stop at the Public Relations Office for information on local walks and trails. Your choices range from a city historic walk to longer treks into the nearby hills. The Dun Line Walkway, part of the countryside network, follows the scenic route of New Zealand's first railway line.

North along Tasman Bay

Below Richmond, Highway 60 branches northwest along the shore of Tasman Bay. Blossoming apple and pear orchards brighten the countryside in October. The coastal road (via Mapua and Ruby Bay) cuts through the heart of the apple district. In season you'll pass roadside stalls piled high with produce. Collectors find interesting seashells along the shore of Ruby Bay.

Near Motueka, wire-hung hopfields and bright green fields of tobacco mark the center of New Zealand's hop and tobacco-growing industries. Fishing boats operating from Port Motueka land scallops and oysters from August to early November. North of Riwaka, a short side road branches off to Kaiteriteri, a sheltered bay bordered by a curve of beach. Boat trips along the coast (page 87) depart from Kaiteriteri.

Inland routes. From Motueka, Highway 61 follows a sleepy river route south through the Motueka Valley farming country to meet Highway 6 at Kohatu.

Another road heads southeast from Motueka up the Moutere River. Lower Moutere is the site of the Riverside Community, a family-operated commune founded by pacifists during World War II. Upper Moutere, settled by German immigrants in the 1840s, retains a faint Bavarian aura.

Takaka Hill. Northwest of Motueka, a side road leads inland from Highway 60 at the base of the hill to a wooded picnic site near the source of the Riwaka River. Often, you'll see anglers dipping their lines here.

As the highway curves and climbs Takaka Hill, pull off the road to take in the panorama of the Motueka Valley and Tasman Bay.

Marble quarried on Takaka Hill (also called Marble Mountain) was used in the construction of some of New Zealand's most imposing buildings, including Nelson's cathedral and Wellington's Parliament Buildings. Near the summit you'll notice strange marble outcroppings and unusual funnel-shaped rock basins. In summer you can see the delicate formations inside Ngarua Caves, near the top of Takaka Hill.

Craft shopping in Nelson

Attracted by Nelson's sunny climate and superb scenery, artists and craftspeople have flocked to the area, giving the city claim to the title of New Zealand's crafts center. Excellent clay in the district has drawn potters for many years; more than 60 now have studios in the Nelson area. They've been joined by weavers, silversmiths, woodworkers, dollmakers, and artisans who create in glass and fabric. Many of them welcome visitors by appointment. But the best way to see the variety of handiwork available is to visit the city's craft shops, exhibitions, and craft fairs.

To follow Nelson's arts and crafts trail, stop first at the Nelson Public Relations Office, at the corner of Trafalgar and Halifax streets. Here you can pick up a guide to craftspeople all over the province who invite visitors; it also lists the shops and galleries that specialize in the arts of the region.

In Nelson, numerous galleries exhibit work by local artists. One—the South Street Gallery, near the cathedral—displays pieces rustically in one of Nelson's historic 19th century cottages. Some craftspeople showcase their wares in the town's cooperative stores. Chez Eelco, a coffeehouse and gallery on Trafalgar Street at the foot of the cathedral steps, is a favorite gathering place with changing exhibitions by local painters, potters, weavers, and photographers.

On Friday and Saturday, you can browse through assorted crafts at the Market Bazaar, an indoor market at 109 Hardy Street.

Takaka Valley. Continuing north, the highway twists down the mountain's steep northern slope to the dairy country of the Takaka River Valley. Until this road was completed, Golden Bay was relatively isolated from the rest of the province.

Tame eels in the Anatoki River are fed daily (10 to 11 A.M. and 3 to 5 P.M.), weather permitting, from the end of August to early May. To reach Anatoki, turn west off Highway 60 just south of Takaka.

Northwest of Takaka is Waikoropupu (Pupu) Springs, where an estimated 266 millions gallons of pure cold water flow from fresh-water springs each day. The road to the springs leaves Highway 60 north of Takaka.

Abel Tasman National Park

New Zealand's smallest national park honors the country's first *pakeha* visitor, Dutch explorer Abel Tasman, who sailed these waters in 1642. A memorial overlooking Ligar Bay commemorates the site where he anchored.

The town of Takaka contains several motels and motor camps, convenient for visitors making a day trip into Abel Tasman National Park. You'll find the park information office in Takaka (open daily during the summer holidays); there's a visitor center at Totaranui Beach.

Park information is available from the chief ranger in Takaka (P.O. Box 53; phone Takaka 58026) or from the ranger in Motueka (phone Motueka 78110).

Takaka to the coast. The 33-km/20-mile route from Takaka to the beach at Totaranui is the only access road into the park. Along the way you'll spot good beaches at Pohara, Ligar Bay, and Tata. Adjacent to Pohara Beach are a campground and recreational facilities.

The first 11 km/7 miles of the road from Takaka to the park are paved, but the surfacing ends at Tata Beach. The winding, graded road (not recommended for vans) soon begins to climb into the forested hills. Spreading tree ferns rising above you shade the road; streams cascade down gullies toward the bay. Trails wind through the park's primeval rain forest and along the shore.

At Totaranui, bush-covered headlands frame the golden sand beach and deep blue bay. Here you'll find a small campground and the visitor center, which features displays on the park's vegetation, sea and land birds, and other natural features.

Guided treks. Three and four-day group treks depart from Motueka from the beginning of February to mid-December. Winter days in this area are usually calm, crisp, and clear.

After a short coach trip to Kaiteriteri, the group boards a launch and cruises north along the coast to Tonga Bay, where the first day's walk begins. Heavy packs are left on board the launch. After tea, hikers turn south and follow the shore to a lodge at Torrent Bay, where hot showers and comfortable beds await them. Next day, guides offer a choice of shorter walks or other activities—fishing, boating, or snorkeling. (Four-day trekkers spend another day at the lodge.) On the final day, the group hikes down the coast to Marahau and returns to Motueka by coach. The trips are operated by Abel Tasman National Park Enterprises, Green Tree Road, R.D. 3, Motueka, Nelson.

Golden sands and clear waters draw vacationers to the sheltered beach at Kaiteriteri. Summer boat trips cruise north from here along the Abel Tasman park coast.

Day cruises. From late December through March, launch trips depart from Kaiteriteri daily at 10 A.M. for a scenic 6-hour cruise along the coast. The launch makes brief stops at several bays to deliver supplies to campers and isolated cottages; tides permitting, it also journeys up the forest-rimmed Falls River. During a 2½-hour stopover at Torrent Bay, you have a chance to explore a small corner of the park.

Tramping through luxuriant bush

Many backpackers have discovered the Heaphy (Hee-fee) Track, a one-time prospectors' trail cutting across the grassy downs and subtropical valleys of northwest Nelson province.

Beginning southwest of Collingwood (via Bainham), the 72-km/45-mile trail climbs through rimu and beech forest and then descends through the red tussock country of the Gouland Downs to the fern-filled valley of the Heaphy River. Here you'll find not only luxuriant stands of nikau palms but also giant sandflies—insect repellent is a "must" for hikers.

The magnificent final section of the track follows the bush-bordered seacoast south to end at the Kohaihai River north of Karamea. Hikers can arrange taxi service at both ends of the trail.

Tramping groups generally take from 4 to 6 days to make the trek, staying overnight in trail huts along the route. Most hikers prefer the months of February and March, after the summer rains. But be prepared for all kinds of weather in this region—it receives up to 200 inches of rain annually.

Experienced trampers who prefer a more challenging and less popular route seek out the Wangapeka Track, another miners' trail south of the Heaphy. It goes westward from Wangapeka through mountains and river valleys to end south of Karamea near Te Namu.

Check with New Zealand Forest Service rangers in Nelson or Takaka for current information on track conditions before setting out on either trek.

Collingwood and the northern tip

From Collingwood you can arrange four-wheel-drive trips to Farewell Spit and other off-road destinations near South Island's northern tip. Collingwood Safari Tours organizes daily trips from mid-December to early February. The rest of the year, trips leave only on Wednesday; groups can make special arrangements for other times.

Heading for the beach? You'll find safe swimming and easy boat launching at Paton's Rock and alluring shells and colored pebbles at Parapara; both are south of Collingwood. Surfcasting, swimming, a campground, and a store are to be found farther north at Pakawau. On the north coast near Cape Farewell, Wharariki Beach offers wave-cut rock formations, a seal colony, and sea birds.

For an inland summer destination, drive southwest through the rich dairy land of the Aorere River Valley to see limestone formations and glowworms in Te Anaroa Caves (open during the summer holidays). Take along picnic supplies—including some Collingwood Cheddar cheese—for lunch beside the river.

Nelson Lakes National Park

In the southern part of the province, dark beech-covered mountains rise steeply from the water to enclose a pair of slender glacial lakes—jewel-like Rotoiti and Rotoroa—in Nelson Lakes National Park. Recently increased in size, the park extends south from Highway 63 to the rocky crags of the Spenser Mountains and east to the St. Arnaud Range. Nelson Lakes includes the northern part of the great alpine fault that dominates South Island.

Two routes lead to the park. From Blenheim and Renwick, Highway 63 heads up the Wairau Valley to Nelson Lakes. From Nelson, you travel south on Highway 6 to Kawatiri Junction, then turn east and follow the Buller River upstream.

Swimming, boating, water-skiing, and picnicking attract many visitors to Lake Rotoiti. More isolated Lake Rotoroa draws anglers, hunters, and hikers. In winter, skiers flock here to enjoy the fine runs on Mount Robert.

Along the Buller River

Lake Rotoiti's outflow becomes the Buller River, the principal river on the West Coast. For most of its route, the Buller churns through a steep, wooded gorge — one of New Zealand's most beautiful river drives.

Murchison, near the junction of highways 6 and 65, serves both nearby farmers and travelers. Originally a gold mining settlement, Murchison has been rebuilt since 1929, when it stood near the epicenter of a devastating earthquake. Exhibits from the earthquake and the town's mining days fill the local museum. Maruia Falls, about 22 km/14 miles south on Highway 65, was created when the earthquake changed the course of the Maruia River.

About 14 km/9 miles west of Murchison, Highway 6 crosses the line of the Murchison earthquake fault. Look for evidence of land displacement across the river. At Inangahua Junction, Highway 69 branches south to Reefton; Highway 6 continues through the scenic Lower Buller Gorge to Westport. Evergreens, beech, and ferns blanket the slopes of the gorge.

The West Coast

When New Zealanders refer to "The Coast," they're talking about the wild, wet West Coast of South Island, a slim strip of land hemmed in between the jagged peaks of the Southern Alps and the rough waters of the Tasman Sea. Highway 6 follows the shore for most of its length.

Though Maoris traveled here over difficult mountain routes in search of greenstone, early European visitors found few attractions. Only the lure of gold could stimulate migration to this long-isolated region.

In the mid-1860s, prospectors swarmed to the Coast. Boom towns appeared overnight, and fortunes were won and lost by hard-working, hard-drinking miners. The West Coast's main towns — Westport, Greymouth, and Hokitika — date from gold rush days, when supply ships anchored near the mouths of the larger coastal rivers to trade with the miners. Travelers lured by the magnificent scenery of the area began arriving in the late 19th century.

Averaging only about 50 km/30 miles in width, the narrow coastal strip offers great variety in geography, climate, and terrain. Lofty peaks, snow covered the year around, tower along the spine of the Southern Alps. Icy glacial fingers inch slowly down the alpine valleys, terminating at relatively low elevations only a short distance from the sea. Luxuriant native rain forest covers the lower slopes. Since coastal weather tends to be unpredictable, always be prepared for rain.

Renowned for their friendliness and hospitality, today's "Coasters" reflect the lively spirit and camaraderie of gold rush days. No group represents this fun-loving region better than the colorfully dressed Kokatahi Miners Band, a musical aggregation whose travels and outrageous exploits are well documented in coastal folklore.

West Coast—the essentials

The main towns along this rugged coastline are Westport, Greymouth, and Hokitika. Primary lure for travelers is spectacular Westland National Park; another favorite attraction is Shantytown, a replica mining town south of Greymouth.

Getting there. Most visitors travel to the West Coast by rental car or motorcoach, but air and rail service is also available. Air New Zealand serves Westport and Hokitika from Christchurch and Wellington. New Zealand Railways trains link Christchurch and Greymouth via Arthur's Pass. Newmans Coach Lines provides service between Nelson and Greymouth. Railways Road Services motorcoaches travel from Christchurch to Westport and Greymouth, between Westport and Fox Glacier, and from the glaciers area via Haast Pass to Queenstown.

Accommodations. Though many travelers stay in Westport, Greymouth, or near the glaciers, modest accommodations and camping areas are available in smaller towns as well.

Westport has a number of hotels (largest is the DB Westport) and motels. In Greymouth, Revington's is a comfortable older hotel in the center of town. Other accommodations include the DB Greymouth Hotel, Ashley Motel and Motor Inn, King's Motor Hotel, and numerous small motels. Hokitika also offers both hotel and motel rooms. Fishing enthusiasts enjoy Mitchells Hotel at Mitchells, 47 km/29 miles southeast of Greymouth on the shore of Lake Brunner.

Activity in the glaciers area centers around the excellent THC Franz Josef Hotel and the Westland Motor Inn at Franz Josef, and the Vacation and Fox Glacier hotels at Fox Glacier. Motel accommodations and motor camps are also available. The DB Haast Hotel is at the western end of scenic Haast Pass.

Getting around. Rental cars and taxis are available at Westport, Greymouth, and Hokitika. Flightseeing trips, glacier walks, and other alpine excursions can be arranged at both Franz Josef and Fox Glacier.

Tourist information. For specific information on West Coast attractions, inquire at local information offices in Greymouth and Hokitika. Visitor centers in Westland National Park are located at Franz Josef and Fox Glacier.

Westport, coal shipping center

Though gold brought prosperity to Westport, coal — "black gold" — has sustained it. Bituminous coal mining began in the Paparoa Range in the 1870s. Westport, located at the mouth of the Buller River, continues as the country's major coal shipping port. Large freighters anchor at riverside wharves to load coal, timber, and cement.

Along the main street, intricately detailed ironwork decorates the pillars and façades of vintage buildings. City parks include Victoria Square, a grassy gathering spot near the center of town, and Westport Domain, a section of subtropical bush at the upper end of Palmerston Street.

Coaltown Trust. Housed in a converted brewery at the upper end of Queen Street, this community museum highlights the area's coal mining industry. Open daily from 9 A.M. to 4:30 P.M., it includes a simulated coal mine, displays of old-time mining equipment and artifacts, and a model of the famed Denniston Incline coal conveyor. Other exhibits depict the area's pioneering and transportation history and the early New Zealand brewing industry.

To Cape Foulwind. From the Buller bridge, a road runs west from Highway 6 past the airport and Carters Beach (a popular swimming and sunning spot) to Cape Foulwind. Topped by a lighthouse, the headland is New Zealand's closest land point to Australia.

Farther south at dune-backed Tauranga Bay, low tide uncovers fascinating tidepools. Walk up the headland at the north end of the beach for a look at the seal colony just offshore.

Visit a coal mine. If you want to learn more about the local coal mining industry, you can arrange to visit an operating coal mine. For information, stop at the Mines Department office in Westport.

One of the most renowned coal towns was Denniston, once a settlement of 2,000 but now a virtual ghost town. To reach the site, about 25 km/16 miles northeast of Westport, take Highway 67 north to Waimangaroa and veer off on the twisting road that climbs eastward into the Paparoa Range. From here the famed Denniston Incline conveyed millions of tons of coal from the mine bins some 600 meters/2,000 feet to the railway below. Acclaimed as an engineering feat when it was established in 1880, the Incline operated until the late 1960s. Now coal from several underground mines is trucked to Waimangaroa and then transported by rail.

Farther north at Granity, also a Buller coal center, another mining road climbs past Millerton's burning mine to the hilly site of Stockton. Here an 8-km/5-mile-long aerial cableway carries coal from Stockton's open cast mine down to Ngakawau.

Karamea and the "winterless north"

From Westport, Highway 67 heads north along the coast toward the remote community of Karamea, an isolated dairy center about 98 km/60 miles north of Westport. Cradled between the mountains and the sea, the district is known for its mild climate; subtropical fruits flourish here.

Along the route to this "winterless north," you can hunt for gemstones, go surfcasting along the beach, or enjoy short walks through the bush. North of Ngakawau you'll pass between steep hills and the sea, then turn inland across the Mokihinui River to wind slowly through thick forests atop Karamea Bluff. Stop at the top for a memorable panoramic view. Short trails lead to a giant matai tree and to tiny Lake Hanlan.

If time permits, continue about 15 km/9 miles north of Karamea to the road's end at the Kohaihai River. Cross the footbridge there and walk part of the spectacular coastal section of the Heaphy Track.

Gold rush memories and scenic grandeur

South of Westport, Highway 6 curves southwest across Addisons Flat; little remains of the gold diggings that once lured thousands of miners here.

In Charleston, the European Hotel keeps the gold rush era alive with its collection of photographs and mining relics. Charleston's tiny roadside post office serves an extensive area of the Coast.

After climbing into the hills south of Charleston, the highway hugs the shore as it cuts through some of the wildest shoreline scenery in New Zealand. Subtropical greenery blankets the slopes of the craggy coastline to the very edge of the Tasman Sea. Large nikau palms, tree ferns, flax, and hebe species border the exposed coast; just inland rise rimu, miro, beech, and rata trees. Bush birds include the bellbird, tomtit, and weka.

The stratified Punakaiki Pancake Rocks, one of the Coast's best-known features, jut into the sea on Dolomite Point about midway between Westport and Greymouth

Coping with sandflies

In many wet lowland areas, "getting away from it all" means walking straight into the domain of the sandfly.

During his May, 1773, sojourn at Dusky Sound on the southwest coast, Captain James Cook noted in his log that sandflies were "so numerous and . . . so troublesome that they exceed everything of the kind that I have met with." The tiny pests are still with us today.

Thriving in moist and humid regions up to 3,000 feet in elevation, these silent and persistent insects appear when the air is calm, particularly at dawn, dusk, or before rain. The small, black sandflies are least belligerent in hot sunshine, in cold weather, or during strong winds or heavy rain.

Only the females bite. In many people these bites set up a series of reactions, often resulting in an allergy to subsequent bites. Vulnerable hikers rely on a powerful insect repellent or vitamin B_1 tablets to discourage the flies from biting. Antihistamine drugs minimize side effects from the bites.

(page 94). Centuries of surf action at this spot have tunneled out rocky grottoes, surge pools, and blow holes beneath the thinly layered limestone headland. On clear days you can see the Southern Alps from here. At the visitor center across the highway in Punakaiki, you'll find tourist facilities and displays explaining features of this geologic anomaly. A modern campground is nearby, and trails lead into the bush and along the coast.

Greymouth, gateway to Shantytown

The largest town on the West Coast is Greymouth, hub of a coal and timber-producing district and the western terminus of Highway 7. Like most other coastal communities, it flourished during the 1860s gold rush. Today, visitors flock to nearby Shantytown, a replica gold mining town. For local tourist information, stop at the West Coast Public Relations Office in the Regent Theatre.

The Grey River carves a broad valley—known as The Gap—through coastal limestone to the sea. On clear days you can gaze eastward to a snowy panorama of the high peaks of the Southern Alps; the best view is from the south breakwater. Another memorable vista is from King

Domain; the steep track starts from Mount Street (leave your car in Smith Street if you're driving) and climbs to several lookouts.

During the spring whitebait season, you may see local anglers netting for the tiny transparent fish in the Grey River and other West Coast streams. Tuna boats call at Greymouth from January to May.

You can see wild game in a natural setting at Hunting and Safari (N.Z.) Ltd.'s wildlife park at Paroa, south of Greymouth; it's open daily.

Highway 73, the Arthur's Pass Road across the mountains (page 96), reaches the coast south of Greymouth.

Coal miners' train. You can board the Rewanui coal miners' train weekdays at 12:30 P.M. at Greymouth's Riverside Station for a ride into the Paparoa hills to an operating underground coal mine. Ask at the ticket office for the Rewanui Miners' Train brochure; it includes a map of the area.

The train travels northeast to Runanga and Dunollie, then climbs steep Seven Mile Canyon to Rewanui. During the short stopover, you'll have time to poke around the mine buildings, coal bins, and conveyor belts of the Liverpool Mine. The train arrives back in Greymouth about 3:05 P.M. (2:35 P.M. on Friday).

Shantytown. Popular Shantytown offers a glimpse of life in a West Coast gold mining town of the 1860s. Set amid native bush 13 km/8 miles southeast of Greymouth, it's open daily from 8:30 A.M. to 5 P.M.

A century-old church, general store, hotel-saloon, and typical shops line the main street. A few buildings have been moved here from other sites; others are reproductions of earlier structures. Among the sights you'll see are an 1837 printing press, an excellent gemstone display, vintage vehicles and equipment, and a replica Chinese den containing articles used by these early miners.

You can climb aboard a stagecoach for a tour of the grounds or ride through the bush on the Kaitangata steam railway. A short trail leads to the gold sluicing area, where you can pan for gold.

West Coast gold country

Discoveries of gold along West Coast streams triggered a massive rush as prospectors of all nationalities flocked to the Coast. Full-fledged towns—complete with hotels, banks, bars, and shops—sprang up almost overnight. In late 1864 only 800 people had settled here, but a year later the population had boomed to 16,000. By the end of 1866, some 50,000 miners had arrived in search of riches.

Miners struck gold in such places as Blackball and Moonlight. In the Ngahere region, Nelson Creek, Red Jacks, and Notown were all thriving gold sites. But the boom collapsed almost as suddenly as it had begun. After the rush to Addisons Flat in May 1867, most prospectors moved on to the new Coromandel gold fields, though mining continued in Westland on a sizable scale until the

mid-1880s. And all activity is still not over—the Kaniere electric-powered dredge continues to recover gold from the Taramakau River.

For information and brochures on side trips from Greymouth to former mining centers, inquire at the Public Relations Office in Greymouth. Forest Service rangers in Hokitika and Totara Flat (on Highway 7 southwest of Ikamatua) can also provide information.

Grey Valley. An enjoyable loop trip from Greymouth follows the north bank road up the Grey River to Blackball, continues on to the timber and rail center of Ikamatua, and returns to the coast on Highway 7.

Coal miners still live in Blackball, where you'll see the old mine's dilapidated outbuildings. Several roads and trails—including the Croesus and Moonlight tracks—head into the Paparoa Range from Blackball. On Highway 7 near Ngahere, roads and trails border the creeks where miners panned for gold a century ago. Waiuta, in the hills southeast of Hukarere, was productive as recently as 1950.

Lake Brunner. Another inland destination is Lake Brunner, a favorite of anglers, yachters, and hikers. There's a picnic area at Moana on the northern shore (accessible from Highway 7). Mitchells, on the southern shore, is a fishing and boating center and the departure point for bush walks. The road to Mitchells veers north from Highway 73 at Kumara and follows part of the old 1865 miners' route through the Greenstone Valley. In Kumara you can examine historic items in the Holy Trinity Anglican Church; built by gold miners, the church has been in continuous use since 1878.

Hokitika for greenstone

Boisterous "capital of the gold fields" in the lively 1860s, today Hokitika is Westland's administrative center and headquarters of the greenstone processing industry. Tourist information is available at 29 Weld Street.

Mining displays and early photographs at the West Coast Historical Museum on lower Tancred Street recall gold rush days. Exhibits include scale models of a gold dredge and a mining shaft. Museum hours are 9:30 A.M. to 4:30 P.M. weekdays, 2 to 4:30 P.M. weekends.

Northeast of town on the airport road, a plane table identifies more than 50 peaks visible in a panorama of the Southern Alps. For a closer look, scenic flights are available.

Crafts. Early Maoris obtained highly prized jade, called greenstone, from the nearby Arahura Valley; from it they carved their weapons, cutting tools, and personal ornaments. Modern craftsmen fashion the hard stone into jewelry, *hei-tiki* pendants, and other decorative objects. On weekdays you can watch greenstone carvers working at two Hokitika factories — Westland Greenstone Company on Tancred Street and Hokitika Jade Company Ltd., 110 Revell Street.

Ski-equipped planes land skiers on an icy glacier after an exhilarating trip over the rugged peaks of the Southern Alps. Nonskiers experience similar thrills on flightseeing trips.

Visitors can also watch glassblowers demonstrate their craft on weekdays at Hokitika Free Form Glass Co., Ltd., 130 Revell Street.

Excursions. At the Blue Spur Gold Mine, about 5 km/3 miles east of Hokitika, you can visit a working gold sluicing operation, pan for gold, and even enter some of the mine shafts and tunnels. The mine is open daily.

Lake Kaniere — one of Westland's loveliest — often mirrors a view of forested hills backed by the snow-topped Southern Alps. Located 18 km/12 miles southeast of Hokitika, the lake is popular for boating, swimming, and water-skiing. Yachting and speed boat regattas ruffle the waters on summer weekends.

Back country explorers and trampers can follow the Hokitika River upstream via Kokatahi and Kowhitirangi. For trail information, check with the Forest Service ranger in Hokitika.

South to the glaciers

From Hokitika, Highway 6 crosses the Hokitika River on a long combined road/rail bridge and curves inland up the valley. Franz Josef lies 147 km/91 miles southwest, Fox Glacier another 25 km/16 miles beyond.

Lake Mahinapua, west of the highway a few kilome-ters south of Hokitika, attracts picnickers and yachters. You can walk in (30 minutes) from the highway or follow a loop road and approach the lake from the west through a tunnel of lush greenery. Ross, a former gold town located south of the turnoff for the lake, is noted for the cherry trees that flower along its main street each spring.

From the Waitaha River south to Lake Ianthe, you wend your way through a forest corridor of tall rimu, lush ferns, and other dense bush. West of Lake Wahapo, a signposted road forks 13 km/8 miles to the coastal settlement of Okarito. From September to February, a white heron colony nests at Okarito Lagoon.

Westland National Park

On the western slope of the Southern Alps, some of New Zealand's most spectacular alpine country has been set aside in Westland National Park. Most visitors focus on Franz Josef and Fox glaciers, a pair of broad, icy tongues that push steeply down from permanent snowfields to within a few kilometers of the sea. And there's more—the park's rain forests, lakes, and coursing rivers, all backed by the range of snow-clad peaks, are equally captivating.

Accommodations and tourist facilities are concentrated in the communities of Franz Josef and Fox Glacier. Park visitor centers feature exhibits on park geology, bot-

Hiking and climbing amid superb scenery

Whether you enjoy a quiet stroll along a short nature trail or go in for strenuous hiking through mountain wilderness, you'll find New Zealand's network of trails one of the country's special treats. Dedicated hikers (called "trampers" in New Zealand) and mountaineers head for the verdant bush and alpine parks, but even the casual walker can enjoy many rewarding short routes.

Many trails are suitable for walkers wearing street shoes; other paths require sturdy walking shoes or hiking boots. Sandy sections of some trails may be soggy after a heavy rain.

New Zealand Walkways. From Cape Reinga in the north to Invercargill in the south, trails offer access to the countryside for Kiwis and visitors alike. Frequently located near urban centers, many of the trails are part of the New Zealand Walkways project, an ambitious and imaginative network of routes. Designed for the walker rather than for the serious backpacker, the trails traverse the scenic areas of the country. In length, they range from an hour's easy walk to a strenuous full-day excursion.

Local tourist offices can provide trail information—and often a descriptive leaflet with a map of the route.

Bush walks. Many of the best short forest walks wind through scenic reserves and national parks. Trees are identified on some nature trails. At park visitor centers, you can study exhibits on local trees, flowers, and birds; park officials can suggest special points of interest and provide trail information. Elsewhere, inquire at Forest Service offices and local tourist centers.

Longer treks. Best known of the longer hikes is the famed Milford Track (page 119), a challenging tramp through South Island's Fiordland National Park; it begins at the head of Lake Te Anau and ends at Milford Sound. Not far away, the Routeburn Track (page 115) traverses the impressive alpine country of Mount Aspiring and Fiordland national parks. A third face of Fiordland National Park may be seen on the low-level river route through the Hollyford Valley (page 118) to Martins Bay.

At the northern end of South Island, the Heaphy and Wangapeka tracks (page 87) wind through native forest and tussock to the lush greenery of the West Coast.

North Island routes range from a coastal trek around Cape Reinga and down Ninety Mile Beach (page 39) to wilderness trails into the Wanganui country (page 57).

Backpackers should check in with the nearest Forest Service ranger before departing to obtain the latest information on weather and track conditions.

Group excursions. Organized group trips on the Milford, Routeburn, and Hollyford routes allow hikers to travel into isolated areas with only lightweight packs. Lodging and meals are provided in huts along the route, and each hiker carries only personal gear in a backpack.

Less strenuous is the South Island excursion that takes hikers from Motueka, northwest of Nelson, into Abel Tasman National Park (page 86); accommodations are provided in a waterfront lodge on Torrent Bay.

Group trips also probe the untamed areas in the central part of North Island. Maori guides lead 5-day tramping adventures into the Urewera country southeast of Rotorua (page 60).

Venturetreks (P.O. Box 3839, Auckland) organizes 5-day guided excursions in the Wanganui Valley (the Wanganui River Walk, page 59), and in the wilderness of Kaimanawa and Kaweka state forest parks east of Tongariro National Park (the Kaimanawa Wilderness Walk, page 53), and the Alpine Walk around Tongariro National Park (page 55).

Mountaineering. New Zealand's high peaks attract experienced mountaineers, and some—such as Sir Edmund Hillary—have won worldwide fame. In the Southern Alps, more than a dozen peaks top 3,050 meters/10,000 feet; highest of all is Mount Cook.

Major climbing areas on South Island lie along the slopes of the Southern Alps. Mount Cook and Westland national parks flank the range's main divide and offer superb alpine scenery. Other high peaks in Mount Aspiring, Arthur's Pass, and Fiordland national parks lure mountaineering enthusiasts.

North Island's mountains are lower than those of South Island, and the major peaks are either extinct or mildly active volcanoes.

Equipment and information. You can purchase or rent equipment for serious hiking and mountaineering in the main towns and alpine resort hotels.

Write to the New Zealand Tourist Office for the brochure *New Zealand Tramping and Mountaineering*. For more specific information, inquire at the park headquarters of each national park or at outdoor clubs. Hikers and trampers can contact the New Zealand Federation of Mountain Clubs, P.O. Box 1604, Wellington. For mountain-climbing information, write to the New Zealand Alpine Club, P.O. Box 41038, Eastbourne, Wellington.

any, and wildlife. You can obtain trail information and park publications at the visitor centers or from the chief ranger in Franz Josef (P.O. Box 14; phone Franz Josef 727) or the ranger in Fox Glacier (P.O. Box 9; phone Fox Glacier 807).

Walking on a glacier. Hikers in good physical condition can join one of the guided glacier excursions departing daily from Franz Josef and from Fox Glacier. Walking on the glacial ice involves fairly strenuous hiking over terminal moraine and ice. Guides outfit participants with well-oiled boots, heavy socks, and—in rainy weather—knee-length slickers. Do not attempt to hike on the ice without proper equipment. A 2½-hour guided trip departs at 9:30 A.M. and 2 P.M. from Fox Glacier.

Popular heli-hike excursions take off from Franz Josef Airfield. During the summer season, visitors can choose either a half-day or a full-day trip. The rest of the year, heli-hike excursions operate on demand, weather permitting. A helicopter takes passengers up the glacier, where the aircraft lands; guides then escort groups of outfitted hikers down the ice. You'll see pinnacle blue ice, crevasses, and ice caves. The full-day trip takes participants up to Victoria Falls under the glacier's main ice fall.

On sunny days, it's essential to protect your eyes and skin against glare from the snow. For comfort on the walk, plan to have both hands free.

Occasionally, you may hear the sound of grinding and cracking ice; it's a sign that the glacier is inching forward under tremendous pressure from the vast ice field above.

Flying through the Alps. Many travelers consider a flightseeing trip through the snowy peaks of the Southern Alps one of the most exciting and memorable experiences of their trip.

Ski-equipped Mount Cook Line planes depart frequently during periods of good weather from airports at Franz Josef and at Fox Glacier. Because demand is great, sign up as soon as you arrive so you won't be disappointed. On most flights, the pilot lands the small plane on a glacial snowfield so passengers can walk on the ice, take photographs, and throw a snowball or two. On longer trips, you fly over the divide and down the Tasman Glacier on the eastern slope of the Alps.

Guided alpine trips. Mountaineering courses and excursions into the Southern Alps are conducted from November to mid-March by Alpine Guides–Westland (P.O. Box 38, Fox Glacier). Winter mountaineering and ice-climbing training and a number of alpine ski tours are scheduled from June through October.

A pause at Franz Josef

Named by explorer Julius von Haast in 1865 for the emperor of his native Austria-Hungary, Franz Josef is the shorter and steeper of the two glaciers; it descends the western slope of the Southern Alps some 11 km/7 miles to terminate about 300 meters/980 feet above sea level.

If you approach from the north, you'll get your first view of the glacier from across Lake Mapourika. Another vista comes as you cross Tatare Bridge north of town. Closer views loom above the THC Franz Josef Hotel

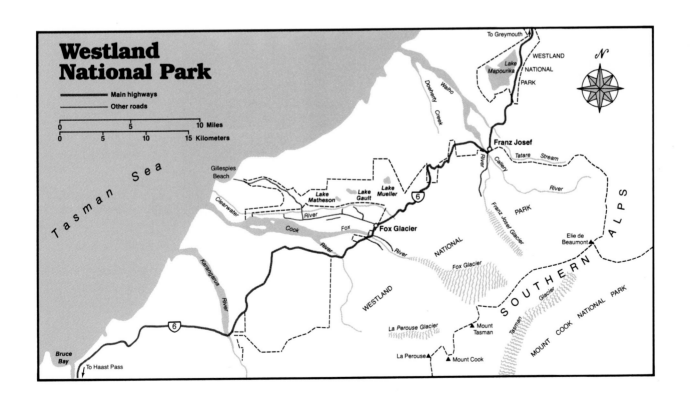

grounds and from Glacier Road, which branches off Highway 6 just south of the Waiho River.

After you've stopped at the park visitor center, be sure to visit nearby St. James' Church to see the alpine view framed in the chancel window.

If you have time for only one walk, take the Terrace Track through the rain forest to historic Callery Gorge, stop at the warm springs, and return along the Waiho River. A booklet, available at the visitor center, describes natural features and points out traces remaining from gold mining days on the Waiho.

From Glacier Road, a 5-minute walk leads to Peters Pool, a "kettle" lake with a glacier reflection. You can continue on the Douglas Track past the swing bridge over the Waiho, then return through bush and moraine areas to the road.

Fox Glacier's walks and views

The curvy, 24-km/15-mile route from Franz Josef to Fox Glacier winds over spur ranges before descending into the broad valley known as the Cook River Flats. The cozy

settlement of Fox Glacier is headquarters for excursions into the southern part of the park. The glacier was named for Sir William Fox, one-time premier of New Zealand.

Stop at the visitor center to see its exhibits of park plants, birds, and geology and for printed information on trails and other park features.

Bush walks. Trails offer enjoyable hikes through luxuriant bush, spectacular views of snowy peaks and tree-rimmed lakes, and a close look at evidence of the glacier's advance and retreat. Leaflets available at the visitor center describe points of interest and help you identify trailside plants.

The walk to Lake Matheson is delightful any time of day, but the classic panorama—Mount Cook and Mount Tasman reflected in the lake's dark waters—is most striking at sunrise, when the first rays streak the clouds and strike the snowy peaks. It's an easy 30-minute walk to the lake and about another 30 minutes on a rock trail to the "view of views" at the far end of the lake. The Lake Gault trail branches north from the Matheson trail.

Just south of the township, the Minnehaha Track is a

Thin layers of limestone create the Pancake Rocks at Punakaiki. Lush greenery, grottoes, blowholes, and a visitor center lure travelers to this coastal curiosity.

20-minute loop from the highway through the bush to the edge of the quiet Minnehaha stream. Several other tracks begin along the South Approach Road (Glacier View Road) south of the river.

If Westland mists lift, some of the most inspiring glacier views come along the steep switchback track up Cone Rock. In less than an hour, you'll climb some 300 meters/980 feet above the Fox River for a grandstand view of the large glacier. After a rain, though, handholds are slick, and you'll dodge one waterfall after another.

A shorter and less strenuous track, also offering splendid views, leads to the Fox Chalet Lookout.

The effects of the glacier's advance and retreat are particularly noticeable on the Moraine Walk through the Fox Valley. Along the way you see forests of varying ages, terminal moraines marking the glacier's advance in earlier centuries, and erratic boulders pushed along by the ice.

Other attractions. You'll discover breathtaking vistas of Fox Glacier and the high peaks from several viewpoints. One of the best is from the Clearwater River bridge on the road to Gillespies Beach. From the South Approach Road, you see the glacier framed by trees, and there's a good view of Mount Tasman from the Fox River bridge.

After dark, you can walk to the glowworm grotto signposted just south of town. Here, glowing iridescent green lights attract night-flying insects. (For more on glowworms, see page 40.)

Gillespies Beach, west of Fox Glacier, was once an isolated gold mining settlement. Gorse now covers the old tailings behind the dunes. Captivating coastal scenery and alpine views await visitors.

If you plan to hike north to the seal colony (1 to 1½ hours round trip), check first at the park visitor center, since part of the beach route is passable only at low tide. An alternate path takes you inland over sections of the old miners' road.

Down the South Westland coast

From Fox Glacier, Highway 6 continues 118 km/73 miles south to Haast Junction. Forest lines much of the route; in summer, white plumes of toe toe, scarlet-blooming rata, and yellow gorse add accents of color.

You can picnic beside the sea at Bruce Bay, where the road briefly skirts the coast before turning inland, or farther south at Lake Paringa or Lake Moeraki, both good fishing lakes. Just north of the Moeraki River bridge, a short side road leads to the start of the Munro Track, a 40-minute walk to the beach through a forest thick with large tree ferns and native fuchsia.

The highway meets the coast again at Knights Point, where a windy viewpoint high above the sea offers vistas of bush-covered headlands, golden sand beaches, and jagged offshore rocks.

About 5 km/3 miles south of Knights Point, you can walk to the beach along Ship Creek; remains of ship-wrecks are sometimes visible below the bridge at low tide.

Lonely road to Jackson Bay

After crossing the Haast River bridge, longest of New Zealand's single lane bridges, most motorists turn inland on Highway 6 to cross Haast Pass, 64 km/40 miles distant. A hardy few continue along the coast toward Haast township and Jackson Bay. Experienced trampers head up the Okuru River into Mount Aspiring National Park.

Just south of the Arawata River bridge, a signposted, unpaved side road leads 4 km/2 miles to the start of the Ellery Track. The 45-minute forest walk beside the outlet stream brings you to secluded Lake Ellery.

Jackson Bay, 48 km/29 miles below Haast Junction, provided a sheltered anchorage for early whalers and sealers. The bay was also the site of one of Westland's most isolated early settlements.

Across rugged Haast Pass

Originally an old Maori route to the West Coast, Haast Pass, at 563 meters/1,847 feet, links the West Coast with the Southern Lakes district and forms the boundary between Westland and Otago.

Geologist-explorer Julius von Haast crossed the pass in 1863 and named the route after himself. In the late 1800s and early 1900s, pack horses carried supplies across the pass to isolated West Coast settlers. Cattle had to be driven up the coast or over the tortuous Haast Pass track, freight came and went by ship, and radio and later aircraft provided the primary means of communication. Not until 1960 did completion of the Wanaka-Haast route end a century of virtual isolation for the people of Haast.

Snow seldom closes the highway, but rainfall is abundant. All too often for visitors, clouds obscure the scenery. Waterfalls pour from hanging valleys into the glacier-cut gorges of the Haast and Makarora rivers.

Camping areas, picnic tables, and rest rooms are located at several roadside points, but you may have to share facilities with aggressive sandflies.

West of the divide. Silver beech trees populate the wet forests on the western slope of the mountains. Southeast of the Pleasant Flat picnic area, a short track leads to Thunder Creek Falls. At the Gates of Haast, the clear, pale blue waters of the Haast River foam over immense boulders wedged into the narrow gorge. The old bridle trail used by prospectors, cattle drovers, and other early travelers parallels the highway near the pass.

Eastern slope. Mountain beech predominates on the drier eastern side of Haast Pass. You descend on an unpaved road along the Makarora River through the northern part of Mount Aspiring National Park. Side roads lead to high-country sheep stations.

The highway cuts through brown tussock lands to skirt the northeastern shore of Lake Wanaka, then angles across The Neck—where the ancient Hawea and Wanaka glaciers met to gouge out the lake beds—and continues south along Lake Hawea to Wanaka.

The Southern Alps

Often shrouded in clouds, the magnificent peaks of the Southern Alps form New Zealand's snow-capped backbone. Towering majestically above western rain forest and eastern plain, they extend some 650 km/400 miles along the western edge of South Island.

Few roads cut through the high alpine valleys. At the northern end, Highway 6 links Nelson and Westport through the Buller River Gorge (page 87); it recrosses the Alps near the southern end through Haast Pass (see page 95). The Milford Road (page 118) links Te Anau and Milford Sound.

In the central part of the range, highways follow old Maori greenstone routes through Lewis Pass and Arthur's Pass to the West Coast.

Lewis Pass Road

Constructed during the Depression of the 1930s, the Lewis Pass Road (Highway 7) begins at Waipara, north of Christchurch, and passes south of Hanmer Springs. Canterbury farmlands give way to rolling golden foothills and beech forests as you follow the Waiau Valley northwest across 864-meter/2,840-foot Lewis Pass. The road then descends through rugged greenery to the West Coast.

At Maruia Springs, just west of Lewis Pass, you can swim in hot pools in an alpine setting. East of Reefton, the Blacks Point Museum — housed in a wooden former church — displays local mining memorabilia. The highway follows the Grey River toward the sea and meets the West Coast highway at Greymouth.

Across Arthur's Pass

Shortest, steepest, and most spectacular of the routes across the Southern Alps, Arthur's Pass Road (Highway 73) is the main link between Canterbury and Westland. Construction of the route began in 1855, boosted by the efforts of Christchurch businessmen seeking to direct the flow of gold from West Coast mines through the Canterbury capital.

From the Canterbury Plains, the road climbs into the mountains and curves around Craigieburn State Forest Park. In winter, inhabitants of Christchurch and the surrounding area enjoy tobogganing at Porters Pass, ice skating at nearby Lake Lyndon, and skiing at Porters Heights and Temple Basin skifield.

Headquarters for Arthur's Pass National Park is located in Arthur's Pass township, just east of the 922-meter/3,029-foot summit.

West of the divide, the highway descends steeply to the railway settlement of Otira; no vans are permitted on the Arthur's Pass-Otira section of the road. At the settlement of Jacksons, a wayside tavern recalls its early years as a stagecoach inn before the rail line was pushed through the mountains; historic photographs evoke this colorful period. The road continues down the Taramakau Valley to meet Highway 6 near Kumara.

A bird's-eye view of nature's wonders

One of the most thrilling adventures for visitors in this air-minded nation is flightseeing—sightseeing by small airplane. These maneuverable, low-flying aircraft have opened up remote and rugged parts of New Zealand formerly inaccessible to most travelers. From the air, New Zealand's fabled scenery takes on a dramatic new perspective.

In most of the country's main tourist centers you can climb aboard a single or twin-engine plane, float plane, or helicopter for a bird's-eye view of the region's lakes, mountains, fiords, or coastline. Photographers will find the most expansive views from the seats beside or immediately behind the pilot.

Perhaps the most spectacular trip is the flight through the rugged white wonderland of the Southern Alps. Ski-equipped planes leave from Mount Cook, Franz Josef, and Fox Glacier. You thread through snowy peaks, fly over gaping crevasses, and then land briefly on one of the high snowfields.

In Rotorua, Taupo, and the southern lakes district, you soar above bush-rimmed lakes. Gaping volcanic craters and steaming geothermal valleys assume new dimensions from the air. Flights from Queenstown and Te Anau take you over Fiordland's dense bush and above hikers' huts along the Milford Track.

For an aerial view of bush-covered headlands bordering an azure sea, consider a flight over the Marlborough Sounds waterways (from Picton) or the Bay of Islands (from Paihia). Above Auckland you look down on Waitemata Harbour and the islands of the Hauraki Gulf. From Kaitaia, fly along Ninety Mile Beach to Cape Reinga—and see Northland's kauri gum fields and mangrove swamps, as well.

Arthur's Pass National Park

Spanning both slopes of the Southern Alps, the park encompasses a broad cross section of alpine flora. Mountain beech forest predominates on the eastern slope, and dense forest covers the western side. Waterfalls tumble from glacier-cut valleys. Alpine wildflowers bloom from mid-November through February; the brilliant crimson flowers of the rata turn the mountainsides ablaze with color. Above the tree line, the scenery is cold and severe. In winter, snow blankets the slopes.

Park activities are concentrated in Arthur's Pass township, about 154 km/95 miles northwest of Christchurch. At park headquarters here, you'll see exhibits depicting the history of the park and the difficult construction of the road and railway. You'll also see one of the old Cobb & Co. stagecoaches that transported passengers and freight across the rugged route before the completion of the Otira tunnel in 1923. Other displays identify local plants and birds. Evening programs are presented here in summer.

Descriptive leaflets are available for several of the park's trails. Popular routes include the Dobson Nature Walk and trails to Bridal Veil Falls, Devil's Punchbowl, and Bealey Valley. All-day climbs lead up nearby peaks, where you can often spot novice rock climbers learning mountaineering skills.

Near the highway summit, a memorial honors Arthur Dobson, the surveyor-engineer who discovered the pass in 1864.

Magnificent Mount Cook

Travelers approach Mount Cook either by air — over the green and golden patchwork farms of the Canterbury Plains — or by road across the tussock-covered hills of the Mackenzie Country or Lindis Pass. On the western horizon, the snow-draped Southern Alps rise majestically.

The heart of this spectacular alpine country — extending some 65 km/40 miles along the eastern slope — has been protected in Mount Cook National Park. Renowned for its craggy beauty, it's a magnet for mountaineers who pit their climbing and skiing skills against its challenging peaks and glaciers. Less energetic visitors are attracted by the park's alpine scenery, its wildflowers and wildlife, and its network of trails. Visitor facilities and accommodations are located in Mount Cook village.

Lofty peaks. Smallest of South Island's four major alpine preserves, Mount Cook National Park encompasses the highest peaks of the Southern Alps. More than 140 mountains rise above 2,100 meters/7,000 feet. Of these, over a dozen top 3,050 meters/10,000 feet. Looming above them all is the range's mighty monarch, the highest peak in Australasia. The Maoris called it *Aorangi* (the cloud piercer). Later explorers named the 3,763-meter/12,349-foot peak in honor of Captain James Cook, first European to set foot on New Zealand soil.

Largest of the park's glaciers is the Tasman, 29 km/

Southern Alps — the essentials

Though Mount Cook National Park attracts the most visitors, you can also experience and enjoy the rugged alpine country in Arthur's Pass and Mount Aspiring national parks. For information on Nelson Lakes National Park, at the northern end of the Alps, see page 87; Westland National Park, located on the western slope of the mountains, is described on page 91.

Getting there. Paved roads penetrate each of the parks. Newmans Air and Mount Cook Line planes and motorcoaches provide transportation to Mount Cook from Christchurch, Queenstown, and other towns. Travelers can reach Arthur's Pass township by train or by Railways Road Services motorcoaches from Christchurch or Greymouth. To reach Mount Aspiring National Park, most visitors travel by air or motorcoach to Queenstown, then continue on to the park by bus or car.

Accommodations. Advance reservations are essential at these remote sites. At Mount Cook, many visitors stay at The Hermitage, one of New Zealand's fine THC hotels, or at Glencoe Lodge; motel flats, chalet units, and a youth hostel are also located in the village. Informal camping is available near Glentanner Park. At Arthur's Pass, motels, a youth hostel, and other accommodations are available in Arthur's Pass township; the park has no formal camping areas. Mount Aspiring visitors stay in hotels, motels, and motor camps in Queenstown, Wanaka, or smaller towns. Mountain huts (for hikers and climbers) are scattered throughout the parks; information on huts and camping regulations is available from each park's chief ranger.

Getting around. At Mount Cook, visitors can arrange for flightseeing trips, coach excursions, rafting trips, and ski-mountaineering expeditions. Guided walks and nature programs are scheduled in summer. Rental car agencies are located in larger towns outside the parks.

Tourist information. A factual guide on all national parks is available from the New Zealand Tourist Office. Park visitor centers are in Mount Cook village, Arthur's Pass township, and Wanaka (for Mount Aspiring National Park). Also serving Mount Aspiring visitors are ranger stations (open weekdays only) at Glenorchy in the Dart Valley and at Makarora on the Haast Pass Road (Highway 6).

18 miles long and up to 3 km/2 miles wide. Other main glaciers include the Mueller and Hooker, both within relatively easy walking distance of park headquarters, and the more distant Murchison and Godley glaciers.

Alpine flora and fauna. Botanists have identified more than 300 species of native plants in the park; labels identify many trees and shrubs along park trails. Small alpine plants flower in high rock crevices. Wildflowers bloom from October to January; best known is the mountain buttercup (often mistakenly called the Mount Cook lily). In December, lupines stretch in a colorful midsummer carpet on the slopes below The Hermitage.

Native birds, including the inquisitive and raucous kea (mountain parrot), inhabit the forests, river beds, and rocky crags. Introduced animals — thar, chamois, and deer — browse in alpine and subalpine scrublands.

Enjoying your visit to Mount Cook

This splendid alpine park attracts people who love the mountains — both vacationers who come primarily to enjoy the scenery and mountaineers who expend their energies striving for the heights.

Allow time to pause and let the mountains enfold you in their beauty and serenity. Listen to the bird songs, let the sun's heat warm your body, watch Mount Cook's sharp peak turn to glowing pink and purple in the sun's waning rays. On an after-dinner walk, enjoy the moonlight on the snow or gaze at a multitude of stars.

Obviously, all that snow and ice doesn't arrive in the sunshine. When rain clouds settle over the mountains, far too many visitors succumb to the cozy lure of the fireplace. Even on threatening days you can stop at the visitor center and walk some of the shorter trails.

Blending in with its alpine backdrop, the steeply roofed visitor center, located just below The Hermitage, is the park's administrative headquarters and major source of information (P.O. Box 5, Mount Cook; phone Mount Cook 819). Photographs, relief maps, and other displays add to your knowledge of the park's history, terrain, plants, and wildlife. You can ask about park trails and guide services or check road conditions or the weather forecast. During holiday periods, park rangers conduct nature walks and evening programs.

At The Hermitage or Glencoe Lodge, you can arrange for sightseeing flights or guided excursions.

Sightseeing flights. One of the "don't miss" experiences in New Zealand is a flight by ski-plane over the icy peaks and glaciers of the Southern Alps. Weather conditions permitting, ski-equipped aircraft operate from the Mount Cook Airport. Helicopter trips depart from the Glentanner Park Helipad.

Within a few minutes after takeoff, your small plane is flying above the gleaming slopes, saw-edged ridges, and jumbled icefalls to the head of Tasman Glacier. If your flight includes a snowfield landing, the pilot lowers the plane's retractable skis, and the craft skims to a gentle stop on the granular ice. You step out onto terrain once accessible only to experienced mountaineers.

Snowy peaks of the Southern Alps tower above Lake Tekapo. Small stone church honors the pioneers who homesteaded the remote Mackenzie Country.

Hiking park trails. Even if clouds move in to obscure the mountains, you can get out and walk some of the paths fanning out from park headquarters. As long as you dress for it and watch for worsening conditions, a brisk hike can be invigorating—even in wet weather.

At the visitor center, you can obtain printed trail information on several of the walks. Boots, heavy socks, and other equipment can be rented at The Hermitage.

The Governor's Bush trail begins below Glencoe Bridge and loops through silver beech forest behind the post office. Even shorter is the Bowen Bush trail, a 10-minute walk on the knoll south of Glencoe Stream. It offers a view up the Hooker Valley to Mount Cook.

Longer hikes take you into the mountains. The Kea Point Nature Walk begins in front of The Hermitage and ends with a view of Mueller Glacier. In summer, hikers favor the Sealy Tarns trail, which leads to small mountain lakes where you can swim. The track to Red Tarns and Mount Sebastopol begins behind Glencoe Lodge.

Other trails lead up the Hooker Valley. The main route forks off the Kea Point path, crosses the Hooker River on a pair of swing bridges, and continues to the lower edge of the Hooker Glacier; experienced mountaineers and guided parties continue up to Hooker Hut and Copland Pass. Beginning at the Ball Hut Road bridge, the Wakefield Track runs along the Hooker River and follows the trail used by parties traveling to the Tasman Glacier in the early 1900s. Short trails lead from Ball Hut Road to Blue Lakes and to a viewpoint of Wakefield Falls.

Tasman Glacier trip. Each morning and afternoon a bus departs from The Hermitage for the 2½-hour trip up rocky, single-lane Ball Hut Road to a viewpoint of the Tasman Glacier and the surrounding peaks.

Rafting on the Tasman River. For a different kind of wilderness experience, consider a raft trip down the Tasman River, the runoff of the Tasman Glacier. On the 3-hour trip, you'll enjoy fine views of the glacier, bounce through rapids, and stop for billy tea and biscuits.

Alpine climbs. Though climbers began arriving at Mount Cook in the 1880s, the peak was not conquered until 1894. Mount Cook National Park encompasses one of the world's most challenging moutaineering areas, where ardent mountaineers find a wealth of demanding climbs. At least one experienced climber should accompany each party, and groups should always notify a park ranger of climbing plans before starting out.

You can arrange for climbing instruction and guide service at The Hermitage, where equipment is available for hire or purchase. The mountaineering school operates from November through March. Full-day guided trips to Hochstetter Icefall, Hooker Hut, Mueller Hut, and other destinations can be arranged. On overnight trips, mountaineers stay in alpine huts.

Skiing the high country. Ski-equipped planes and helicopters allow experienced alpine skiers accompanied by guides to enjoy the pristine white slopes of the glaciers and high snowfields. Generally, skiing is excellent from July to October.

In recent years ski-touring and ski-mountaineering have become popular; groups bunk overnight at high-country huts. At The Hermitage, visitors can rent equipment, arrange for instruction, or hire an alpine guide.

Mount Aspiring National Park

Southernmost of South Island's alpine preserves, Mount Aspiring National Park encompasses the high slopes on both sides of the divide between the Haast and Te Anau-Milford highways. Its highest and most magnificent peak is 3,035-meter/9,957-foot Mount Aspiring.

A mountaineer's park, Mount Aspiring draws hikers and climbers who probe its remote river valleys and ascend through beech forest to rugged, glaciated peaks. Numerous alpine huts offer shelter from variable mountain weather.

Cutting across the northern end of the park, Highway 6 offers hikers access to the Wilkin Valley and other tributaries of the Haast and Makarora rivers. From Wanaka, motorists can follow a lonely road (unpaved beyond Glendhu Bay) up the scenic Matukituki Valley to the park boundary for views of Rob Roy Glacier, Mount Avalanche, and Mount Aspiring's pyramid-shaped peak. To reach the Dart, Rees, and Routeburn valleys, follow the Glenorchy road from Queenstown.

Park information is available at the visitor center in Wanaka; or contact the chief ranger (P.O. Box 93; phone Wanaka 7660). At the center you can check the current status of trails and weather, as well as view displays on the park's flora, fauna, and history. Ranger stations are open weekdays only at Makarora (on Highway 6, the Haast Pass Road) and at Glenorchy (near the head of Lake Wakatipu).

Exploring South Canterbury

From Christchurch, Highway 1 stretches across the checkerboard farmlands and sheep pastures of the Canterbury Plains and turns south toward the coastal resort of Timaru, a touring base for exploring the region. Highway 72 veers farther inland, passing through the Rakaia Gorge to Geraldine and on into the lonely hills of the Mackenzie Country; it's hard to surpass this route for scenic variety.

Bordered on the south by the Waitaki River and on the west by the imposing Southern Alps, South Canterbury is a land of contrasts. Inland from the coastal beaches, you'll see spacious farmlands, the rolling tussock-covered hills of the Mackenzie Country, and the glacier-gouged Tekapo, Pukaki, and Ohau lakes. Trees planted by English settlers more than a century ago border roads and shade stately homesteads. On the southern boundary, the Waitaki River is marked by a series of massive hydroelectric dams and reservoirs.

Anglers come to South Canterbury for the plentiful trout in the lakes and streams, for the hefty (to 30 lbs.) quinnat salmon migrating up the Rangitata and Opihi rivers in late summer, and for the salt-water fish north and south of Caroline Bay. In winter, skiing and ice skating claim the sports spotlight.

The Canterbury Plains

From Christchurch, the flat Canterbury Plains extend inland to the foothills of the Southern Alps. Viewed from above, the plains form a vast rural patchwork of green and gold farmlands, criss-crossed by country roads and cut by broad rivers. The plains are New Zealand's granary, a rich agricultural region renowned for its wheat, wool, and livestock. Sheep and cattle farms abound. More than a century ago, Australian sheepmen began grazing their flocks on the open plains, and today Canterbury lamb has a worldwide reputation. On the big, isolated sheep stations in the high country, sheep are raised for wool, rather than for meat.

South Canterbury—the essentials

South of Christchurch, farming centers such as Ashburton and Geraldine dot the rich Canterbury Plains. Visitors can relax at the popular beach resort of Timaru, then head inland to explore the lonely Mackenzie Country and the austere but beautiful Waitaki lakes.

Getting there. Christchurch International Airport is the terminus of most flights, though Timaru has a small airfield. From Christchurch, New Zealand Railways and Railways Road Services provide daily train and motorcoach service to main towns along the South Canterbury and Otago coasts. Mount Cook Line motorcoaches serve inland towns between Christchurch and Queenstown (including Geraldine, Twizel, and Cromwell) and also between Timaru and Mount Cook.

Accommodations. Timaru has numerous hotels and motels. Elsewhere in the region, overnight facilities are limited and often modest. You'll find accommodations in Methven, Ashburton, Geraldine, Fairlie, Lake Tekapo, Twizel, and at Lake Ohau. Many farm families welcome overnight visitors (page 124).

Getting around. Motorcoaches provide daily service between the larger towns (see above). Rental cars are available in Christchurch, Timaru, and Ashburton. From Christchurch, you can take a day-long excursion to Erewhon Park.

Tourist information. Canterbury touring information is available at Christchurch tourist offices (page 73). Timaru also has a local Public Relations Office at 7 The Terrace.

The main route across the plains is Highway 1, which crosses the Rakaia River on the country's longest bridge. Massive trees shade the brick buildings of Ashburton, the district's farming center. Anglers fish the Rakaia, Ashburton, and Rangitata rivers for salmon and sea-run trout.

Other routes from Christchurch head west across the plains to Windwhistle, gateway to the Rakaia Gorge and Canterbury lakes. Gouged out by long-departed glaciers, these mountain lakes attract local sports enthusiasts. Lake Coleridge is popular for fishing and boating. In winter, tiny Lake Ida freezes to become a natural outdoor ice rink. There's skiing at Mount Hutt and in the Craigieburn Mountains.

One of New Zealand's best ski areas, Mount Hutt is only 104 km/65 miles from Christchurch. From its slopes, skiers enjoy panoramic views over the Canterbury Plains. Skiing begins in May and continues through November. Whether you're a beginner or an expert, you'll find runs suitable for your level of ability. Rental equipment and ski school lessons are available at the area. Advanced skiers can arrange for guided helicopter skiing in the surrounding basins. There's transportation to the resort from Methven and Christchurch.

Methven, 84 km/52 miles from Christchurch, is a fast-growing resort town serving the Mount Hutt skifield; it's also a base for mountaineering, fishing, and other back-country activities. Jet boat and raft trips travel through the scenic gorge of the nearby Rakaia River.

Timaru, a holiday town

Located midway between Christchurch and Dunedin, the coastal town of Timaru is one of South Island's most popular seaside resorts. An easy, 160-km/100-mile drive across sheep-covered plains southwest of Christchurch, Timaru is a departure point for exploring the spectacular highlands of the Waitaki-Mackenzie Basin.

Built on gently sloping hills facing Caroline Bay, Timaru attracts visitors the year around with its mild climate, fine tourist and conference facilities, and protected beach.

A long breakwater shelters Timaru's artificial harbor, the only port between the Banks Peninsula and Oamaru. Center of a large farming region, Timaru is a major shipping port for the province's grain and meat, as well as home port for a fishing fleet. North of the breakwater, fine sand has accumulated at the old whaling cove of Caroline Bay to form a sweeping beach. Thousands flock here for Timaru's annual New Year's beach carnival.

Laid out by rival surveyors, Timaru has an irregular street grid. Winding Stafford Street follows an old bullock track near the waterfront. Local bluestone was used in the construction of many buildings.

You can stroll along the Centennial Park Walkway, which parallels a stream through the park, or visit the Botanic Gardens bordering Queen Street. Part of the city's scenic drive winds through the gardens; inquire at the Public Relations Office, 7 The Terrace, for a map showing the route. Fine paintings and touring exhibitions are housed in the Aigantighe Art Gallery, 49 Wai-iti Road. At the South Canterbury Historical Museum on Perth Street, you can learn about local history and port development.

In the countryside, more than 200 wild animals roam the rolling hills at Hadlow Game Park. Temuka, just north of Timaru, is known for its earthenware pottery and good fishing streams.

Highway 8 heads up the Tengawai River toward Fairlie. Along the way, stop at Pleasant Point to see a restored steam locomotive and railway museum. In the village of Cave, the old stone Church of St. David is a hand-built memorial to Mackenzie Country pioneers.

Waimate, south of Timaru on the slopes of the Hunters Hills, is the center of a varied agricultural district.

Autumn color in Geraldine

Located inland at the edge of rolling downs, Geraldine once supplied isolated sheep stations. Today it serves a flourishing agricultural district. English settlers planted trees in profusion here—not the pines of the plains, but elm, larch, oak, poplar, ash, and willow. In autumn, the golden foliage is a feast for the eyes. You can picnic beside the Waihi River, which flows through town. From Geraldine Downs behind town, the panorama extends over mountains, across tree-studded plains, and along the coast from the Port Hills south to Waimate.

River gorges. North of Geraldine, roads follow the Orari, Waihi, and Hae Hae Te Moana rivers to historic buildings, riverside picnic areas, and hiking trails.

At Orari Gorge Station, the New Zealand Historic Trust has restored the original homestead buildings. Both Waihi Gorge and Te Moana Gorge have fine recreation sites, and you can swim in the Waihi River. In Pleasant Valley you pass rustic St. Anne's Anglican Church, built in 1862 of pit-sawn native timber. Horses can be rented for saddle trips up the Waihi Gorge. In Woodbury, the slate-roofed, Norman-style St. Thomas' Anglican Church contains carved oak furniture and memorial tablets.

Up the Rangitata. North of Geraldine is Peel Forest park, a pocket reserve of native bush favored for its easy walks, waterfalls, and abundant birdlife. Families picnic and camp here, and anglers fish the Rangitata River. A short distance beyond Peel Forest stand the historic buildings of Mount Peel Station.

West of the coastal hills lies another world, one where treeless expanses of greyish brown tussock extend to the rugged slopes of the Southern Alps. An unpaved road, fording tributary streams, continues another 46 km/ 29 miles beyond to the isolated station of Mesopotamia. This remote sheep run inspired pioneer runholder Samuel Butler to write the classic 19th century satirical novel *Erewhon*, in which he describes the utter loneliness of the rolling tussock country and the dwarfing vastness of mountains and plain.

North of the Rangitata River is Erewhon Park, accessible from Highway 72 at Mount Somers; it caters to

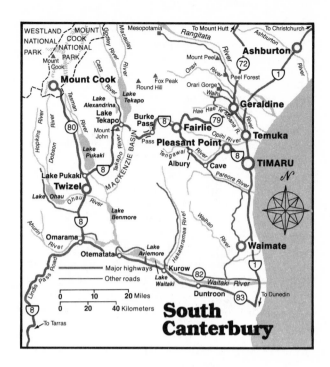

visitors who enjoy the outdoors. Anglers, climbers, hunters, and horseback riders enjoy this remote country in summer; skiers and ice skaters come here in winter.

The lonely Mackenzie Country

This great upland plain first came to general notice in 1855 with the capture of James McKenzie, a Scottish rustler who discovered it while spiriting away sheep stolen from the lowlands. Though sparsely populated, the remote back country supports vast pastoral runs with thousands of hardy sheep.

Set in rolling, tree-dotted downs, Fairlie is gateway to the Mackenzie Country. About 5 km/3 miles northeast is Strathaven Clydesdale Stud, where working teams pull horse-drawn farm implements in much the same way as was done in pioneer days. Fairlie's historical and transport museums offer an interesting look at the past. The Mackenzie Country Carnival is a big event during the Christmas-New Year holidays.

From Fairlie you follow the Opihi River upstream, climbing through a wooded valley to Burke Pass.

As you enter the Mackenzie Country, the transformation is abrupt and total. Spread before you is a vast, shimmering sea of tussock grasslands merging into a distant purple wall of snow-capped peaks. Sunlight glints off the light blue waters of glacier-fed lakes. You'll want to breathe deeply and enjoy the pure air.

The Mackenzie Basin provides access to the high mountains, and its lakes feed the upper Waitaki hydroelectric power project.

The Waitaki lakes. Fed by melting glaciers and snow, the milky turquoise Waitaki lakes occupy the lower ends of glaciated valleys in the shadow of the Southern Alps. Walled in by moraines, these austerely beautiful lakes feed the great Waitaki River.

Lake Tekapo. On still days, Tekapo is a vast mirror reflecting the majestic mountain panorama. Acres of wild lupines in brilliant shades of bluish purple, pink, and yellow brighten the lake shore in summer. During bad weather, savage alpine winds churn the lake into a maelstrom and slice across the exposed hills.

Silhouetted against the mountains, the solitary little Church of the Good Shepherd conveys the isolation and endurance of the Mackenzie Country pioneers in whose memory it was erected. Inside, a large window above the altar frames a splendid view of lake and mountains.

Farther along the shore, a bronze collie monument honors the devoted and hard-working sheep dogs. Atop Mount John are an observatory and a U.S. satellite tracking station.

West of Tekapo, smaller Alexandrina and McGregor lakes offer good trout fishing, swimming, and camping.

Lake Pukaki. Fed by the Tasman River, icy Pukaki points north toward Mount Cook. The scene is a paradox of wild beauty and forbidding solitude — the pale blue lake and golden tussock contrasting with the snow-capped Alps, purpling in the western shadow. The road to Mount Cook National Park follows the western shore of the long lake.

Lake Ohau. Anglers, hikers, boaters, and skiers enjoy this beautiful back-country region. Unpaved roads closely follow Lake Ohau's shore, and trails lead into the nearby beech forest.

The Waitaki Valley

Marking the boundary between Canterbury and Otago, the broad Waitaki River drains the high snowfields of the Southern Alps. Rivers flowing from the Waitaki lakes meet in the Mackenzie uplands above Benmore Dam. A series of dams and canals store and redirect lake waters to the project's power generating stations. As the Waitaki River flows eastward, it broadens into three manmade lakes — Benmore, Aviemore, and Waitaki — and then meets the ocean north of Oamaru.

A side road from Highway 83 leads to an observation area overlooking Lake Benmore, the largest of New Zealand's manmade lakes. The giant 110-meter/360-foot-high Benmore Dam created a vast reservoir bordered by some 110 km/68 miles of shoreline. Power boats and water-skiers cut white swaths, and sailboats glide across the water. Fishing is good, and in summer, visitors can take sightseeing boat trips. Below the dam, a sheltered recreation area attracts picnickers and swimmers.

Farther east, a scenic 19-km/12-mile road loops north from Otematata around Lake Aviemore. Here extensive tree planting and landscaping have softened the harsh effects of construction.

Early wandering hunters and fishermen drew pictures on the rock walls of the Waitaki Gorge; many are now submerged beneath the lakes, but some Maori rock drawings are visible beneath a large limestone bluff just west of Duntroon (signposted over a stile).

Omarama, Otematata, and Kurow are centers for anglers who come to fish in the lakes and in some of South Island's best trout streams. In late summer, migrating quinnat salmon are caught below Waitaki Dam. Omarama also attracts glider pilots, who gather here in summer to take advantage of the area's favorable air currents.

From Omarama, the Lindis Pass Road (Highway 8) follows an old Maori trail south and links the Waitaki Valley with Central Otago. Stretching over the lonely hills are vast sheep stations, some in operation for more than a century.

Gracious, dignified Dunedin

Spread over the hills at the head of one of the country's loveliest harbors, Dunedin was envisioned by its Scottish founders as the "Edinburgh of the South." The Presbyterian settlement was colonized by settlers who landed at Port Chalmers in 1848.

After gold was discovered in Central Otago in the 1860s, the tiny frontier colony thrived. Prosperity ushered in a golden era in architecture, culture, and industry. Dunedin soon became the wealthiest and most influential town in Victorian New Zealand — the model for the rest of the country.

A gracious and dignified city, Dunedin has a special charm. Its Scottish heritage is evoked in its street names and in the sturdy appeal of its handsome stone buildings. You'll find the country's only kiltmaker and whisky distillery here, and a statue of Scottish poet Robert Burns overlooks downtown activity from the Octagon, a small grassy park in the heart of the city.

Getting settled in Dunedin

Dunedin is a planned city, its streets and suburbs fanning out from the Octagon. Bisecting this downtown oasis is Dunedin's main thoroughfare, named George Street north of the park, Princes Street to the south. Most of the major downtown stores, banks, hotels, and restaurants are concentrated along or near this street. Stuart Street branches at right angles from the main street.

You'll find restaurants in the larger hotels and motor inns and others specializing in English, Italian, or continental cuisine scattered throughout the city. For an experience a little out of the ordinary, dine in an atmosphere reminiscent of a turn-of-the-century railway station at Carnarvon Station, housed in the historic Prince of Wales Hotel, 474 Princes Street. Vintage train carriages and equipment combined with handsome architectural features from one of the city's early mansions recall Dunedin's golden age.

Gothic clock tower rises above the slate-roofed bluestone buildings of the University of Otago. The country's first university moved to this site in 1878.

Most evening entertainment revolves around the hotels. Concerts are presented at Town Hall, and visiting artists perform at the Regent Theatre.

A walk around town

If you enjoy exploring a city on foot, you'll like Dunedin's compact central district. In an hour or two, you can stroll many of the downtown streets, enjoy a few of the city's parks and architectural gems, and absorb a bit of Dunedin's history. Ask for leaflets that indicate points of interest.

Many fine Victorian buildings give the city its distinctive character and recall the era when Dunedin was the most important settlement in the country. In older parts of the city, houses reflect the Scottish heritage of its early settlers.

The Octagon. Heart of the city is the grassy Octagon, where you stand beneath aging trees and survey the passing scene alongside the statue of Scotland's bard, Robert Burns. Shoppers pause here to chat, and office workers eat lunch on the grass on pleasant days.

Facing the park are the impressive St. Paul's Cathedral, the Municipal Chambers with its adjacent Town Hall, and the Regent and Fortune theaters. Daily at 12:30, 6, 7:30, and 9 P.M., the Star Fountain puts on a colorful display utilizing water jets, music, and lighting effects.

First Church. Walk east down Stuart Street, detouring a block south on Moray Place for a look at the First Church of Otago. One of the country's finest churches, it was designed by R. A. Lawson, architect of many of Dunedin's most distinctive buildings, and dedicated in 1873. Interior features include a lovely rose window and imaginative plant and animal motifs carved in Oamaru stone.

Railway station. Returning to Stuart Street, continue east past the Law Courts to Dunedin's elegant old railway station, built in 1904. Its facade features granite pillars supporting an arched colonnade, and heraldic lions ornament the copper-lined tower. A delightful touch is the New Zealand Railways' motif (NZR) used with abandon — etched in glass, patterned in mosaic floor tile, even created in stained glass (in the second-floor windows depicting a smoke-belching train).

Early Settlers' Museum. Follow Anzac Avenue south to the Early Settlers' Museum, noteworthy for its collection of vintage vehicles (steam locomotives, a cable car, a Cobb & Co. stagecoach, and Dunedin's first fire engine), old paintings and photographs, and relics of whaling and mining days. The museum is open weekdays from 9 A.M. to 5 P.M., Saturday from 10:30 A.M. to 4 P.M., and Sunday from 1:30 to 4:30 P.M.

Angle a block south on Cumberland Street past Queens Gardens, a tranquil island in a sea of traffic. Then walk west on Rattray Street to the ornate Gothic Cargill Monument at Princes Street.

Dunedin — the essentials

Dunedin is the country's fourth largest city and the capital of Otago, the largest province. A commercial and manufacturing center, a busy port, and a transportation hub, Dunedin is the gateway to Central Otago and the Southern Lakes district.

Getting there. Air New Zealand and Mount Cook Line planes land at Dunedin's attractive airport, located 29 km/18 miles southwest of the city near Mosgiel. Trains and Railways Road Services motorcoaches provide service to Dunedin from the larger east coast towns between Christchurch and Invercargill. Other motorcoaches link Dunedin with inland towns, including Alexandra, Cromwell, Wanaka, Queenstown, and Te Anau.

Accommodations. Downtown accommodations within walking distance of the Octagon include the Town House, City Hotel, Southern Cross, and DB Wain's Hotel. Cherry Court Lodge enjoys a garden setting a few blocks north of the park, and Leisure Lodge borders the Leith waterway near the Botanic Gardens. Pacific Park Motor Inn overlooks the Town Belt and harbor. The Shoreline Motor Hotel is located in south Dunedin. At Larnach Castle on the Otago Peninsula, the stables have been converted to overnight accommodations.

On the North Otago coast, Oamaru has many hotels and motels; small motels are scattered along the coast.

Getting around. A bus tour of the city and Otago Peninsula departs daily at 1:45 P.M. in front of the Government Tourist Bureau. Taxis and chauffeur-driven cars are available in Dunedin for local transport and touring. You can rent cars in Dunedin or Oamaru.

Tourist information. Stop at the office of the Otago Council Inc., 119 Princes Street, for information about Dunedin and Otago province. For travel reservations and tour information, visit the Government Tourist Bureau, 131 Princes Street. Local tourist information is also available in Oamaru.

Classic buildings. Some of the city's well-designed 19th century buildings are still in use in the stock exchange area. Many are constructed of Port Chalmers or Oamaru stone and include interior furnishings of native and imported woods.

Among buildings of special note are these on Princes Street: the 1874 Lawson-designed A.N.Z. Bank, built in classical Greek style; DB Wain's Hotel, built in 1878 and embellished with carvings above its street-level bay windows; and the 1883 Bank of New Zealand, noted for its fine ceiling in the banking hall. Another century-old building is St. Matthews Church on Stafford Street; it contains a rebuilt 1880 organ.

To return to the Octagon, return to Princes Street and walk north for several blocks.

Dunedin's hilly green belt

To fully appreciate Dunedin's harbor setting, head for the hills. Framed between rugged peninsulas, narrow Otago Harbour cuts inland. At its head, Dunedin's buildings rim the water and climb the encircling hills.

Dunedin's planners reserved a band of greenery — called the Town Belt — on the higher slopes of the hills facing the harbor. Queens Drive, a 7-km/4-mile scenic road winding through this wooded retreat, offers motorists and walkers a succession of magnificent vistas.

Favorite close-in viewpoints include Unity Park, Bracken's Lookout (Northern Cemetery), and Southern Cemetery. For sweeping panoramas of Dunedin, the harbor, and the Otago Peninsula, head north of the city to Signal Hill or Mount Cargill.

One of the city walks (map brochure available) takes you through part of the reserve. It starts near Queen and Regent streets and follows Queens Drive north through Prospect Park and the Woodhaugh Gardens.

Other Dunedin highlights

Dunedin's handsome architecture not only delights the eye but also provides tangible evidence of the prosperity and talent that enriched the burgeoning town during the late 19th century. It was then that wealthy residents began assembling some of the country's outstanding collections of art and historical items.

Otago Museum. One of the finest museums in the country, the Otago is noted for its Pacific collections of Oceanian art, Polynesian and Melanesian cultural displays, marine life and maritime exhibits, and fine arts collections. In Maori Hall, you'll see a reconstructed meeting house and storehouse, along with exhibits of Maori wearing apparel, tools, carvings, and greenstone articles. The adjacent Hocken Library is a repository of historic New Zealand books, manuscripts, maps, photographs, and art.

Located at 419 Great King Street, the museum is open weekdays from 9 A.M. to 4:30 P.M., Saturday from 10:30 A.M. to 4:30 P.M., and Sunday from 1:30 to 4:30 P.M.

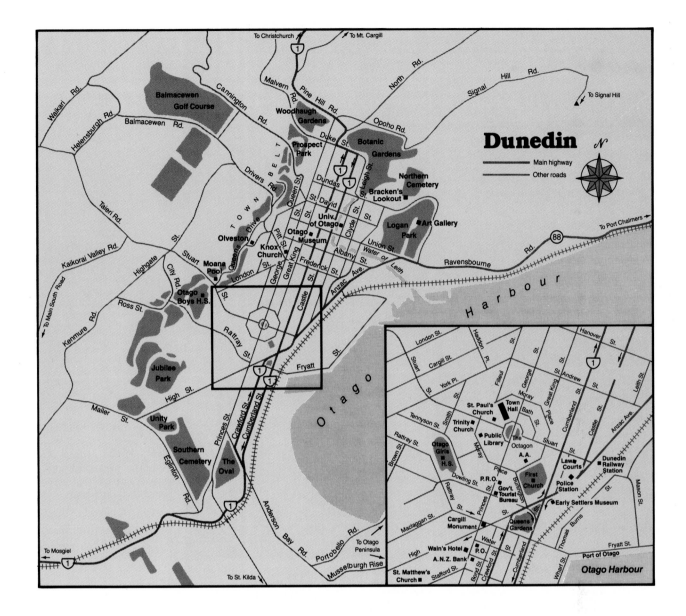

Botanic Gardens. Established in 1868, this north Dunedin showplace is lovely in any season but at its best in spring when the rhododendrons and azaleas bloom in profusion and daffodils pop out of the lawn. Colorful autumn foliage brightens the upper area during April. The main entrance to the gardens is at Pine Hill Road and Great King Street; walking paths wend through the gardens.

Art Gallery. Located in Logan Park, the gallery is noted for the Smythe Collection of watercolors, paintings by Frances Hodgkins, and frequent special exhibitions. The museum is open weekdays and Saturday and Sunday afternoons.

University of Otago. New Zealand's first university was founded in 1869; it moved to its present site 9 years later. Walk through the stone archway and the quadrangle and

savor the old stone buildings, the mature trees, and a placid stream called the Water of Leith. About 7,000 students attend school here.

Olveston. Built for a wealthy and well-traveled Dunedin businessman and bequeathed to the city by his daughter, this 35-room mansion depicts a bygone era of gracious living. The Jacobean-style house, completed in 1906, stands on a landscaped acre and is sheltered by tall trees. A showplace of Edwardian grandeur, the house contains antique furniture, paintings, and elegant household articles shipped here from all parts of the world.

Located at 42 Royal Terrace (at the corner of Cobden Street off Queens Drive), the building is open daily for guided tours.

The beach scene. Sunworshipers head for St. Clair and St. Kilda, two beach communities south of Dunedin. You

Fishing boats moor at a wharf near Port Chalmers. Curving around a deep-water bay, the historic port town is an important container shipping center.

can watch surfers ride the waves, play a round of golf, swim in a heated salt-water pool, or follow the horses at Forbury Park Raceway.

From St. Kilda, a short, scenic drive cuts across the sand dunes to a lookout at Lawyers Head.

Day trips from Dunedin

Short excursions from Dunedin offer visitors a look at the hilly Otago Peninsula with its numerous attractions, the deep-water harbor at Port Chalmers, and the North Otago coast.

The Otago Peninsula loop

Northeast of Dunedin, the hilly Otago Peninsula offers a delightful rural excursion. Small settlements and weekend cottages dot the harbor's sheltered slopes, in contrast to the wild and lonely beauty of the Pacific side. Dry stone walls, tinted with moss and lichen, lace the peninsula. Sea birds abound, not only the famous royal albatross but also shags, yellow-eyed penguins, godwits, and oystercatchers.

Take the Portobello Road along the harbor, then return along the high road that follows the crest of the peninsula hills to take in panoramic views of the rugged coastline and secluded bays.

Glenfalloch Gardens. Nestled in a fold in the hills above the harbor, this 27-acre woodland garden reflects a century of loving care. The original 1871 homestead still stands. Now owned by the Otago Peninsula Trust, the garden peaks in spring when primroses bloom under English oaks and azaleas and rhododendrons burst forth with color. Bush walks lead up the glen; a small stream trickles down the hill to the harbor.

Larnach Castle. Set in 35 acres of trees and gardens and crowning a wooded hill, this sumptuous residence was built in the 1870s by Dunedin banker W. J. N. Larnach for his first wife, a French heiress.

Building the hilltop mansion far from town was an audacious project. Designed in Scotland, the 43-room neo-Gothic castle took 3 years to build, another 12 to complete the handsome interior. Master craftsmen were brought here from around the world, as were materials—marble and Venetian glass from Italy, tiles from England, woods from many countries. The 40,000-square-foot house required 46 household servants to maintain. Larnach added the 3,000-square-foot ballroom as a 21st birthday present for his favorite daughter.

Furnished in the grand manner, the house is open daily to visitors. After completing your self-guided tour of the interior, take the spiral stone stairway up to the battlements for a commanding panorama from Dunedin across the harbor to the headlands and open coast. Before leaving, stroll through the gardens and visit the dungeons (used by Larnach for storing firewood). The castle's brick-paved stables have been converted to accommodations.

Harborside attractions. The Portobello Marine Biological Station occupies a site facing Otago Harbour. Part of the University of Otago, it maintains a variety of marine life in tanks and pools.

Otakou—corrupted by early whalers to Otago—was the site of an ancient Maori settlement from which the province took its name. A plaque near the water marks the location of the 1830s whaling station. Behind the Otakou Maori Church, built in 1940 to replace an earlier structure, are a small museum and a cemetery. Three important South Island Maori chiefs are buried here.

Albatross colony. The world's largest sea bird — the royal albatross — breeds in a mainland colony at Taiaroa Head at the northern tip of the Otago Peninsula. Adult birds have a wing span up to 3½ meters/11 feet long. During high winds, you sometimes see the giant birds circling above their nesting grounds.

The birds begin to arrive at Taiaroa in early spring. At the beginning of November they build their nests; each female lays a single white egg about 13 centimeters/ 5 inches in diameter. Males and females share charge of the egg during incubation. Chicks hatch in January.

By prior arrangement, small groups may visit the colony from late November through September; best months for viewing are December to May. Inquiries and reservations are handled by the Government Tourist Bureau in Dunedin.

On the peninsula's southeast coast, yellow-eyed penguins come ashore to nest at Penguin Place, and seals bask on a rocky isle just offshore. Access is from Taiaroa Head.

Port Chalmers, Otago's seafaring town

Otago's first settlers arrived by sea, landing at Port Chalmers in 1848. The town faces a sheltered, deep-water bay on Otago Harbour's northern shore about 14 km/9 miles northeast of Dunedin.

Thousands of fortune hunters debarked here in the 1860s on their way to the gold fields. New Zealand's first export cargo of frozen meat was shipped from Port Chalmers in 1882. Antarctic explorers Scott, Shackleton, and Byrd called here on their expeditions to the southern continent.

Today, Port Chalmers's prosperity rests on its modern wharf and container shipping facilities.

Overlooking the town is St. Iona's Presbyterian Church, its spire-topped stone clock tower commanding the skyline. On the headland dominating the harbor stand a restored flagstaff — erected in 1862 to regulate harbor traffic—and a lookout.

Dotting the old seafaring town are numerous 19th century buildings, many of them constructed of Port Chalmers stone. At 55 Harrington Street is Stonehenge, best preserved of four remaining stone houses built in the 1880s. Holy Trinity Church, dating from the mid-1870s, has a hammer-beamed ceiling, stone walls, and an unusual organ. St. Mary's Star of the Sea Church opened in 1878; its interior reflects the town's link with the sea.

The local fishing fleet anchors at Careys Bay, just north of Port Chalmers. At low tide the rotting hulks of several old sailing ships become visible just off the shore of Deborah Bay. The coastal road continues to Aramoana, where vacation homes face an ocean beach; flocks of sea birds feed here.

Along the Otago coast

North of Dunedin, Highway 1 parallels the coast for 125 km/78 miles to Oamaru. Swimming off sandy beaches, river and surf fishing, and other water-related activities draw visitors to the many small beach communities along the coast. Near Oamaru, notice the use of the local white stone in buildings, bridges, walls, and chimneys.

North of Waitati, a coastal road skirting the shore of Waikouaiti Bay offers marvelous vistas and ocean beaches. The pleasant seaside village of Karitane is a holiday retreat for Dunedin families, who come here to swim in the river and ocean, fish, go boating, and frolic on the sandy beach. Near the flagstaff is the homestead of Sir Truby King, a medical reformer who founded the Plunket Society, an organization dedicated to educating mothers in the care of infants.

Otago's oldest European settlement (dating from 1840) and an early port, Waikouaiti today attracts visitors to its sandy beach and coastal bird sanctuary. The settlement has several old churches, and local historic artifacts are displayed in a roadside museum. At Palmerston, Highway 85 (known as The Pigroot) heads inland to Central Otago. Farther north, sea birds congregate on the rocks at Shag Point.

A landmark of the Otago coast, the Moeraki boulders are a geological curiosity. Strewn on the sand along Katiki Beach and north of the fishing village of Moeraki, the spherical, gray rocks weigh several tons each and extend up to 4 meters/13 feet in diameter. Geologists say they were formed on the sea floor millions of years ago when lime salts accumulated around a center core.

The white stone city of Oamaru

North Otago's thriving commercial center is Oamaru, noted for its wide, tree-lined streets and many handsome stone buildings. Built of the local creamy white limestone (quarried at Weston), they give the town its special appearance and unity.

From the war monument in the center of town, walk south along Thames Street to admire the classic stone buildings — among them Brydone Hotel (1880), Waitaki County Council Chambers (1882), Borough Council Offices (1880), courthouse (1883), post office (1884), National Bank (1870), and Bank of New South Wales (1884). The two banks were designed by R. A. Lawson, architect of Dunedin's First Church. Even earlier buildings line waterfront streets.

Public gardens off Severn Street provide a pleasant urban retreat, and on the city outskirts, country lanes cut through large market gardens.

For a view of Oamaru and the surrounding country, take Tyne Street south to Tamar and turn uphill to the lookout reserve.

Golden days in Central Otago

Sun-baked in summer and numbingly cold in winter, "Central" is a grand and desolate region of craggy ranges, stark ravines, fruit orchards, and tawny tracts of wind-rippled tussock stretching toward the distant horizon. Sleepy old mining towns and abandoned stone cottages drowse in the golden sun beneath brilliant blue skies.

Sheep runholders who opened up this parched hinterland in the late 1850s earned their wealth by enduring lonely isolation and hardship. A few years later, prospectors established the first settlements; colorful names bestowed during mining days still identify many towns, hills, and gullies.

Settlers transformed the once-barren landscape by planting trees along river banks and roadways and in windbreaks; in April, travelers delight in the vibrant displays of autumn color visible in the area today.

More recently, dams on major rivers and a network of irrigation channels have made farming feasible and added hydroelectric power. Development is currently underway in the Clutha Valley.

Up the Clutha River

About 60 km/37 miles southwest of Dunedin near Milton, Highway 8 branches off the east coast road and cuts northwest into the bare, brown, and beautiful hills of Central Otago — gold country.

Lawrence. Poplars and birch trees line the highway as you approach Lawrence, a once-raw mining town that has grown old gracefully. Its Victorian buildings reflect its history — prosperity followed by gradual decline. Lawrence lies at the convergence of two gold-bearing streams: Gabriels Gully, where Gabriel Read discovered gold in May, 1861, triggering the Otago gold rush; and Wetherston, also the scene of feverish activity.

Roxburgh. Commercial fruit orchards and a massive hydroelectric power dam dominate Roxburgh's site. Most of the peaches, apricots, apples, and strawberries harvested here are airlifted to northern markets. Sea-

Central Otago — the essentials

You can make a 2-day loop trip from Dunedin into Central Otago, or sample the country briefly as you travel between Dunedin and Queenstown.

Getting there. Railways Road Services motorcoaches provide scheduled service to Clutha Valley towns on routes between Dunedin and Queenstown or Wanaka; you can also travel from Dunedin to Cromwell on the Mosgiel-Taieri Valley-Ranfurly route. Mount Cook Line buses stop in Cromwell on the Queenstown-Christchurch run, and Mount Cook planes link Alexandra with Dunedin and Queenstown.

Accommodations. In Alexandra, the region's major town, you can stay in the DB Golden Central Hotel or in one of several small motels. Cromwell, center of the Clutha Valley hydroelectric project, and Clyde also offer a choice of accommodations. Overnight facilities are available in Ranfurly and Roxburgh.

Getting around. Scheduled motorcoach service offers a glimpse of the country, but you'll need a car to do any exploring. Rental cars are available in Dunedin, Queenstown, Wanaka, and Alexandra.

Tourist information. Stop at Dunedin (page 104) or Queenstown (page 112) tourist offices before you depart. There's also an information center in Cromwell.

sonal pickers converge on the town at harvest time, and "pick-your-own" orchards attract Otago families on weekends. Coal mining at Coal Creek and sheep farming are also important.

Alexandra, hub of Central Otago

Prospectors rushed here after gold was discovered in 1862, but for many years Alexandra was outshone by its twin town of Dunstan (now called Clyde). Gold dredging gave the town a new lease on life in the 1890s.

Today, Alexandra is the hub of a prosperous fruit-growing district. Apricots, peaches, nectarines, plums, cherries, apples, and pears are shipped all over the country. Alexandra's spring blossom festival is a major event. In April, deciduous trees are ablaze with autumn colors.

The small Bodkin Museum, southeast of Pioneer Park on Thomson Street, is open on weekday afternoons. Here you'll see interesting gold mining exhibits, including articles used by Chinese miners.

Near Alexandra, side roads lead up many old gold mining gullies, some now planted with fruit trees. Anglers and water-sports enthusiasts head for trout-stocked reservoirs. In winter, local families enjoy ice skating and curling on the frozen lakes behind Idaburn and Lower Manorburn dams.

North of town, giant Roxburgh Dam holds back the waters of the Clutha River. Behind the dam, a narrow lake extends far upriver; it's a boaters' favorite.

The Cromwell Gorge

Upriver from Alexandra, the Clutha and its tributaries drain the great glacier-carved valleys containing lakes Wanaka, Hawea, and Wakatipu. Joined by the Kawarau River at Cromwell, the Clutha funnels into the rocky Cromwell Gorge. For nearly 20 km/12 miles the deep river flows steadily onward between steep, barren slopes, relieved only occasionally by an orchard.

The character of the Upper Clutha basin is undergoing a major change. Construction has begun on the first of several hydroelectric dams planned for the region. When completed in 1987, the dam at Clyde will create a large lake — to be called Lake Dunstan — that will flood the scenic Cromwell Gorge and widen out above Cromwell. Other dams will be constructed upstream on the Clutha and on the Kawarau rivers.

Clyde. Once a boisterous mining town called Dunstan, the settlement of Clyde still has many of its old stone buildings, constructed with rock quarried during road building through the Cromwell Gorge. Mining memorabilia are on display in Goldfields Museum, located in the 1864 stone courthouse on Blyth Street.

Cromwell. Perched above the junction of the swift-flowing Clutha and Kawarau rivers, Cromwell is the center of the construction project. Completion of the Clyde dam will turn Cromwell into a lakeside town; part of its commercial center will be relocated. The information cen-

ter on Melrose Terrace offers a fascinating look at Cromwell's past—photographs from mining days and artifacts unearthed by project archeologists—as well as details of the region's future as Clutha Valley development unfolds.

From December to May, you can learn about mining methods and equipment—from simple gold pan to massive quartz stamper and dredging machinery — at The Goldminer on Main Street. A walk along the Kawarau River begins in the garden by the bridge.

From Cromwell you can visit several deserted gold towns, marked by abandoned stone buildings, piles of waste rock, and scattered trees. Highway 8 follows the Clutha north to Lowburn and Bendigo. South of Cromwell, unpaved roads lead to Bannockburn and old mining sites in the Carrick Range.

Golden ghosts of the Maniototo

To reach the Maniototo Plains head north from Alexandra up the Manuherikia Valley. Settlements are small and scattered. Side roads lead to sheep stations — some stocked since the 1860s—and old mining sites in the foothills of the Dunstan Mountains and Raggedy Range.

Off the main road are St. Bathans and Naseby, both former gold mining centers and worth a detour. About halfway between Alexandra and the coast is Ranfurly, a farming center and the largest town (population 1,000) on the Maniototo Plains. Highway 85 continues east across The Pigroot, a well-worn route to the gold fields.

St. Bathans. A string of tired Victorian buildings, anchored by the Vulcan Hotel, descends the settlement's sloping street. After the miners left, the excavated valley flooded to form Blue Lake. Years of hydraulic mining created the high, fluted cliffs surrounding the deep pool. Nearby Vinegar Hill and Cambrians also saw extensive mining activity.

Naseby. One of the most attractive of the mining towns, Naseby has a peaceful, unhurried charm. Trees shade most of its streets. Some buildings, including the 1863 Ancient Briton Hotel, are built of sun-dried brick. The Maniototo Early Settlers' Museum has memorabilia of mining days and early curling contests, as well as an outdoor display of vintage vehicles. In summer, Naseby is popular with campers; in winter, visitors come here to ice skate and enjoy the Scottish sport of curling.

Northeast of Naseby, the narrow and unpaved Dansey Pass route twists across the Kakanui Mountains to the Waitaki Valley. Heaped tailings and ragged cliffs identify the Kyeburn diggings. The Dansey Pass Hotel, built in the 1880s, provides refreshments and accommodations for travelers in this lonely region.

Ranfurly. No ghost town, Ranfurly is Maniototo's administrative and supply center. It lies in the heart of a vast inland plain broken only by occasional clumps of pines and poplars. South of Ranfurly are isolated stations and scattered farming settlements, some—such as Hamiltons and Patearoa—dating from mining days. The paved road ends at Patearoa, but a gravel route continues to Paerau (formerly called Styx), where you'll see buildings from the early 1860s. Styx was an overnight coach stop on the Old Dunstan Road at the Taieri River crossing.

Over The Pigroot. East of Ranfurly, Highway 85 is known as The Pigroot, an old coach road that linked Palmerston with the Otago gold fields. Vast, lonely expanses of golden tussock stretch toward distant mountains, and a few rough roads lead off to abandoned digging sites and deserted roadside inns.

Across the Taieri Plain

Before The Pigroot stage road to the gold fields opened in the mid 1860s, miners followed the Old Dunstan Road. Highway 87 parallels part of this historic route west from Dunedin.

Mosgiel district. Colonists who settled on the fertile Taieri Plain prospered during the gold rush by supplying provisions for the miners. With their proceeds the settlers built large homesteads and developed farms where they improved stock breeds and pioneered new farming methods.

Many colonial buildings of the 1860s and 1870s are still in use in Taieri farms and communities. The country's oldest woolen factory, operating in Mosgiel since 1871, was the first major industry on the Taieri Plain. The handsome East Taieri Church is another one of R. A. Lawson's many splendid designs; built in 1869, the brick and stone church is elaborate by Presbyterian standards. The 1877 manse and cemetery are nearby.

Outram. Gold seekers forded the Taieri River at Outram; today, you'll find an attractive riverside picnic area here. Taieri Historic Park features colonial buildings, moved here from other sites. In the town itself are a number of restored 19th century buildings.

The road north. West of Outram, traffic to the gold fields took the hilly Old Dunstan Road. Highway 87 follows the prospectors' route northwest to Clarks Junction; from here the rugged miners' track branches off to climb steeply over the mountains to Paerau (Styx) and other former digging sites.

Highway 87 continues north to Middlemarch, tucked in a valley below the Rock and Pillar mountains, then follows the Taieri River toward Kyeburn. In Macraes Flat, 19 km/12 miles southeast of Hyde, sturdy old Stanley's Hotel still serves thirsty travelers as it has since gold mining days.

Scenic Queenstown

Queenstown, South Island's principal resort, is the hub of the Southern Lakes District, a popular recreation area. Visitors come to Queenstown the year around to enjoy its lake and mountain scenery, exhilarating climate, changing seasons, and varied surroundings.

Born as a canvas town during the Otago gold rush, Queenstown prospered as miners uncovered rich finds in the Arrow, Shotover, and Kawarau rivers. When the easily won gold was gone, most of the prospectors moved on to the new West Coast gold fields, and sheepmen staked out the grassy slopes for vast high-country stations.

Close by are the southern lakes, filling deep troughs scooped out by ancient glaciers. From lakes Hawea and Wanaka in the north to Fiordland's beautiful Te Anau and Manapouri, these tranquil, water-filled valleys lure water-sports enthusiasts and anglers. Another favorite lakeside resort is Wanaka, located at the southern end of Lake Wanaka.

Getting settled in Queenstown

Backed by steep mountains, Queenstown nestles in a curve of Lake Wakatipu at the head of a small, horseshoe-shaped bay. Because it's so compact, Queenstown is a perfect walkers' town; most attractions are near the lake.

Evening activity centers around Queenstown's numerous hotels, which often feature music, dancing, or cabaret entertainment during peak seasons. In winter, après-ski activity is lively in local hotels and pubs.

Since outdoor activities dominate life in Queenstown, most restaurants are relatively casual and specialize in hearty food and generous portions. Tourist or hotel staff can direct you to a variety of restaurants.

For dinner with a view, take the gondola to the restaurant at Skyline Chalet on Bob's Peak and enjoy sunset views over the lake and mountains. If you're seeking historic atmosphere along with your food, consider the elegant Packers' Arms, just north of Arthur's Point; it's housed in a stone-walled inn that first served miners during the 1860s gold rush. For a more informal evening, you can dine in a former miner's cottage at Roaring Meg's, 57 Shotover Street.

A stroll around town

Tourist activity centers around the mall at the foot of Ballarat Street, a busy and colorful block where you'll find information and tour-booking agencies, major stores, and several of the town's historic buildings. Eichardt's Hotel, at the foot of the street facing the lake, began serving thirsty travelers in 1871.

Perpendicular to the mall, Marine Parade borders the waterfront. You board the hydrofoil or Kawarau jet boat at the small pier, where children toss bread to tame trout and greedy ducks swimming below. Along the gravelly shore, benches shaded by weeping willows invite you to pause and enjoy the scenery and lake activity.

Lake Wakatipu. Shaped like an elongated S, Lake Wakatipu fills a deep and narrow 83-km/52-mile-long glacial trough. Rugged mountains rise abruptly around its shore. Third largest of New Zealand's lakes, it's noted for its seiche action—a rhythmic oscillation in water level that rises and recedes as much as 13 centimeters/5 inches within 4 or 5 minutes. Scientists say the oscillation is due to mountain-funneled winds or changes in atmospheric pressure. Maori legend claims the motion is caused by the heartbeat of a giant at the bottom of the lake.

Lakeside parks. You'll enjoy a stroll through Government Gardens, a wooded park on a peninsula jutting into the lake and separating Queenstown Bay from Frankton Arm. A small stone bridge arches across the park's lawn-bordered pond. You can watch lawn bowlers in summer. St. Omer Park offers a grassy lakeside promenade along the bay beyond the steamer wharf.

City attractions. Upstairs in the Shotover Arcade on Beach Street, the Sound & Light Museum presents a 30-minute audio-visual show re-creating the sights and sounds of Queenstown in the 1860s.

Vintage touring and racing cars, motorcycles, and pioneer aircraft—all in working order—are on exhibit at the Queenstown Motor Museum on Brecon Street, just below the gondola terminal. The museum is open daily.

Grand old lady of Lake Wakatipu is the coal-burning Earnslaw, last of the steamship fleet that once cruised the lake. Trips depart from Queenstown from late October to mid-May.

Queenstown district—the essentials

Water sports, fishing, and back-country trips attract summer vacationers; in winter, skiing is the main lure. Since Queenstown is popular with visitors throughout the year, travelers are wise to make advance reservations, particularly during the school holidays (page 17), on long weekends, or during the ski season.

Getting there. Mount Cook Line flights link Queenstown's airport with most of the country's large cities and major resorts, and Mount Cook motorcoaches travel daily between Christchurch and Queenstown. Railways Road Services motorcoaches offer scheduled service to Queenstown from Dunedin, from Milford and Te Anau, from Invercargill, and from the West Coast glacier area via Wanaka.

Accommodations. Major Queenstown hotels include the Travelodge, on Beach Street near the steamer wharf; Lakeland Resort Inn, a 10-minute walk from town on the Lake Esplanade; Country Lodge on Fernhill Road; and Hyatt Kingsgate on Frankton Road. Smaller hotels include the Vacation (O'Connells), Wakatipu, and Mountaineer Establishment, all centrally located; and Hotel Esplanade, terraced above the water facing Frankton Arm. Among many excellent motels are the A-Line Motor Inn and the Ambassador, Lakeside, and Modern motels. Arrowtown has several small motels.

Accommodations at Wanaka include the fine THC Wanaka Hotel overlooking the lake, as well as numerous motels. A pleasant campground borders Lake Wanaka at Glendhu Bay.

Getting around. Numerous excursions departing from Queenstown invite visitors to explore the countryside by bus, plane, or four-wheel-drive vehicle, on horseback, or on foot. Rental cars are available in Queenstown and Wanaka.

Tourist information. You can make travel and accommodation reservations at the Government Tourist Bureau, 49 Shotover Street. Information on tours and excursions is available at booking offices facing the Mall at the foot of Ballarat Street. For information on Mount Aspiring National Park, stop at the park's visitor center in Wanaka.

Panoramic viewpoints and walks

The steep slopes rising from the lake offer spectacular views of Queenstown, Lake Wakatipu, and the sawtooth peaks of The Remarkables along the eastern shore.

Take a gondola ride up Bob's Peak in a four-seat bubble car to the Skyline Restaurant and adjoining tearoom, housed in a glass-walled mountainside chalet perched high above the lake. To reach another popular viewpoint, start at Deer Park Heights, a game reserve near Frankton (page 115). The chair lift ride to the summit of Coronet Peak provides a splendid view over the river basin, Crown Range, and other towering peaks.

If you want some exercise as well, take the trail up Queenstown Hill behind town or the longer trek up Ben Lomond. Other tracks lead up river valleys to old mining sites. Tourist officials can suggest routes you'll enjoy.

Excursions from Queenstown

Using Queenstown as your touring base, you can explore this historic district by boat, plane, motorcoach, four-wheel-drive vehicle, gondola, chair lift—even by horseback. Your main problem may be deciding what to do first among the bewildering array of activities.

Popular excursions fill rapidly, so book early. Some tours are seasonal; others require a minimum number of participants. You can obtain current tour information and make reservations at booking offices bordering the Mall at the foot of Ballarat Street.

Sightseeing by bus and plane

After you've explored Queenstown on foot, it's time to venture farther afield.

Half-day bus excursions depart from Queenstown for Coronet Peak, Skippers Canyon, Arrowtown, Waterfall Park, Deer Park Heights, and Goldfields Town. A full-day trip follows the lake road from Queenstown to Glenorchy and on to the Routeburn Valley.

For another full-day sightseeing trip, you can depart from Queenstown on the early Railways Road Services bus, travel through farming country to Te Anau, continue on the Milford Road to Milford, have lunch and take a launch trip on Milford Sound, and return to Te Anau by dinner time (or continue back to Queenstown, if you prefer).

Scenic flights departing from Queenstown's airport fly over Lake Wakatipu and the rugged mountainous country to the west. On a round-trip flight to Milford Sound, you pass over the Milford Track and experience eye-level views of Sutherland Falls and snowy peaks. Helicopter flights range from short trips over Queenstown to an excursion into the high peaks of The Remarkables.

Boat trips galore

You can cruise Lake Wakatipu on a sturdy old steamship, speed across the water on a hydrofoil, skim through scenic river gorges in a jet boat, float leisurely with the current aboard a raft, glide silently in a canoe, or charter a boat for a few hours of fishing.

Lake steamer. The grand old lady of the lake is the T.S.S. *Earnslaw,* a white-painted, coal-burning steamship that

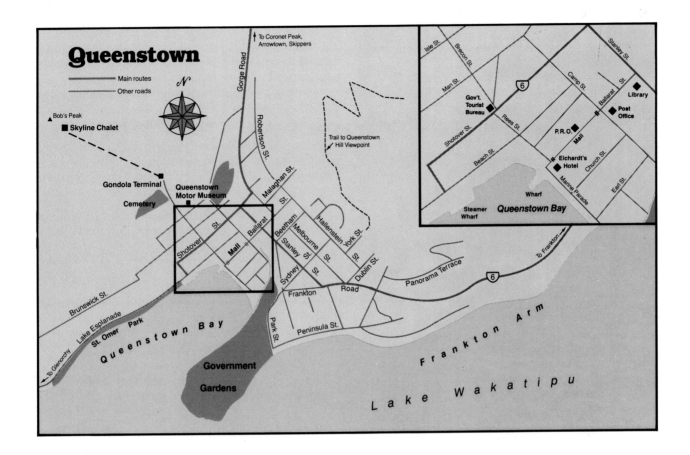

made her debut on Lake Wakatipu in 1912. Last of the steamship fleet that once plied the lake, she makes morning and afternoon cruises to Mount Nicholas Station and a lunch cruise up Frankton Arm from late October to mid-May. A dinner cruise is added in summer.

Jet boat trips. Several Queenstown operators offer an array of exciting trips on Otago's historic gold-bearing rivers. You can shoot white-water rapids through the narrow canyon of the Shotover River or skim the waters of the Kawarau River through the Kawarau Gorge. One excursion combines jet boat travel on both rivers.

If you crave even more excitement, you can choose an outing combining a jet boat ride with helicopter sightseeing, river rafting, or a hydrofoil trip.

Hydrofoil. Departing from the wharf at the foot of the mall, the 17-passenger hydrofoil *Meteor III* takes passengers on a one-hour, 40-km/25-mile cruise on Lake Wakatipu. Speeding along smoothly on its foils with its hull above the water, the boat passes lakeside sheep stations and mountain scenery in the upper reaches of the lake. During school holiday periods, shorter trips depart at frequent intervals.

Raft and canoe trips. From September through May, you can raft down the Shotover or Kawarau rivers on trips ranging in length from 2 hours to a full day. Or you can paddle your own canoe on a 3-hour safari down the

Kawarau. Without noise or fuel fumes, you float downstream past pine-studded cliffs and grazing livestock as you savor views of the valley and distant mountains. Overnight rafting trips on more remote rivers are also available (page 114).

Fishing expeditions. If fishing is your passion, you can charter a boat and guide for a few hours or a full day of trolling on Lake Wakatipu or fly-fishing on one of the local rivers. All equipment is provided by the guide.

Exploring the rugged back country

Four-wheel-drive vehicles provide access to some of the district's scenic and unspoiled valleys. You can raft down remote rivers or ride horseback to old mining areas.

Skippers Canyon. Best known of the back-country excursions is the trip up historic Skippers Canyon. The narrow, single-lane road snakes high above the Shotover River, where a century ago miners panned for gold. Rock monoliths jut above the craggy terrain. Intense sun scorches the parched valley in summer; biting winds and snow ravage the gullies in winter.

You'll see stretches of the pack horse trail to the Upper Shotover gold fields and part of the narrow road built by Chinese workers, who were lowered over the cliff to hammer out the route. Occasionally, you pass the dilapidated remains of a long-abandoned building.

Slender poplar trees in brilliant gold rim Lake Hayes. In autumn, you'll see foliage displays around Queenstown, Arrowtown, and Wanaka.

Other day trips. From Queenstown you can also arrange excursions by four-wheel-drive vehicle to Moke Lake, the ghost towns of Macetown and Sefferton, and up the Rees and Dart river valleys. Most trips stop for billy tea (brewed in a can over an open fire); day-long trips include lunch.

Trail riding. Escorted trips on horseback follow trails used by miners more than a century ago. On half-day and full-day excursions, you ride up the Shotover Gorge and —on longer journeys—into the Moke Valley to the site of Sefferton. Other trips traverse the Wakatipu farmlands.

Hiking and rafting excursions. Danes Back Country Experiences (P.O. Box 230, Queenstown) offers longer outback safaris that explore the remote valleys of the Upper Shotover, Matukituki, Hunter, Dart, Rees, and Landsborough rivers. Operated between October and April, the trips range from 2 to 5 days in length. Participants are transported into the valleys by four-wheel-drive vehicle or helicopter, then continue on foot or by raft. Groups camp in tents and cook over open fires.

See a cattle show

A good opportunity to learn about New Zealand's beef and dairy industry is at the Cattledrome 7 km/4 miles north of Queenstown. Shows are held daily at 9:30 A.M. and 2:15 P.M. at the exhibition center on Skippers Road. You'll see trained pedigreed cattle walk to their places on stage and watch cows being milked with glass milking machines. You can even try your own hand at milking.

Coronet Peak—for skiing and scenery

In winter, Queenstown turns into an alpine skiers' paradise. The challenging terrain of Coronet Peak, an easy 19 km/12 miles north of Queenstown, offers excellent skiing from mid-June until October.

Facilities at Coronet Peak are among the best in Australasia. A double chair lift transports skiers from the cafeteria-restaurant at 1,140 meters/3,800 feet to the 1,650-meter/5,400-foot summit. A triple chair lift provides access to the expert slopes, and other lifts take novice skiers to learners' areas. One fine days, you'll see many skiers soaking up the sun from the restaurant deck.

Coronet Peak has a ski shop and ski school; you can rent skis, boots, and poles in town or at the ski area. Skiers find ample accommodations and plenty of après-ski activity in Queenstown; during ski season, regular coach service operates between Queenstown and the ski area.

In summer, sightseers take the chair lift to the summit station, then climb to a glassed-in viewpoint for a breathtaking panorama over the Lake Wakatipu region and the Southern Alps. On chilly days, army greatcoats help ward off the biting wind during your ride.

A new warm-weather attraction is Cresta Run, a 600-meter/1,800-foot stainless steel toboggan run. Adventurous riders maneuver one or two-passenger toboggans down the curving slide beneath the chair lift.

Mining memories linger in Arrowtown

The 20-km/12-mile trip to Arrowtown is a diverting one. Memories of gold rush days come to mind as you cross the Shotover River and pass rebuilt 1860s inns still serving travelers. Side roads lead to Skippers Canyon and Coronet Peak. As you drive through the peaceful Wharehuanui Valley, you may meet a herd of cattle ambling along the road.

Mellow old Arrowtown has a lively past. After gold was discovered in the Arrow River, a midwinter flood in 1863 wiped out the riverside canvas town. Permanent stone and wooden buildings were built on higher ground; many have been converted into shops. A former bank, thickwalled and barred, houses the mining and pioneer memorabilia of the Lakes District Centennial Museum.

Century-old sycamores form a shady canopy over upper Buckingham Street and its wooden cottages. You'll find the empty Arrowtown jail off Cardigan Street. If you stroll the upper streets, you'll discover old stone buildings mortared with river sand, dry rock fences, attractive village churches, and clapboard houses with pillared porches and ornamental ironwork.

Gravestones in the cemetery record poignant tales of early death—miners who drowned in floods, children "too gentle for this bustling world." You can picnic along the river or under the willows by Bush Creek.

Horseback treks depart from Arrowtown on half-day excursions up the Arrow River; full-day trips continue on to Macetown.

Return to Queenstown past Lake Hayes, its glassy surface reflecting the pastoral countryside and mountain backdrop. Poplar trees ringing the lake turn brilliant gold in autumn.

Along Frankton Arm

East of Queenstown, Highway 6 skirts Frankton Arm, outlet of the Kawarau River into Lake Wakatipu. A small zoological garden borders the river near its outlet. The Kelvin Peninsula marks the arm's southern shore.

Located 3 km/2 miles east of town on the Frankton road, Goldfields Town seeks to re-create life in a mid-19th century mining village. Typical gold rush buildings are furnished in period style. Outside displays feature mining equipment and old vehicles.

One of the best views of the lake district comes from a private game reserve atop Deer Park Heights on the peninsula. Plan ahead — to enter the reserve you'll need to purchase a token at the Queenstown Public Relations Office or at small grocery stores in Frankton.

From Frankton, the road to Deer Park Heights climbs to a viewpoint high above Frankton Arm. On the drive you'll see several kinds of deer, as well as thar, chamois, mountain goats, and wapiti (elk), roaming the grassy park. From the summit you look down on Queenstown, nestling in its own bay, and mountains rising steeply around the rim of Wakatipu's waters. Coronet Peak looms high over pastoral valleys and several small lakes.

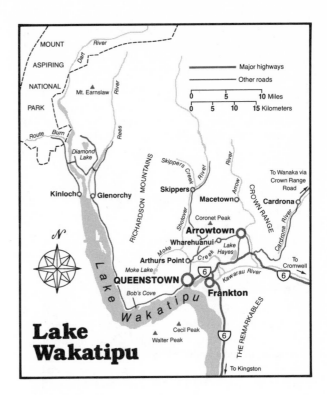

Visit a sheep station

You can combine a cruise on Lake Wakatipu with a visit to a high-country sheep and cattle station. Located on the far shore of the lake and inaccessible by road, the isolated stations are reached from Queenstown by station launch or the steamship *Earnslaw*.

Homesteaded during the 1880s, the stations now cater to day visitors from Queenstown. Homestead buildings have been restored or rebuilt and furnished with articles of historic interest. Visitors learn about the station's past and current farming activities, enjoy tea (or a meal on longer trips), tour some of the early buildings, and watch demonstrations of shearing and wool spinning. You'll also see sheep dogs at work.

Trips operate the year around to Cecil Peak Station (overnight accommodations also available) and Walter Peak Station; launches transport visitors from Queenstown Wharf. Visitors to Mount Nicholas Station board the *Earnslaw* for the trip across the lake; this excursion operates from late October to mid-May.

Hiking the Routeburn Track

Queenstown is the departure point for hikers following the Routeburn Track, a 40-km/25-mile alpine trail winding through the magnificent country of Mount Aspiring and Fiordland national parks. The trail cuts along river valleys and through untouched beech forest, past cascading waterfalls and saucerlike alpine tarns, and across a challenging 1,280-meter/4,200-foot mountain pass. Portions of the trail are exposed and can be dangerous in bad weather. Huts provide overnight shelter for hikers.

The track is usually open from mid-November to late April, though snow may still cover parts of the trail early in the season.

You can hike the trail independently or with a guided group from either end—beginning at road's end north of Kinloch or from the Divide on the Milford Road near the Hollyford junction. You can arrange to connect with hiking trips on the Milford or Hollyford tracks.

For those who prefer not to carry a heavy pack, Routeburn Walk Ltd. (P.O. Box 271, Queenstown) conducts 4-day guided excursions over the trail. Hikers carry only their personal gear; all food, utensils, and sleeping equipment are provided. Parties are small — usually 12 hikers and 2 guides. Huts at Routeburn Falls and Lake Mackenzie are complete with down sleeping bags, mattresses, and hot showers.

The Wanaka country

Many travelers know Wanaka only as a brief stopover on the Haast Pass route linking the West Coast with Otago and South Canterbury destinations. Other visitors linger to indulge in the lake resort's amenities and sports facilities. Wanaka draws water-sports buffs who come to boat, swim, water-ski, and fish on long and narrow Lake Wanaka, neighboring Lake Hawea, and their tributaries.

Wanaka. Clustered at the southeastern end of Lake Wanaka, the resort faces glacier-molded hills. For an overview, walk from the business district to the lookout above town, in front of the white war memorial. Outside town, the 3D Maze of intricate passageways is a popular family attraction.

In season, you can arrange for lake sightseeing and fishing trips, raft trips on the Clutha River, and scenic flights. Rental bicycles, boats, and fishing equipment are available. At the Gin and Raspberry Stables in the Cardrona Valley, you can rent horses for day or overnight treks through the historic gold fields.

In summer, Wanaka is the departure point for hikers heading into Mount Aspiring National Park (page 99). Winter visitors head for the ski fields at Treble Cone and Cardrona, and for heli-skiing in the Harris and Richardson mountains.

Day excursions. Short drives lead to sheltered Albert Bay, pleasant for a picnic and afternoon swim, and to Glendhu Bay and West Wanaka, center of water-sports activities. Willows and poplars along the lakeshore form an attractive golden border in autumn. Hiking trails lead up Mount Iron and Mount Roy.

Lake Hawea is a favorite of anglers for its rainbow trout and landlocked salmon. Many boat owners come here in summer to escape Wanaka's crowds. Small vacation homes hug the cliffs above the shoreline.

Crown Range Road. A scenic alternative to Highway 6 from Wanaka to Queenstown is Crown Range Road (Highway 89), an unpaved 70-km/44-mile route (closed in winter). Not recommended for nervous drivers, the road wends south from Wanaka through the Cardrona Valley, passes Cardrona's sagging old hotel, and continues to the summit of the Crown Range. From the crest you survey the entire Wakatipu Valley. The road then plunges in zigzag curves to the valley, where it crosses the Arrow River and meets Highway 6 northeast of Queenstown.

All aboard the Kingston Flyer

Every summer a shrill whistle and the hiss of escaping steam herald the approach of the Kingston Flyer, New Zealand's vintage steam train, as it chugs leisurely through the wooded hills and farm country south of Lake Wakatipu. Children wave as the train passes scattered homes and villages, and grazing sheep scurry in alarm as the smoke-belching engine nears.

Beginning in the 1880s and continuing for many years, express passenger trains transporting tourists to scenic Lake Wakatipu and its surrounding mountains provided fast service between Gore and Kingston via Lumsden. A few years ago a pair of the old coal-fired locomotives and some of the historic dark green carriages were brought out of retirement, carefully restored, and redecorated to 1920s elegance.

You can choose your seat in the combined first-class car and guard's van, the "birdcage" or gallery carriage, the refreshment car, or the passenger carriages. Brasswork gleams and woodwork is varnished to high luster. Match-striker plates, ornate luggage-rack brackets, and gas lamps add a nostalgic touch. The traditional spittoons have been removed, though, and in some carriages horsehair seats have been replaced with foam-padded vinyl. You can buy light refreshments and souvenirs in the refreshment car.

From October to mid-May, the Kingston Flyer makes three round trips daily between Kingston and Fairlight. Each one-way trip takes about 25 minutes.

Rugged, remote Fiordland

New Zealand's largest and most remote national park, Fiordland encompasses the entire southwestern corner of South Island. Incredibly beautiful and wild, the region is an intriguing combination of rugged mountain ranges, dense rain forest, solitary alpine lakes, sparkling rivers, and splashing waterfalls. Majestic fiords indent its western coast. Much of Fiordland is virtually unexplored wilderness, still inhabited by such rare birds as the takahe and kakapo.

Sports enthusiasts come here for boating, hiking and climbing, fishing for trout and salmon, and hunting deer and wapiti. You can arrange for fishing or hunting guides and for float planes to transport your party to one of the remote lakes. Many visitors enjoy scenic flights and launch trips; others join hiking groups on the Milford, Hollyford, or Routeburn tracks.

Te Anau, gateway to Fiordland

Largest of the southern lakes is Lake Te Anau, which marks Fiordland's eastern boundary for some 60 km/38 miles. Its three long fingers probe deeply into the park's thickly wooded mountains. Near the lake's southern end is the town of Te Anau, gateway to this wilderness country and base for excursions south to Lake Manapouri and Doubtful Sound and north to Milford.

From Te Anau, visitors can cruise on the lake, visit a glowworm cave, or go flightseeing. If you prefer more leisurely pursuits, you can rent a bicycle, stroll along the lake shore, or enjoy a day of fishing or golf. Arrangements can be made in town for guided back-country fishing or hunting trips. To see some of Fiordland's rare birds, including the takahe, visit Te Anau's wildlife park.

Te Ana-au Caves. Launches make regular trips the year around from Te Anau to the glowworm caves. Located about 16 km/10 miles north of Te Anau on the far side of the lake, the site can be reached only by boat.

Maoris probably discovered and named this "Cave of Rushing Water," but it was not rediscovered until 1948. Geologically young, it's known as a "living cave," since the limestone cavern is still being eroded. A powerful underground stream cascading from Lake Orbell continues to hollow out the limestone cliffs of the Murchison Mountains.

A short boat ride takes you into the cavern, where lighted walkways guide you past frothing waterfalls and limestone formations. A punt transports visitors along the cave's underground river into the glowworm grotto.

Boat trips. Jet boat and rafting trips depart from Te Anau for the Upper Waiau River. You can enjoy white-water thrills on the jet boat excursion, drift leisurely down Fiordland's largest river aboard a raft, or even combine the two.

Fiordland—the essentials

Spectacular scenery and outdoor activities attract visitors to this corner of New Zealand. You'll find few commercial diversions here. The region's most accessible destinations are majestic Milford Sound and the lakes of Te Anau and Manapouri.

Getting there. Mount Cook Line planes connect Te Anau with major South Island cities and resorts; flights operate on demand, weather permitting, between Queenstown and Milford, less often between Te Anau and Milford. Railways Road Services buses travel to Te Anau from Dunedin, Queenstown, and Invercargill, and provide daily service to Milford from Queenstown and Te Anau.

Accommodations. Te Anau, headquarters for most Fiordland excursions, offers a variety of accommodations, including the THC Te Anau Hotel, Vacation Hotel, and Campbell Autolodge (all facing the lake), Fiordland Motor Lodge, and Luxmore Inn. At Manapouri, most motorists stay at the DB Manapouri Motor Inn.

On the Milford Road, accommodations are available at the Te Anau Downs Motor Lodge at Te Anau Downs, 27 km/17 miles from Te Anau, and at Cascade Lodge at Cascade Creek. Campsites with fireplaces and toilets are located along the Milford Road. Facilities at Milford are limited to the THC Hotel Milford, facing the sound, and the Milford hostel, used mainly by Milford Track hikers.

Getting around. Scheduled motorcoach service links the main destinations. Scenic Fiordland flights depart from Te Anau; anglers and hunters can charter float planes for trips to remote lakes and fiords. Weather permitting, small planes fly between Queenstown and Milford and between Te Anau and Milford, offering a spectacular aerial view of the lush and rugged country. Many Milford visitors travel one way by road, the other by air.

Boat trips and other excursions depart from Te Anau, Manapouri, and Milford. Rental cars are available in Te Anau for independent exploring.

Tourist information. Details on excursions are available from Fiordland Travel Ltd. or Mount Cook Travel Bureau in Te Anau. For information on Fiordland National Park campsites, trails, and activities, contact park headquarters in Te Anau.

From November to early April you can take a trip to the head of Lake Te Anau. A motorcoach delivers visitors to Te Anau Downs; the trip continues aboard a launch to Glade House, start of the Milford Track. You return later in the day by the same route.

It's possible to arrange launch or water taxi trips from Te Anau to such lakeside destinations as Gorge Falls, on the lake's south fiord, or Brod Bay (for swimming, picnicking, a nature walk, or a hike up Mount Luxmore). Yacht charters can be arranged for one-day or overnight trips exploring Lake Te Anau's fiords, bays, and islands.

Flightseeing excursions. Several carriers operate scenic flights over this rugged countryside by float plane, land-based aircraft, or helicopter. You fly above the lakes and rivers, through uninhabited valleys, and over thick forests and hidden waterways to the western fiord country. Helicopters transport hikers and skiers to Mount Luxmore.

Float plane and helicopter trips depart from the Te Anau lakefront; other flightseeing excursions leave from the Te Anau/Manapouri Airport.

Aerial views of Fiordland National Park, its splendid scenery, and the recovery of live deer by helicopter are shown in an audio-visual program at the Fiordland Flights Theatre, 90 Te Anau Terrace.

Fishing and hunting trips. Experienced guides are available for one-day or longer fishing and hunting trips into Fiordland National Park. Permits, available at park headquarters in Te Anau, are required to hunt in the park. Chartered float planes transport anglers and hunters to remote sites.

Fiordland National Park

Less than 15,000 years ago this region was locked in thick ice. Glaciers sculpted the land on a larger-than-life scale, gouging out long, narrow lakes, carving out coastal fiords, and shearing high mountain valleys. Captain James Cook sailed along the coast in 1770 and returned here in 1773, putting in at several fiords and anchoring at Dusky Sound for rest and ship repair.

The best of Fiordland lies off the roads, to be experienced in solitude, on foot or by boat. The region's appeal is not only in its awesome beauty but also in its isolation and challenging terrain.

Park headquarters is in the town of Te Anau (P.O. Box 29, Te Anau; phone Te Anau 819); the visitor center is open daily. Permits for backpackers planning an independent trek on the Milford Track (page 119) are available here.

At the visitor center you'll learn about park wildlife, accessible attractions, and current activities. Nature programs are scheduled in summer. You can also get current information here on road, trail, and weather conditions.

By air to Milford

You can reach Milford by air over the rugged Fiordland wilderness, through mountain valleys along the Milford Road, or on foot along the Milford Track. Each approach offers an unforgettable experience.

The flight over Fiordland to Milford Sound gives travelers a thrilling perspective of this rugged and remote region. It's a good idea to book space ahead, especially in summer.

In Queenstown or Te Anau, you board a small plane for an aerial look at Fiordland's mountains, forests, and waterways. You fly over the route of the Milford Track, gazing down on hikers' huts along the trail, past 580-meter/1,904-foot Sutherland Falls plunging in a spectacular triple cataract from Lake Quill's glacier-carved basin, then down the Arthur Valley to land at Milford's small airstrip.

After a brief stop, your plane returns by a different route, soaring high for a bird's-eye view of world-famous Milford Sound, then flying between crinkled icy peaks and down alpine gorges that broaden into river plains.

The memorable Milford Road

If you travel from Te Anau to Milford by car or bus, you'll follow the 119-km/74-mile Milford Road (Highway 94), an alpine route cutting through some of New Zealand's most untouched country. The route is maintained in good condition; a section about 20 km/12 miles long — from Cascade Creek over the Divide to Marian Corner — is graded gravel. During bad weather, the road may be closed temporarily due to snow, ice, or flooding. You can get current road information and a leaflet describing roadside points of interest at Fiordland National Park headquarters.

If you're driving, plan to leave early so you can have a leisurely trip. Allow at least 2½ hours for the journey to Milford — more if you want to stop or make side trips. By late morning, fast-moving buses speeding along the route raise clouds of dust on the unpaved parts of the road. Camping vans and trailers are not permitted beyond Cascade Creek.

The Eglinton Valley. From Te Anau you follow the shore of Lake Te Anau north to Te Anau Downs, then veer up the broad wooded valley of the Eglinton River, popular for fly-fishing. Beech-covered mountains frame a view of distant peaks, and colorful lupines brighten the valley floor in summer. You'll find picnicking and camping sites scattered throughout the valley.

You pass the tiny Mirror Lakes, where photographers capture mountain reflections in calm weather, before arriving at Cascade Creek, the only travelers' oasis (rustic accommodations, meals, gasoline) between Lake Te Anau and Milford. If you want to stretch your legs, take the short self-guided nature walk that begins across the creek from the lodge.

Continuing past lakes Gunn, Fergus, and Lochie, you cross the Divide, the lowest pass (534 meters/1,752 feet) in the Southern Alps. From here hikers depart for Lake Howden and the Routeburn and Greenstone tracks to Lake Wakatipu.

Down the Hollyford Valley. A side road follows the Hollyford River, a sparkling stream that empties into the Tasman Sea at Martins Bay. About 8 km/5 miles from the highway at Gunns Camp, a small museum displays a fascinating collection of mementos, old photographs, and yellowed clippings on various aspects of Fiordland lore

Float plane lands on Milford Sound, rippling the mirrored reflection of Mitre Peak.
Visitors can fly over the fiord or cruise past waterfalls all the way to open sea.

—ill-fated settlements, legendary local characters, ship-wrecks and plane crashes, early Milford Track hikers, the construction of the Homer Tunnel.

From late October to mid-April, guided groups take the Hollyford Valley Walk from road's end to Martins Bay. You hike the first 14 km/9 miles, then travel by jet boat about 38 km/23 miles down the lower river and across Lake McKerrow. Groups bunk in comfortable riverside lodges. At Martins Bay you can visit a seal colony, see sites of pioneer settlements, or go fishing or beachcomb-ing. Participants on the 4-day trip depart on a scenic flight terminating at Milford Sound. On the 5-day excursion, hikers retrace the valley route by jet boat and on foot. For more information, contact Hollyford Tourist & Travel Co. Ltd., P.O. Box 216, Invercargill.

Through the Homer Tunnel. Mountains crowd closer as you continue climbing toward the Homer Tunnel, a single-lane, rough-hewn bore piercing the Darran Range. Sharp-eyed travelers can spot signs of glacial activity and avalanches.

One-way traffic moves through the narrow tunnel—westbound to Milford from the hour to 25 minutes past, eastbound to Te Anau from the half-hour to 55 minutes past. If you have a short wait, take a stroll or just relax

and enjoy the scenery. At both ends of the tunnel, walks lead through natural alpine gardens, where wildflowers bloom in December and January.

Cleddau Valley. West of the tunnel, the switchback road descends the steep upper Cleddau Valley. Sheer walls rise from the valley floor; after a rain, the cliffs are curtained by waterfalls. About 7 km/4 miles below the tunnel, a signposted trail leads to the Chasm. Take the 5-minute walk through beech forest to a railed platform overlook-ing the turbulent Cleddau River as it thunders through a narrow rocky gorge and drops in frenzied cascades on its route to the sea.

"The finest walk in the world"

Hikers find the Milford Track more than just a scenic adventure—it's a total experience. Thousands have tra-versed this wilderness trail between Lake Te Anau and Milford Sound. Yet each feels a sense of achievement gazing down from the summit of Mackinnon Pass or catching the first glimpse of awesome Sutherland Falls.

Trampers experience many of the same challenges the pioneer Milford hikers did in the 1890s—rivers to be crossed, a mountain pass to be conquered, the caprices of rain and weather to be endured. Yet today's walkers take

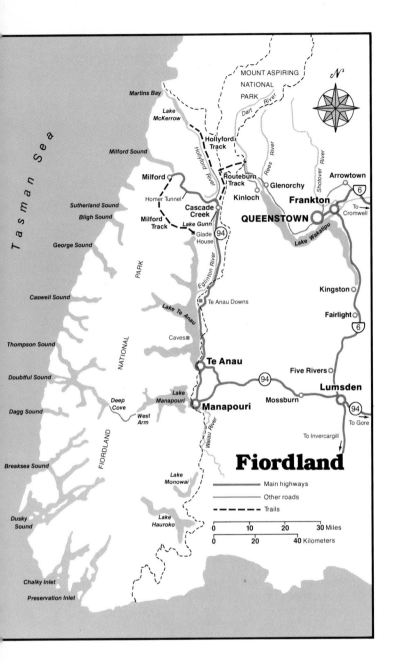

Organized group trips. From mid-November through March, parties depart Te Anau three times a week (daily in midsummer) on the 53-km/33-mile tramp to Milford Sound. Along the route hikers stay in huts equipped with bunks, electricity, hot showers, and toilet facilities. Meals are provided.

You must book space months in advance (through the New Zealand Tourist Office) for these popular 5-day excursions. Hikers carry only clothing and personal articles needed on the trail; "city clothes" are sent ahead.

Along the Milford Track. Hikers depart from Te Anau by motorcoach, then cross Lake Te Anau by launch to reach Glade House, start of the trail.

Though it is "good going," the trail is challenging even in fine weather, for you must ford numerous streams and cross a 1,067-meter/3,500-foot alpine pass. In bad weather, it's a difficult and demanding route, even for experienced, physically fit hikers.

The trail is divided into three sections; hikers do a section a day at their own pace. From Glade House the route climbs through native beech forest along the Clinton River to Pompolona Hut. Next day comes the most challenging part of the trip: a steep climb through open alpine country to Mackinnon Pass, followed by a switchback descent to Quintin Hut. From here, a trail leads to the bottom of famous Sutherland Falls. On the final day of hiking, you follow the Arthur River downstream, skirting Lake Ada, to Sandfly Point, where a launch transports hikers the final step across Milford Sound. The trip ends after lunch the following day at Milford.

The grandeur of Milford Sound

Milford Sound leaves an indelible impression in the memories of many travelers. Far from any population center, it's a destination renowned solely for its beauty.

From the head of the fiord, one of New Zealand's classic views unfolds before you. Steep granite peaks, wooded on their lower slopes, frame the glacier-carved inlet and cast mirrored reflections on its dark, calm waters. Dominating the scene is the triangular pinnacle of mile-high Mitre Peak, Milford's landmark. Along the sheer cliffs, several waterfalls tumble more than 150 meters/500 feet into the sheltered sound. Only a few moored boats and a scattering of buildings at the head of the sound break the unity of mountains, forest, and water.

The grandeur of Milford's unspoiled setting is best appreciated from the water. Launches depart from the Milford wharf several times daily on 1 and 2-hour cruises; if you have time, take the longer trip—it goes all the way to the open sea. You'll glide past Mitre Peak and glacier-topped Mount Pembroke. Spray blows over you as the boat noses close to Stirling and Bowen falls. Often, you'll spot a seal or two basking on sun-warmed rocks.

Overnight visitors can experience Milford's quiet moods. In early morning, shafts of sunlight pierce the mist to illuminate Mitre Peak. At day's end, pastel sunset

for granted comforts beyond the dreams of those early tourists, one of whom called this footpath through Fiordland "the finest walk in the world."

You can hike the track independently, packing all your equipment and supplies, or join a group and carry only personal items. Trail access is controlled by Fiordland National Park headquarters in Te Anau (P.O. Box 29, Te Anau; phone Te Anau 819). Since only a limited number of independent hikers (called "freedom walkers") are permitted on the Milford Track, advance reservations are necessary. Because of variable weather and trail conditions, only experienced hikers with proper equipment are allowed on the trail. All hikers walk the track in one direction—from Lake Te Anau to Milford Sound.

tints streak the cloud-strewn sky. In any season, passing clouds can bring drenching rainstorms, which create dozens of new waterfalls.

Information on walks is available at the hotel reception desk. The Bowen Falls trail begins near the wharf and follows the shore along the cliff face; wear a raincoat or waterproof parka. The Lookout Track starts behind the hotel. A 5-minute climb gives you a view over the hotel to the water. Beyond this point, you'll need agility and sturdy footwear to clamber over exposed roots and rocks on the slippery slopes.

Island-studded Lake Manapouri

Many New Zealanders consider Manapouri, south of Te Anau, the most beautiful lake in the entire country. Thick forests border its meandering shoreline, and some 30 bush-clad islets stud its expanse of blue. Flanking the lake on three sides are high mountains, their snow-tipped peaks mirrored in lake waters.

Boat excursions depart from Pearl Harbour on the Waiau River. You also can rent a rowboat or arrange for water taxi service here. A favorite destination for a beach picnic is Stockyard Cove, one of the lake's loveliest bays, where you can walk through conifer forest.

From Manapouri you can take a half-day trip to the power station at West Arm, or a full-day excursion that continues on to Doubtful Sound for a cruise on this unspoiled fiord. Trips operate daily from late August to mid-May, three times weekly in winter.

Manapouri Power Station. To visit the power station, visitors cross the lake to West Arm, where a bus whisks them down a steep, spiraling tunnel to the powerhouse, 213 meters/700 feet below ground. Hewn from solid rock, it houses seven turbines, each driving a powerful generator. Water from the lake enters vertical penstocks, plunges through the turbines, and then is channeled through a 10-km/6-mile-long tailrace tunnel for release into the sea at Doubtful Sound, located on the other side of the mountains. The station furnishes power for the aluminum smelter at Bluff.

On to Doubtful Sound. Construction of the power station opened up some of New Zealand's most spectacular scenery. Visitors can now see at close hand virtually untouched country.

From the power station, travelers board a motorcoach and ride on an upgraded construction road over 671-meter/2,200-foot Wilmot Pass to Deep Cove on Doubtful Sound.

Here you board a launch for a 2-hour cruise on Doubtful Sound, one of the region's most majestic fiords. Noted by Captain James Cook (as Doubtful Harbour) in 1770, it is 10 times larger than Milford Sound. As you cruise into Hall Arm, you'll gaze at vertical cliffs thrusting high into the sky. Mighty waterfalls plunge over the sheer rock faces. In fine weather, mountains and greenery are reflected in the protected waters of the fiord.

On foot in Fiordland

Fiordland's tracks offer opportunities for hikers to escape urban pressures and enjoy the special qualities of this intriguing area.

The types of country you can traverse here vary greatly, but the tramps have much in common. Routeburn concentrates on the high country (above sandfly level); Milford ranges from open alpine terrain to lush rain-forest valleys; Hollyford is a low-level river track. Their proximity and complementary nature make it possible to combine two—or all three—walks on an extended hiking vacation.

A hiker's adventure. Hiking the Milford or Routeburn track is a tramping adventure, not a tourist excursion. The trip can be difficult for the inexperienced or out-of-condition hiker; sections of the trail are demanding and strenuous, particularly in foul weather.

On the trail you enter a remote world almost untouched by man. Dwarfed by gigantic mountains, you follow a twisting track through dense forest, across alpine grasslands, along swift-flowing rivers, and past cascading waterfalls. Naturalists delight in the varied flowers, trees, ferns, and shrubs. Tumbling streams glint in the sun like molten silver, and only the liquid trill of a forest songbird or the shrill call of a kea breaks the quiet.

You cross the deeper streams on suspension bridges or large fallen trees; smaller streams are forded. Be prepared for wet weather; a short rainstorm can suddenly deepen creeks and create dozens of new waterfalls.

Along with your trail companions you'll carry a "cut lunch" and share "scroggin," a high-energy mix of nuts, raisins, and ginger, and hot "billy tea" brewed from the water of snow-fed streams. Evenings are a time for the comfortable camaraderie of shared experiences.

Keep your pack light. If you're joining one of the group trips, you'll receive a recommended packing list. Each hiker carries personal gear; you can rent a backpack, but your own will probably be more comfortable.

One hiker's formula: "Be prepared for bad weather, carry a minimum amount of clothing, and be very fit." You'll want a waterproof hooded jacket and comfortable footwear. Lightweight boots (well broken in), worn with two pairs of woolen socks, provide shock absorption and traction. A complete change of warm clothing and underwear is essential insurance against a downpour.

Miscellaneous equipment includes a small flashlight, adhesive tape, sunglasses, and insect repellent. Milford hikers can purchase evening refreshments and small items at hut shops.

Exploring Southland

Though whalers roved the southern seas as early as the 1840s and pastoral runholders had claimed most of Southland's grazing lands by the 1860s, real settlement got a late start in this region. During the Otago gold rush, most Southland residents prospered only indirectly by providing food and other supplies for the miners.

Southland's future lay in less spectacular but more enduring assets — primarily its rich grasslands, but also its timber and coal reserves. Wool and meat are exported from here to markets around the world; dairy products add their share to Southland's wealth. Mills began to ship timber to Dunedin in the 1860s, and coal has been mined in the Ohai-Nightcaps district since 1880.

Though legally Southland has no provincial standing, its boundaries cover the southernmost part of South Island, skimming the south shore of Lake Wakatipu and stretching from the east coast to the western fiords. Off the South Island "mainland" is unspoiled Stewart Island.

Roaming the interior

Between Lake Wakatipu and the south coast, only scattered small farm towns break the open plains. Sheep and cattle munch on the rich grasslands; they'll provide wool and meat for the export market. Deer farming is an increasingly important industry. Anglers come here to enjoy well-stocked trout streams, among them the Aparima, Oreti, and Mataura rivers.

From the junction town of Lumsden, highways radiate in all directions — north to Queenstown, west to Te Anau and Milford Sound, south to Invercargill, and east to Gore and Balclutha. Near Mossburn to the west, red deer browse in the tussock and manuka at the West Dome Deer Ranch.

Coal mines. West of Winton, rich deposits of coal in the foothills above Ohai and Nightcaps have been mined for nearly a century. Coal from underground and open-cast mines fuels many Southland industries. For more information stop at the state Coal Mines Office in Ohai.

Southern Fiordland. Lying near the Waiau River in limestone cave country, Clifden is the gateway to Lake Hauroko and southern Fiordland. At the Fiordland National Park ranger station in Clifden you can obtain trail information and hunting permits.

One of the park's southernmost lakes, Hauroko occupies a wild and beautiful bush setting. There's a camping area near the park boundary. Trails beginning near road's end follow the lake shore and lead into the park. Remains of a Maori burial cave have been discovered on Mary Island.

Timber country. Tuatapere, a timber town in the Waiau Valley, is the principal lumber milling center for Otago and Southland markets. Anglers come here to fish for trout and salmon. You can picnic or camp in a wooded park on the riverbank. On New Year's Day, axmen from around the country converge here to compete in wood-chopping contests.

Country driving offers the unexpected. Here, drivers meet a flock of sheep on the road. Sheep dog (at far right) maneuvers strays with the rest of the group.

Hokonui Hills. Southland's second largest town is Gore, surrounded by lush rolling pastures and fields of grain. West and south of Gore are the Hokonui Hills, for decades synonymous with illicit whisky. The Scottish sheepmen who settled this district brought with them knowledge of whisky distilling, as well as a taste for the brew. Until World War II, moonshiners and Customs officials engaged in a continuous battle of wits over the stills.

South of Gore, at the foot of the hills, Dolamore Park has a pleasant, forest-rimmed picnic area and trails winding through the bush. The Mataura Plain farther south is cattle and dairy country; its main centers are Mataura, Edendale, and Wyndham.

The southeast coast

From Balclutha, center of the rich South Otago sheep farming area, Highway 92 follows a slow and winding coastal route southwest to Invercargill. Side roads turn off to unspoiled beaches and seaside points of interest, some best observed at low tide. An unpaved stretch of roadway cuts through nature reserves where trees and ferns spill down to the sea.

South of Balclutha, you can follow a scenic coastal road to Port Molyneux, where you'll enjoy a magnificent view. Kaka Point is a favorite family vacation retreat just north of the lighthouse at Nugget Point.

In Owaka, farming center of the Catlins district, the small Catlins Historical Society Museum on Waikawa Road contains displays on whaling, early industry and transport, and other facets of the region's colorful history.

South of Owaka, side roads lead to Jacks Bay Blowhole, impressive at high tide and in stormy weather, and to Penguin Bay, where in late afternoon penguins come ashore to nest in the bush. An easy walk through beech forest takes you to Purakaunui Falls, where a stream cascades over a series of broad terraces. Farther south, Tautuku Beach is a superb sandy strand backed by trees.

Southeast of Chaslands, a steep trail leads down to Waipati Beach and the Cathedral Caves. Accessible only at low tide, the interconnected, high-ceilinged sea caves cut far back into the cliffs. Check tide times before exploring and take a flashlight if you plan to venture into the caves.

Visible at low tide, Curio Bay fossil forest contains the petrified logs of a subtropical forest, buried by volcanic ash millions of years ago. When the land mass re-emerged from the sea, waves cut the sandstone to reveal the petrified stumps and broken logs.

At the east end of Toetoes Bay, hidden reefs extend beyond the Waipapa Point lighthouse to mark the eastern entrance to Foveaux Strait.

Invercargill, Southland's market center

Thriving economic center of Southland, Invercargill spreads across the open plains along the New River estuary. The city shares Dunedin's Scottish origins. Broad

A & P shows— a warm look at rural life

Enjoy a festive glimpse of New Zealand's rural life style by attending one of the Agricultural & Pastoral Society shows held in farming communities throughout the country. Most take place on Saturdays from October through March. Tourist information offices, local newspapers, and word-of-mouth alert you to upcoming shows.

The smaller A & P shows are the most fun. From outlying farms and ranches, families bring their prize livestock, produce, and handmade crafts to the show grounds. Activities are informal, and the whole family participates.

Early in the day, most men congregate near the livestock exhibits, where they stand in small groups discussing the merits of different breeds of sheep and cattle. Youngsters nervously groom their animals before the livestock judging and riding events. In the exhibit building, women arrange their preserved and baked goods, sewing and knitting projects, garden produce, and cut flowers. Children's art work is displayed on the walls.

Sheep dog trials and horse-jumping events are afternoon highlights. Burly wood choppers and skillful sheep shearers have their own competitions. Food vendors, amusement rides, and displays of new farm equipment vie for attention. Children scamper about trying to see everything at once.

Later, thirsty participants may gather at a local pub to rehash the day's events.

streets—many named for Scottish rivers—and numerous parks mark its level site.

Invercargill was a busy river port during the late 1850s and 1860s, but during later decades Bluff gradually gained dominance as the principal coastal shipping port. Today, Invercargill is New Zealand's eighth largest city and the market center for the surrounding district. Ringing the city are massive freezing works that prepare fat Southland lambs for world markets.

Lovely parks enhance Invercargill's appeal. The city's showplace is Queens Park, a large reserve north of the business district. Its magnificent gardens flourish in Southland's equable climate. In season you'll enjoy extensive displays of irises, rhododendrons, and roses. Tropical plants thrive under glass in the Winter Garden. Nearby, sleek bronze animal statues rim the shallow children's pool. Sunday concerts attract families in summer.

Stay with a
farm family

Spending a night or two with a hospitable farm family is a wonderful way to meet New Zealanders. Throughout the country, congenial families open their homes to visitors who want to sample the friendliness of farm life or just relax for a few days in a rural setting. Other than during the main holiday periods, arrangements can usually be made on short notice.

A farm visit offers a relaxing change from the usual hotel room and fast-paced touring itinerary. In addition to getting acquainted with a friendly Kiwi family, you also get a first-hand look at the backbone of the country's economy. Some stations have been farmed for more than 100 years.

Usually you stay in a cozy guest room in the family homestead (frequently, though not always, with private bath) and eat hearty, country-style meals with the family. During informal evenings at home, you share conversation with your host family. Most families take only a few guests at a time to keep the experience on a personal level.

If you like, you can join in farm chores and watch sheep dogs go through their paces. Perhaps you'll want to lend a hand with the mustering, join the haying crew, learn to operate a spinning wheel, observe sheep shearers at work, or ride along with your host to the local stock sale.

If you prefer, you can use the farm as a base for touring or just relax on the veranda.

Other activities vary by station—often you can ride horseback around the farm, fish for trout in a nearby stream, go swimming, hunt for deer in the hills, or picnic out in the countryside.

Accommodations range from farms just a few miles from main roads and country towns to high-country stations off the beaten track. If you're traveling by public transport, your host family can usually meet you at the nearest sizable town.

You can obtain details on individual farms and arrange for accommodations at offices of the Government Tourist Bureau in major New Zealand cities (page 12). Of the organizations promoting farm visits, the largest is Farm Holidays Ltd., P.O. Box 1436, Wellington; they also have reservation centers in Auckland and Christchurch.

Sports fields include an 18-hole golf course, hockey and cricket grounds, lawn bowling and croquet greens, and tennis and squash courts.

Near the southern boundary of Queens Park, the Southland Centennial Museum and Art Gallery contains excellent displays on the region's Maori culture and natural history, as well as collections of whaling and pioneer relics and Victoriana.

The City Art Gallery is located in Anderson Park, about 7 km/4 miles north of Invercargill. Works by early and contemporary New Zealand artists hang in the former home of Sir Robert Anderson, whose family gave the city the house and its well-tended gardens and surrounding bush.

Other parklands lie south of the main shopping district, where greenery lines Otepuni Creek as it flows through the city, and near the city's northern boundary. Here, Thomsons Bush, an 85-acre scenic reserve of native trees, borders the upper Waihopai River; in summer, you can rent canoes and paddle along the quiet stream.

Horse racing is presented at Southland Racecourse, on the city's eastern boundary, throughout the year.

Along Foveaux Strait

The protected waterways and coastal beaches lining Foveaux Strait are Southland's playground. Just west of Invercargill, weekend boaters race, row, and water-ski on the long, straight stretches of the Oreti River and New River estuaries, and anglers cast for trout. Yachts and power boats cruise the strait and its sheltered bays.

Beaches border Foveaux Strait from the estuary west to Riverton. On warm weekends and during long summer twilights, local families converge on Oreti Beach west of Invercargill. Toheroas are taken from the beach during the short winter clamming season.

Riverton exudes the mellow charm of an unpretentious seaside resort; families come here on holiday, particularly during the New Year carnival period. Fishing boats and pleasure craft moor along the estuary's south shore. Flanking the seaside road to Howells Point are The Rocks, a local landmark. Farther west on Highway 99, the village of Colac Bay faces the strait and Centre Island.

Bluff and the southern tip

Built on a natural harbor, Bluff is Southland's seafaring town. The port is a major meat and wool exporting center. Storage tanks and coolstores rim the sheltered inlet. Ferry service links Bluff with Stewart Island.

Across the water on Tiwai Point gleam the silver buildings of the large Comalco aluminum smelter. Oxygen is extracted from aluminum oxide shipped here from Queensland, Australia, and the molten aluminum is cast; some is alloyed with other metals before being exported. The Manapouri power project (page 121), developed in conjunction with the smelter, provides the massive amounts of electricity needed for the process.

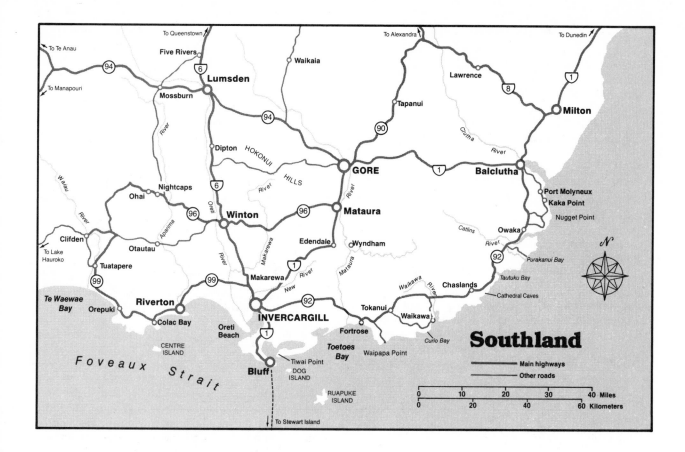

Bluff is home port of a large commercial fishing fleet, including the sturdy boats that dredge Foveaux Strait for the succulent Bluff oysters. The country's oyster lovers anxiously await the opening of the March-to-August season; the shellfish are air freighted from here to all parts of New Zealand.

Houses cover the low slopes of Old Man Bluff, the hill that gave the town its name. Turn uphill by the post office and follow the road to the summit, where a wind-swept panorama over Bluff Harbour and the town, sprawling Southland plains, and Foveaux Strait islands opens before you.

Highway 1 ends at Stirling Point lookout, where a signpost gives kilometer distances to various worldwide points. A walking track begins at road's end; the 2½-hour Foveaux Walk follows the coast as it winds around the bush-covered bluff toward the island's southern tip. It gives fine views across Foveaux Strait to Stewart Island.

Unspoiled Stewart Island

Separated from South Island by the waters of Foveaux Strait, Stewart Island is less a destination than a way of life. For residents and visitors alike, its attractions lie in its virtually untouched beauty, glowing skies, and unhurried pace. Time is unimportant; only the tide governs daily activities. You'll find few cars, few roads, and little tourist development here. Most of the island is a nature reserve, rich in birdlife.

Since warm currents sweep eastward through Foveaux Strait, the island, about 32 km/20 miles from the mainland, enjoys a mild — if frequently wet — climate despite its southerly latitude; temperatures are seldom very high or very low. But on the southern tip, raw icy blasts sweep north from the Antarctic. Year-round rain-fall provides most of the island's water supply. Brilliant dawns and sunsets streak these southern skies, and occasionally the aurora australis — the "southern lights" — adds special radiance.

Visitors come in all seasons, but most prefer the summer months, when the whole island is alive with native birds and the scent of flowers perfumes the air. But even in winter the skies retain their glow, and coastal waters lure fishing enthusiasts.

First impressions

Mountainous and heavily forested, Stewart Island is roughly triangular in shape, and about 60 km/40 miles long and 30 km/20 miles wide. Steep, wooded promontories rise sharply from the clear waters. Many fine harbors and beach-rimmed coves indent its irregular shoreline. Off the coast lie numerous islets, including the Mutton-bird (Titi) Islands off the southwest cape, where Maoris traditionally collect many young birds each autumn.

Stewart Island's only sizable settlement is Halfmoon Bay (also called Oban), a fishing settlement bordering a scenic bay. Low buildings ringing the bright blue water blend into the wooded hills behind. Sheltered from westerly winds by the island's forested ranges, the tranquil village basks in the sun. Only a tiny stretch of the northern coast has been touched by roads and habitation.

Southland — the essentials

At the country's southern tip, Invercargill is the region's commercial center and largest town. South of Bluff, across Foveaux Strait, is unspoiled Stewart Island, a popular summer destination.

Getting there. Air New Zealand flights land at Invercargill's airport, about a 5-minute drive west of the business district. The Southerner train and Railways Road Services motorcoaches provide regular service to Invercargill from Christchurch, Dunedin, and other east coast towns. Motorcoaches also link Invercargill with the lake resorts of Te Anau and Queenstown.

Stewart Island, about 32 km/20 miles from the mainland, is a 15-minute flight from Invercargill or a 2½-hour ferry trip from Bluff.

Accommodations. Most travelers stay in Invercargill, where accommodations include the centrally located Kelvin Hotel, the gracious older Grand Hotel, Don Lodge Motor Hotel, and Ascot Park Hotel/Motel. You'll also find many smaller hotels and motels in town. Anglers on fishing forays to Southland rivers may want to make Gore their headquarters. Bluff's small hotels cater to travelers taking the Stewart Island ferry.

On Stewart Island, you'll find simple but comfortable accommodations at the South Seas Hotel, the world's most southerly pub; the small Rakiura Motel; and well-equipped camping vans at Ferndale Caravan Park. Cabins and campsites are available at Horseshoe Bay. There's also a youth hostel on the island. Summer accommodations on Stewart Island must be booked months ahead.

Getting around. Trains and motorcoaches stop in Milton, Balclutha, and Gore on east coast routes; buses also serve the inland towns of Winton and Lumsden on routes to the lake resorts. Anglers and hunters can charter float planes for trips to remote lakes. Taxis and rental cars are available in Invercargill.

On Stewart Island, visitors can take a short coach tour of the main settlement and nearby attractions; in summer, a launch trip operates to Ulva Island.

Tourist information. Visitors can obtain local information at the office of the Southland Progress League, Oreti House, 120 Esk Street, Invercargill.

The island has about 450 permanent residents; many are descendants of European whalers who intermarried with the island's Maori inhabitants. They ride their fishing boats westward into the heavy swells in search of the crayfish and cod that provide the residents' main source of income.

Most visitors come for just the day; to experience the island's special appeal, though, plan to stay for several days. A mini-bus transports visitors on a short tour of the northern hills and bush-fringed bays.

Stewart Island Museum, on Ayr Street near the shore, contains a fascinating collection of relics from the island's past, when whaling, sealing, and timber milling were the main industries. You'll also see exhibits of island plants and birds.

Exploring the island

To enjoy Stewart Island's special attractions, you'll want to explore its coastline and forest reserves.

Cruising the coast. In summer, regular launch trips operate for fishing and sightseeing. You can also charter a launch for a day of cruising; inquire at the general store on the waterfront or check the notice board outside.

Only a thin strip of land divides Halfmoon Bay from Paterson Inlet, the large, landlocked harbor on the northeastern side of the island. Wooded to the water's edge, the inlet is a favorite of sailboats and other pleasure craft. You can cruise into Price's Inlet — perhaps stopping to see relics of a Norwegian whaling base at Surveyors Bay — or venture farther up Paterson's southwest arm.

Enchanting Ulva Island, near the inlet entrance, is a popular stopping point. Its sandy beaches are ideal for a picnic; trails wind through unspoiled forest, and birdlife abounds. Nearby Native Island was the site of a Maori settlement.

Hiking island trails. Numerous walking tracks hug the coastline and cut through the bush. Shellhounds head for Ringaringa Beach, about a mile from Halfmoon Bay, or for Horseshoe Bay. Other easy walks lead to Garden Mound or Lee Bay; day-hike destinations include Butterfield Beach, Golden Bay, Thule, and the lighthouse.

Ambitious hikers enjoy the walking tracks in some of the more remote and wild parts of the island. Forest Service huts offer overnight shelter on the longer routes; you bring your own food and equipment and replace the firewood you use.

The island has a wealth of unique native plants and rare birds. Rimu, rata, miro, and totara trees stretch skyward from the mossy floor. All birdlife is protected; you may see tuis, parakeets, bellbirds, kakas, and perhaps a rare weka or kiwi searching for insects in the dense undergrowth. Deer also roam the island.

Information on island trails is available at the Forest Service information center at Halfmoon Bay. A light waterproof jacket and sturdy footwear come in handy any time of year.

Index

Maori entertainers perform in Rotorua, where visitors can tour Maori villages, learn about their crafts, and sample foods at a *hangi* feast.